W9-BEP-110

THE
PENINSULA
YEARS

to John Webster
with "trans-continental friendship"!

Xmas 2005

THE PENINSULA YEARS

BRITAIN'S REDCOATS IN SPAIN AND PORTUGAL

by

D.S. RICHARDS

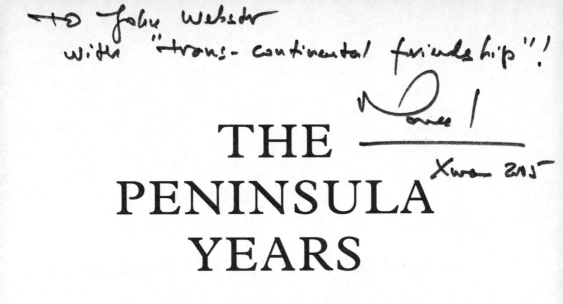

LEO COOPER

TO RICHARD GUILDEN CLARKE

First published in Great Britain 2002 by
LEO COOPER
an imprint of Pen & Sword Books Ltd
47 Church Street
Barnsley, South Yorkshire, S70 2AS

Copyright © 2002 by D. S. Richards

ISBN 0 85052 919 0

A CIP record for this book is available from The British Library

Typeset in 10.5/12.5 Plantin by
Phoenix Typesetting, Ilkley, West Yorkshire.

Printed by CPI UK

CONTENTS

Chapter 1   'The fragrant heaths of Portugal'.   1

Chapter 2   The Battle for Vimiero.   13

Chapter 3   'For this country we can do nothing'.   22

Chapter 4   An infamous retreat.   31

Chapter 5   The welcome sight of Vigo.   43

Chapter 6   Corunna.   50

Chapter 7   Talavera.   60

Chapter 8   Busaco Ridge.   76

Chapter 9   'I will insure you all now, for half a dollar by God!'   89

Chapter 10   'Never in this world was so cruel and distressing warfare waged'.   99

Chapter 11   'Whore's ar Arthur? Aw wish he wore 'ere'.   113

Chapter 12   'Soldiers! The eyes of your country are upon you'.   122

Chapter 13   The breach at Badajoz.   135

Chapter 14   Salamanca summer.   146

Chapter 15   'This cursed castle'.   158

Chapter 16   Rich rewards at Vitoria.   170

Chapter 17   Battle for the Pyrenees.   180

Chapter 18   Advance into France.   189

Chapter 19   Crossing the Adour.   201

Chapter 20   'No more fighting, lads. Now for our homes, wives and sweethearts'.   211

Bibliography   223

Index   225

DRAMATIS PERSONAE

Sergeant James Anton.	1st Batt. 42nd Regiment.
Ensign George Bell.	2nd Batt. 34th Regiment.
Captain Charles Boothby.	Staff Corps Engineer.
Lieutenant William Bragge.	3rd Light Dragoons.
Captain Robert Blakeney.	28th Regiment.
Ensign Thomas Bunbury.	2nd Batt. 3rd Regiment.
Thomas Bugeaud.	French observer.
Major Charles Cadell.	28th Regiment.
Ensign Edward Close.	48th Regiment.
Captain John Cooke.	43rd Regiment.
Rifleman Edward Costello.	1st Batt. 95th Regiment.
Sergeant John Cooper.	1st Batt. 7th Fusiliers.
Private Joseph Donaldson.	94th Regiment.
Lieutenant Robert Fernyhough.	3rd Batt. 95th Regiment.
Lieutenant W. Field.	Brigade of Guards.
Ensign William Gavin.	71st Regiment.
Lieutenant George Gleig.	85th Regiment.
Captain Alexander Gordon.	15th Hussars.
Lieutenant William Grattan.	88th Regiment.
Private John Green.	68th Regiment.
Rifleman John Harris.	1st Batt. 95th Regiment.
Sergeant James Hale.	9th Regiment.
Captain John Harley.	47th Regiment.
Ensign William Hay.	52nd Regiment.
Lieutenant Peter Hawker.	14th Light Dragoons.
Sir Richard Henegan.	Field Train Dept.
Lieutenant Henry Hough.	Royal Artillery.
Surgeon Walter Henry.	2nd Batt. 66th Regiment.
Ensign William Thornton Keep.	28th Regiment.
Lieutenant Robert Knowles.	2nd Batt. 7th Fusiliers.

Captain John Kincaid.	1st Batt. 95th Regiment.
Captain Jonathan Leach.	2nd Batt. 95th Regiment.
Sergeant William Lawrence.	40th Regiment.
Captain Harry Ross Lewin.	1st Batt. 32nd Regiment.
Joseph Maemphel.	Serving with the French.
Lieutenant John Malcom.	1st Batt. 42nd Regiment.
Captain McCarthy.	50th Regiment.
Ensign John Mills.	1st Batt. Coldstream Guards.
Major Charles Napier.	50th Regiment.
Major George Napier.	1st Batt. 52nd Regiment.
Adam Neale.	Physician.
Captain John Patterson.	50th Regiment.
Private Thomas Pococke.	71st Regiment.
Rifleman Thomas PluKnet.	1st Batt. 95th Regiment.
Major Samuel Rice.	51st Regiment.
Sergeant D. Robertson.	92nd Regiment.
August Schaumann.	Commissary with the K.G.L.
Lieutenant Joseph Moyle Sherer.	2nd Batt. 24th Regiment.
Lieutenant George Simmons.	1st Batt. 95th Regiment.
Lieutenant Harry Smith.	1st Batt. 95th Regiment.
Lieutenant John Cowell Stepney.	Brigade of Guards.
Q.M.S. William Surtees	2nd Batt. 95th Regiment.
Captain William Tomkinson.	16th Light Dragoons.
Captain William Warre.	A.D.C. to General Beresford.
Ensign Edmund Wheatley.	King's German Legion.
Corporal William Wheeler.	51st Regiment.

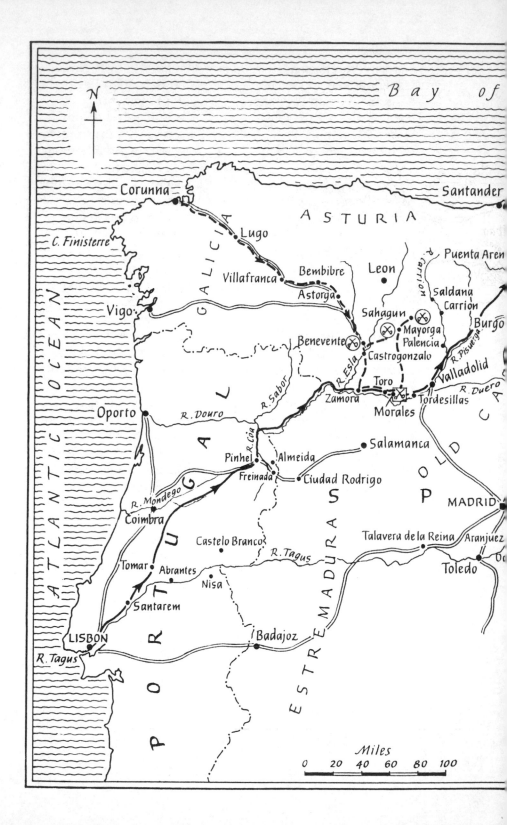

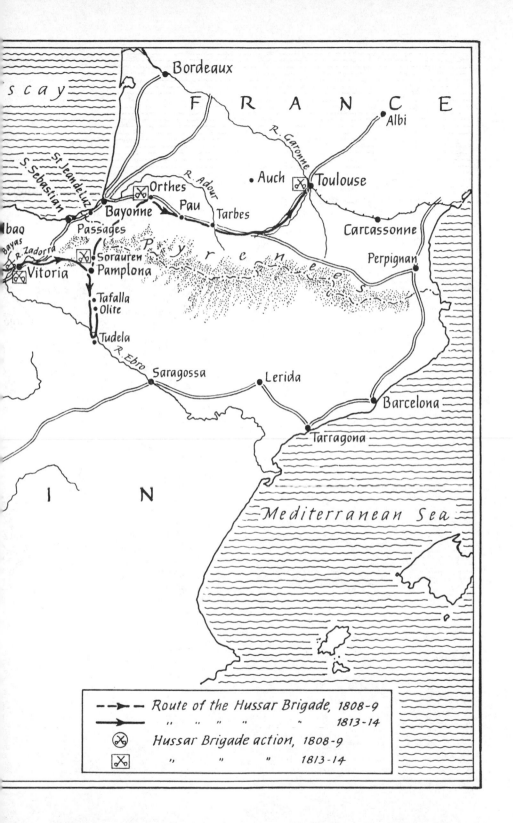

Route of the Hussar Brigade, 1808-9
" " " " " 1813-14

Hussar Brigade action, 1808-9
" " " 1813-14

PREFACE

A wealth of material exists for the student of the Napoleonic Period in the diaries and journals of the junior officers and men who formed the spearhead of Britain's Peninsular army. Many of their memoirs have recently been reproduced in facsimile.

In my description of the campaigns in the Peninsula and the south of France I have drawn upon the experiences of some fifty-six combatants and non-combatants which I am sure will provide added interest and colour to the narrative and give an insight into the vicissitudes of a redcoat's life, including the comradeship, which at times extended even to the enemy.

Previous to Waterloo, Wellington was asked his opinion as to the likely outcome of the battle. Pointing to a private soldier, the Duke replied, 'It all depends on that article whether we do the business or not. Give me enough of it and I am sure.'

Despite the seemingly disparaging terms he employed, Wellington knew full well that the redcoats he had commanded in Spain and Portugal enjoyed a reputation second to none in Europe, never having suffered a major defeat at the hands of the French.

Wellington's other notorious remark, that the army was composed of 'the scum of the earth', is also open to misinterpretation when it is considered that the majority in the ranks was largely recruited from the criminal classes, the impoverished and the many who enlisted for drink. The Duke's true feelings were revealed when he added, 'It is really wonderful that we should have made them the fine fellows they are'.

The contrary nature of the man in the ranks is no better illustrated than during the long and arduous retreat to Corunna and Vigo with its accompanying scenes of drunken and brutal behaviour, in sharp contrast to the feats of outstanding courage demonstrated in the battle of Albuera and the murderous assault against the fortress of Badajoz where even Wellington was reduced to tears after witnessing the destruction of his elite division in the Great Ditch. His redcoats were truly, as that great military historian Sir William Napier described them, 'astonishing infantry'.

In acknowledging the help I have received in the compilation of this work, I would particularly like to thank Mr. Jamie Wilson of Spellmount Publishers for allowing me to quote from the letters of Ensigns William Thornton Keep and John Mills, published respectively in the books *In the Service of the King* and *For King and Country*. The illustrations in this book, together with the jacket cover, are reproduced by the kind permission of the National Army Museum. For his excellent map of the Peninsula as it was in the 19th Century my thanks are due to Mr. John Mollo for allowing me to reproduce it from his book *The Prince's Dolls* and for the detailed campaign maps accompanying the relevant chapters, I am indebted to Lt. Colonel Sir Julian Paget.

I should also like to express my appreciation of the help afforded me by the British Library and the National Army Museum at Chelsea, without whose research facilities this book would never have been completed. My thanks also go to Tom Hartman for bringing the maps to my attention and for his assistance in preparing this book for publication.

Chapter 1

'THE FRAGRANT HEATHS OF PORTUGAL'

For twelve years the Kingdom of Spain had been a close ally of Napoleonic France, an alliance which in 1795 had promised much but had brought Spain nothing but misfortune and a series of humiliating reverses at sea from Cape St. Vincent in 1797 to an overwhelming defeat at Trafalgar eight years later. Since then ties between the two countries had deteriorated to the extent that when, in the winter of 1807, Napoleon, determined to bring Portugal to heel, assembled a mixed force of French and Spanish soldiers at Bayonne in readiness to march through Spain to invade Portugal, resentment at the connivance of the Spanish Court threatened to escalate into open hostility by the Spanish peasantry.

An unprecedented series of victories from December 1805 to June 1807 over the combined armies of Austria and Russia at Austerlitz, the Prussians at Jena, and a Russian army of 90,000 at Friedland, had forced those nations to sue for peace and on 25 June Napoleon met the Czar on a log raft moored on the River Niemen near the town of Tilsit to discuss terms.

The three-hour meeting, subsequently ratified as the Treaty of Tilsit, was remarkable for the degree of goodwill which existed between Napoleon and the 30-year-old Czar Alexander. The two sovereigns embraced before retiring under a canopy for a long private conversation. Indeed, the blond curls and blue eyes of the handsome Russian so intrigued the Corsican that he was said to have afterwards confided to an aide, "Were he a woman, I think I should fall passionately in love".

Whatever flatteries were heaped upon the impressionable young Czar, the terms of an alliance were settled far more rapidly than might have been the case through diplomatic channels. Whilst the treaty deprived Prussia of most of its territory between the Elbe and the Rhine, the rapport which existed between Napoleon and Alexander merely obliged the Czar to close his ports to the one nation whose maritime strength

1

threatened to obstruct the expansionist ambitions of the French Emperor. Unable to match England's naval power, Bonaparte sought to deny her the profitable trade from exporting goods to Europe by creating a 'Continental System' – in effect a coalition of Russia, Austria, Prussia and Denmark, to stifle the commerce of Great Britain.

One important route for British trade to the continent remained open, however. The government of Portugal, which had long maintained close ties with Britain, refused to align herself with the other states and continued to trade, despite the threats, in the knowledge that her seaboard was protected by ships of the Royal Navy.

Portugal's defiant attitude undoubtedly worked to the advantage of many of Britain's commercial enterprises for when the rest of Europe discovered that woollen goods, coffee, sugar and other Empire products were in short supply, contraband running became so widespread that goods were even being smuggled into France.

A furious Bonaparte summoned the Portuguese ambassador in Paris and railed against his country's effrontery in her persistent refusal to align herself with the other European states against Great Britain.

"If Portugal does not do as I wish," he stormed, "the House of Braganza will no longer reign in two months."

Whatever the action contemplated by a weak Portuguese government, which, on 17 October 1807, did expel the British ambassador, it was already too late, for French troops were on the move through Spain. Twelve days later Prince John and the Royal family sailed for Brazil escorted by six British men o'war barely hours before General Junot arrived at the gates of Lisbon.

The 2,000 inexperienced conscripts who limped through the streets of the Portuguese capital on 31 November were just a small part of the 'Observation Corps of the Gironde' which had been 25,000 strong when Junot had crossed the Bidassoa on 18 October. The long march over rain-soaked hills had been notable for an endless trail of footsore stragglers who were everywhere greeted by a cold hostility stopping just short of violence.

Spain in 1807 was a country whose rural population was poverty-stricken and priest-ridden. There were few decent roads, the villages largely a collection of miserable hovels and, with the land divided by mountainous regions, altogether it presented some serious obstacles to campaigning. A report to the Emperor from one of his Generals in 1808 noted that, "There are no roads, no transport, no houses, no shops, no provisions in a country where the people warm themselves in the sun and live on nothing. . . . The Spaniard is brave, daring and proud, he is the perfect assassin."

On 13 November a 'Second Observation Corps of the Gironde', led by General Pierre Dupont, crossed the frontier and advanced on Valladolid, whilst at the eastern end of the Pyrenees another division, commanded by General Duhesme, seized the frontier fortress of Barcelona to enter Catalonia a few weeks later on the slim excuse of protecting the coastline. This invasion of their country gave rise to a dark suspicion that the real intention of the French, far from protecting the Peninsula coast, was to destroy Spanish independence and resentment quickly turned to rage when in February King Charles IV resigned the Crown and with the Queen and Crown Prince Ferdinand joined Napoleon in Bayonne.

On 2 May Marshal Joachim Murat, whose troops had been ordered by Napoleon to adopt "a warlike fashion", attempted to escort the last of the Spanish royal family out of Spain. The sight of the popular young prince Don Francisco in tears and refusing to mount the carriage steps greatly affected the watching crowd which soon moved forward to prevent his abduction. Muskets exploded and knives flashed in the sun as the infuriated Spaniards closed with the Prince's French escort. The protest was quickly overcome by the battalion on duty at the Palace, but the commotion brought crowds on to the streets armed with every conceivable weapon with which to end the life of any Frenchman unwary enough to be caught in the maze of narrow alleys. Murat's troops reacted with commendable speed, for within minutes of the disturbance breaking out every regiment was standing by ready to quell the riotous behaviour by force of arms if necessary.

"We charged into the city by half companies with fixed bayonets," recalled a young German in the service of France, "overthrew everything in our way." But 17-year-old Joseph Maemphel soon discovered that the citizens of Madrid were not to be so easily cowed. "They threw down from the windows and the roofs of the houses everything which they could reach," he recorded, "and killed and wounded a great number of our men."

Murat retaliated with equal ferocity, his cavalry sweeping the streets from end to end wielding their sabres with lethal efficiency.

"The young Spaniards learnt in a new kind of catechism that Satan was in three persons; Napoleon, Murat, and Godoy," wrote Lieutenant Thomas Bugeaud. In a letter to his sister, which spared her most of the gory details, the Lieutenant went on to describe the events of that particular day. "The population of Madrid took a fancy to revolt on the 2nd of May. They seized upon struggling Frenchmen and cut their throats, then ran to the arsenal, took possession of it, dragged out guns, seized upon firelocks, and began a little war in the streets with some French pickets. On our side we were not inactive . . . and their success was but brief. Peace appears to be restored but there is no depending upon it. . . .

3

I assure you that I am not much at ease when walking through the streets."

The insurrection was soon put down and, after a summary trial by a military court, ninety-five Spaniards were shot on 3 May, their execution immortalized by Goya in his masterpiece 'El Trest de Mayo', currently to be seen in the Prado.

In their excitement and anger, the spirit of the Spanish people was undiminished by events in the capital which had also served as a catalyst for the patriotic fervour of the peasantry. In almost every town and village their barely suppressed fury erupted in a series of brutal assassinations of French residents. At Cadiz, Seville, Cartagena, Torquemada, and Valladolid, the streets became stained with the blood of French soldiers and their Spanish sympathizers, often after barbaric torture which in its turn brought savage retaliation from the French authorities. Villages were reduced to ashes and their inhabitants put to death without regard to age or gender.

News of these horrors reached London and on 8 June a delegation from the Asturias was received at the Admiralty where the Spaniards sought material assistance in their struggle against Bonaparte's invasion of their country. The junta's petition was greeted sympathetically by Parliament which until now had lacked an opportunity to launch the full strength of Britain's land forces against Napoleon in Europe.

Oddly enough, many high-ranking officers regarded the affair with mixed feelings. There could be no question of the desire of the army's junior officers to get to grips with the French, but the greybeards in Horse Guards thought it ironic that a country which only a few months before had been actively opposing them in Montevideo and Buenos Aires should now find it necessary to call for their assistance. King George had no such doubts, for in addressing Parliament on the subject, he said, "I view with the liveliest interest the loyal and determined spirit manifested in resisting the violence and perfidity with which the dearest rights of the Spanish nation have been assailed. The kingdom thus nobly struggling against the usurpation and tyranny of France can no longer be considered the enemy of Great Britain, but is recognized by me as a natural friend and ally."

Once the government had pledged assistance to the people of the Iberian Peninsula – for, smarting under the arbitrary rule of General Andoche Junot, the Portuguese had also risen in revolt – the promise was quickly turned into reality. Spanish prisoners of war were clothed, equipped and sent back to their homeland together with the munitions of war and substantial sums of money. It was perhaps a fortunate co-incidence that 10,000 troops under the command of Sir John Moore were at that time returning from an abortive expedition to Sweden, and this force, augmented by an additional 9,000 men assembling at Cork and led by Sir Arthur Wellesley, was put under sailing orders for the Peninsula, the place of disembarkation for the men from Cork being left to the discretion of the General.

Wellesley, the 39-year-old third son of a distinguished Anglo-Irish family, had enjoyed considerable military success in India against the Mahrattas and these victories had certainly been a contributory factor in the Horse Guards commission for him "to bring about the entire and absolute evacuation of the Peninsula by the troops of France".

A few days before sailing Wellesley had been asked what he thought of his chances. "Of the French," he replied, "I have never seen them; they may overwhelm me, but I don't think they will out manoeuvre me . . . because if what I hear of their system of manoeuvre is true, I think it a false one against steady troops. . . . I, at least, will not be frightened beforehand."

Taking passage in the *Crocodile* Wellesley reached Oporto eleven days later where he learnt from the Bishop that a yellow stone fort at Mondego Bay had been seized by patriots and was now garrisoned by 400 marines put ashore by Admiral Cotton. This was welcome news to the British General for not only was the Bay a convenient landing point within easy marching distance of Lisbon, but it avoided the problem of disembarking north of the Tagus where any landing would be opposed by French-manned Portuguese ships. The Bay did, however, suffer from one disadvantage in that, although of ample size to accommodate the twenty-one transports that had sailed from Cork, it was subject to a pounding surf along the entire length of its rocky coastline.

The Atlantic swell that gave rise to that surf occasioned no comment from the experienced sailor but as his vessel pitched and rolled, causing wholesale breakages amongst the regimental crockery, Captain Jonathan Leach of the 2nd Battalion, 95th Foot, felt justified in complaining to the Master that never before had he undergone such discomfort even in the strongest gale. Leach was not alone in his misery. The small craft carrying Lieutenant Peter Hawker of the 14th Light Dragoons rolled so violently from side to side that he found it almost impossible to leave his cabin.

"This together with the continual creaking of the ship, the stifled state we were in having our dead lights up and being without air," wrote Hawker, "kept us the whole night in the very essence of misery."

Disembarkation began on 1 August with flat-bottomed boats leaving the transports closely packed with redcoats clamping their muskets between their knees as they clung desperately to each other for support in the wildly pitching craft. The swell carried them rapidly towards the beach, but spills were frequent as the frail craft were swept between rocks and along the strand in a welter of foam. The reaction of a Commissary in the King's German Legion was no doubt shared by many who were put ashore on that bright August morning: "With beating hearts we approached the first line of surf and were lifted high into the air," recorded August Ludolf Schaumann. "We clung frantically to our seats . . . not a few closed their eyes and prayed."

Despite the skill of the sailors, boats were overturned in the surf, where many of the occupants, encumbered by their equipment, struggled to keep a footing in the receding undertow. Typical of the soldiers' misfortune was the experience of Ensign William Gavin: "Wave succeeded wave, mountains high," he wrote, "and when it approaches the boat the crew abandon their oars and throw themselves flat in the bottom of the boat, invoking the Blessed Virgin and all the Saints in the calendar."

Gavin's craft had been crewed by Portuguese fishermen familiar with the conditions and after a ducking and presumably a terrible fright, the redcoats of the 71st were swept ashore without further mishap.

No sooner had Wellesley's troops recovered their breath before they were assailed by a crowd of Portuguese traders, most of whom were shaded from the rays of a broiling sun by a variety of large umbrellas. The thirsty soldiers readily accepted the delicious grapes, oranges and beakers of wine that were offered for sale, but, as Richard Henegan parted with the last of his English coins, he could not help but marvel how their value could be so well understood and appreciated by the local populace.

As the hours slipped away, the once virgin stretches of sand became crowded with material of every description, ranging from barrels of salted beef to stacks of muskets at irregular intervals. Commissariat officers strove to create some sort of order out of a confused mass of stores, whilst dozens of horses, feeling the touch of firm ground and a strong breeze after a long confinement in a ship's hold, galloped madly up and down or rolled on their backs in the warm sand. Finally, on 8 August disembarkation was completed when the last boatload of redcoats, drenched to the skin, thankfully removed their haversacks to snatch a few hours' sleep before the customary dawn assembly.

"I wrapped myself in a boat cloak, and sank down in repose," confessed the physician Adam Neale, "happy in having exchanged the noisome and damp cabin of a transport for the fragrant heaths of Portugal".

Early the next morning an advance guard formed from companies of the 60th and 95th Rifles moved off along the coast road to Leira accompanied by a choking cloud of sand and the nerve-jarring screech of wooden axles turning in ungreased journals. The Treasury refused to finance a regular transport system and so the army was obliged to rely upon the hire or requisition of carts from civilian sources. In the Peninsula that meant Spanish or Portuguese wagons crudely constructed from a few rough planks bolted together with three or four upright wooden stakes to form the sides. A long pole harnessed a bullock team by its horns. Progress was infuriatingly slow, but since the animals' hooves were shod in iron a team could drag quite heavy loads over the rough tracks with considerable ease.

With an August sun to add to the torment from a myriad sand flies, the march to Leira over soft sandy hillocks imposed a severe test of stamina on troops yet to recover from the discomforts of a week's sea voyage. Each soldier carried a haversack containing 4 lbs of salt beef and 4 lbs of ships biscuit, a canteen of water, a hatchet, a musket 42 inches long and weighing 15 lbs together with eighty rounds of ball ammunition in leather pouches. The light sand churned up by hundreds of boots hung in the air to smother each sweating redcoat, who, with his head pushed forward by the rolled blanket or greatcoat strapped to the top of his haversack, suffered accordingly. It was no small wonder that many should drop out of the line of march suffering from heatstroke. Even so, Wellesley urged the men along at a fast pace. Leira had to be reached before the French General Henri François Delaborde, riding at the head of his troops marching from Lisbon, could join forces with a column hurrying west from the Spanish frontier.

Wellesley's light infantry soon made contact with the French and on the 15th the first engagement of the campaign took place outside the small town of Obidos when the 95th clashed with Delaborde's pickets. The French contested the ground fiercely, but were quickly driven from the town at the point of the bayonet, and Wellesley's men bivouacked for the night only to discover early the next morning that the enemy was ensconced in a strong position near the village of Rolica where they had occupied a hill.

The ridge upon which the village was sited was surrounded by vineyards and olive groves, behind which lay the Azambujeira mountains 15 miles from Lisbon, whose passes afforded the French General a convenient escape route, or should he so choose, a formidable series of defence points. Originally Delaborde's army had been 6,000 strong, but casualties and sickness had reduced its numbers to little more than 4,000, a figure massively outnumbered by the British who could field 13,000,supported by eighteen cannon.

The battle opened in the usual fashion with a cloud of skirmishers moving forward to dislodge the voltigeurs spread across the crest of the hill. Moving to the left and right in pairs, the Green Jackets picked their way between the gorse and dwarf ilex which studded the sandy slope, as Wellesley's artillery opened fire at long range.

For troops yet to become acclimatized to an Iberian summer, it was an exhausting climb and as Captain Leach led his men up the steep side of the hill, every breath he drew seemed to him to come from an oven.

The French put up a spirited resistance and three separate attacks were repulsed before General Delaborde, who had been slightly wounded, gave the order to retire. The British Commander was reluctant to press his advantage. He had very few cavalry and his men were young and inexperienced, but, excited by their successful brush with a formidable enemy, they bivouacked for the night well pleased with their success. A few Staff officers may have thrown anxious glances in the direction of Torres Vedras, the route taken by Delaborde, but although Wellesley had failed to encircle the French, he had prevented Delaborde from joining General Loison who was moving down from the Tagus towards him.

The British General's main objective now was to secure the large harbour at Lisbon which was essential as a base for his future campaign in Spain as well as affording shelter to the fleet from the Atlantic storms. Wellesley had every reason to feel that his operations would be crowned with success, for the discipline and fire power of the British Army was of a remarkably high standard considering the raw material from which it had been formed. Reviled at home, because of the use of troops in the suppression of public disorder, the enlisted man was regarded with contempt if not outright hostility. The formation of a Militia in 1799 lessened public hostility somewhat but did little to swell the ranks of the Line regiments and, as an inducement, the Horse Guards were obliged to offer what they considered to be a generous bounty. Posters were put up in every town and village designed to attract the notice of any impressionable farm hand or labourer.

> WANTED. Brisk lads, light and straight, and by no means gummy; not under 5 feet 6 inches . . . Liberal Bounty, good uniforms, generous pay. . . .

Of those who responded, a few were young farm boys barely out of their teens, but apart from these lads, the poster's promises attracted only the desperately impoverished and the criminal element of the industrial towns. It was perhaps fortunate that, in addition to those recruited in Britain, there existed a rich source of manpower in the villages and country areas of Ireland. William Grattan wrote with pride of his countrymen's characteristics: "Give him his pipe of tobacco and he will march for two days without food and without grumbling; give him in addition a little spirits and biscuit and he will work for a week. . . ." The Irish peasant was also, with few exceptions, illiterate, violent and addicted to drink. But he was also undeniably courageous and hardy – qualities to be welcomed in any army. The tavern, whether in Ireland or England, was looked upon as a profitable area for enlistment by the recruiting party where the smart green uniform and dashing appearance of a sergeant in the 95th so impressed a young shepherd from Dorset that, although a serving member of the Militia and thereby absolved from duty overseas, John Harris nevertheless felt an overwhelming urge to become a Rifleman himself.

Harris's choice of regiment was fortunate as far as the uniform was concerned, for, apart from that worn by the Rifles, the uniform of the early 19th Century soldier was as uncomfortable as it was impracticable. Uniforms varied with the regiment, with the officer obliged to purchase his own without reimbursement.

Usually the soldier wore a black stovepipe shako covered with heel-ball and polished like a mirror. A scarlet jacket on the shoulders of which were sewn two wings of cloth designed to retain the pipe-clayed crossbelts was closely fitted with bright shining buttons and, to complete the uniform, one-piece overall trousers of white cloth usually worn outside the black leather gaiters. A box of black lacquered canvas stiffened with wood and equipped with leather shoulder straps served as a knapsack which often cut into the spine and gave rise to an injury known as 'pack palsy'. An uncomfortable four-inch band of stiff varnished leather worn around the neck completed the uniform which, together with the weight of a rain-soaked blanket folded to the square of his knapsack, must have seemed an abomination to all but the hardiest of men.

Although spared the more uncomfortable items of an infantryman's uniform, John Harris nevertheless resented the burden he had to carry. "Altogether the quantity of things I had on my shoulders was enough and more than enough for my wants," he complained. "Sufficient indeed to sink a little fellow of five feet seven inches into the earth."

Commented John Cooper of the Fusiliers who similarly suffered: 'The government should have sent us new backbones to bear the extra weight."

On the other hand the French infantryman seems to have been far more sensibly attired. "Broad-toed shoes studded with nails, wide trousers of Spanish brown, a hairy knapsack, a broad leather-topped cap, decorated with a ball, and shining scales, and fronted by a brazen eagle, with extended wings," recorded Captain Cooke of the 43rd. "In action they usually appeared in light grey greatcoats, decorated with red or green worsted epaulettes, belts outside, without any breastplates, with short sleeves, slashed at the cuff, to enable them to handle their arms, and prime and load with facility. Their flints were excellent, but the powder of their cartridges coarse; that of the British infantry was remarkably fine, but their flints were indifferent."

Having taken the oath, the recruit in the British army found himself faced with a way of life which, although severe, was little worse than that of the ordinary labourer. Food consisted of a monotonous daily fare of ¾ lb of beef bone and 1½ lb of bread or biscuit. From this he prepared his two meals of the day, usually boiled as a broth or stew thickened with crumbs from his biscuit. In all likelihood it was an inadequate ration, borne out by Sergeant Cooper's remark: "When a man entered upon a soldier's life, he should have parted with half his stomach." Even the doubtful comfort of marriage was denied most recruits for only six women in a Company of 100 men were accepted on the ration strength and allowed to accompany their husbands overseas. "They are, of course, perfectly sure of getting as many husbands as they may choose," commented George Gleig. "Indeed, most bereaved widows married again, sometimes within hours of their loss, to prevent being sent home."

The punishment for serious misdemeanours could be harsh. Private William Lawrence of the 40th Regiment was court-martialled and sentenced to 400 strokes of the cat-o'-nine-tails for absenting himself from guard duty. "I felt ten times worse on hearing this sentence than I ever did on entering any battlefield," wrote Lawrence many years later. "In fact if I had been sentenced to be shot, I could not have been in more despair."

At a battalion parade he was stripped to the waist and tied to a triangle of halberds. The Colonel then gave the order for the regimental drummers to begin the flogging, but after he had received a third of his sentence without crying out, although the blood ran down his legs, the Colonel ordered the Sergeant to "cut the sulky rascal down", and Private Lawrence, who was to bear the scars on his back for the rest of his life, was escorted to the hospital. Lawrence had been fortunate, for there were few commanding officers as compassionate as the Colonel of the 40th Regiment. In some instances half the sentence was carried out and only completed when the offender's back had healed.

Curiously, such punitive measures were accepted philosophically by most soldiers as being necessary to maintain discipline. "I detest the sight of the lash," wrote Benjamin Harris of the 95th, "but I am convinced the British army can never go on without it." "Without it," admitted James Anton, "the good must be left to the mercy of the worthless." Even William Lawrence admitted that in all probability the punishment he had received had prevented him from committing crimes which might well have brought him a more severe sentence.

Viewed from this politically correct age, it seems astonishing that a military life could attract even the most desperate of characters. Certainly the pay, often months in arrears, was not to be equated with a civilian job bringing in a daily or weekly wage. Lawrence received just thirteen pence per diem subject to deductions, and, while a junior officer's pay was considerably more, many Ensigns found that a private income of at least £75 per annum was necessary to enjoy even a basic subsistence. George Bell soon discovered that his five shillings a day was scarcely enough to cover his needs and he came to rely upon the services of an agent from whom he could draw money against promissory notes deposited from home.

With the appointment of Frederick Duke of York in 1795 as Commander-in-Chief considerable improvements in the welfare of the rank and file were introduced. Greatcoats became standard issue, hospital care and schools were established with the laudable objective of teaching the private soldier and his siblings to read and write. Little was done to improve the soldier's weaponry, however, which had hardly changed since the reign of Charles II. The basic infantry weapon was still a smooth-bore muzzle-loading flintlock having a calibre of 0.75 inch and weighing almost 12 lbs. This musket, known as "Brown Bess", was 42 inches long and fitted with a removable bayonet 16 inches long, which, however, was seldom used. Loading the musket was a complicated business opened by the soldier biting off the end of a cartridge containing both ball and powder – an action which in battle often gave the soldier a raging thirst. The black powder contents were then poured down the barrel, the cartridge reversed and together with the lead ball rammed home with the paper wadding by means of a ramrod, the priming pan being filled separately. Rates of fire were consequently low – no more than two to three rounds per minute – but, despite these drawbacks, the British infantryman, because of his calm and steady behaviour under battle conditions, could boast of a fire power in controlled volleys that rapidly became the most destructive in Europe.

By the time of the Napoleonic Wars specialist companies of elite troops had been created under the able direction of Sir John Moore at Shorncliffe. In 1803 the 95th and 60th were merged to form the Rifle Brigade and the nucleus of one of the most famous divisions in Wellington's army. Unlike the Line regiments, the 'Green Jackets' were armed with the Baker rifle, another muzzle-loader but with a rifled barrel which gave it much greater accuracy and, in the hands of a marksman, was lethal at ranges of 200 yards or more. In the battles to come against the French in Spain and Portugal, Sir Arthur Wellesley and his Generals were to perfect a tactical system employing these riflemen as skirmishers which, together with the fire power of the Line regiments, would succeed in neutralizing a method of attack which for almost a decade had enabled French columns to smash through enemy defences with consummate ease.

The British regiments with their esprit de corps, were to prove themselves, as Napier described them, "astonishing infantry".

Chapter 2

THE BATTLE FOR VIMIERO

General Delaborde's withdrawal had left the road to Lisbon open, but, although British casualties had been light, Wellesley was reluctant to follow up his success. He lacked the necessary cavalry for pursuit and he laboured under the disadvantage of having to safeguard his rear against the threat of Loison's column descending from the hills. In the event, his dilemma was resolved when on 18 August a despatch was received at his headquarters reporting the presence of General Anstruther with two brigades and a quantity of supplies off the coast near Peniche. All thought of pursuing Delaborde was abandoned and orders were at once given for a march on the nearby village of Vimiero with the intention of protecting Anstruther's disembarkation.

As he was to demonstrate on numerous occasions, Wellesley was adept at selecting a defensive position which afforded him a tactical advantage over his opponent. The area he now chose to occupy was just such a one, being a chain of hills extending westward to the sea. The village of Vimiero lay in a valley at the eastward end of the ridge with steep rugged gradients to the south and a fine range of hills to the west. In front of the village a plateau studded with chestnut and olive trees through which the Maceira River followed a twisting path presented a difficulty to the French, dominated as it was by the heights which overlooked the river on either side.

Wellesley may have been confident in his ability to beat the French, a view shared by his Staff and the troops under their command, but this assurance did not extend to the Horse Guards in London. Whitehall had yet to be convinced that Wellesley's Indian experience was sufficient to justify a command in a European theatre of war and with the arrival of Anstruther and his 4,000 troops came orders which ended his period of service as Commander of the expedition.

The choice of leader for this Iberian adventure had been the subject of much soul-searching among the authorities in Whitehall. Sir John Moore

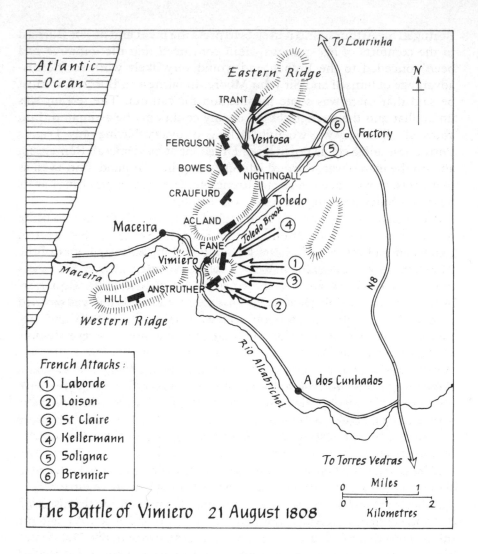

The Battle of Vimiero   21 August 1808

French Attacks:
1. Laborde
2. Loison
3. St Claire
4. Kellermann
5. Solignac
6. Brennier

certainly had the support of the Duke of York, but Moore's opposition to the Government and his reputation as a trouble-maker had not endeared him to those in power and Canning had little difficulty in persuading the Horse Guards to appoint two superannuated Generals over both Moore and Wellesley – Sir Hew Dalrymple, Governor of Gibraltar, and the amiable but incompetent Sir Harry Burrard.

Now that a considerable Reserve was available to strengthen the expeditionary force, Wellesley had high hopes of resuming his advance on Lisbon, but when he argued the case aboard the frigate he found Burrard vehemently opposed to any immediate progress pending the arrival of Sir John Moore whose troops were even then off the coast of northern

14

Portugal. Sir Arthur found it useless to press the point and he left Burrard to the comforts of his spacious cabin convinced that the initiative had been conceded to the French and would very likely work to the disadvantage of himself and Sir John Moore. In fairness to Burrard, it must be said that there was some justification for caution. The terrain was unfamiliar and the strength of the enemy could only be estimated, but, above all, Wellesley was woefully lacking in cavalry, having only Trant's Portuguese and a single regiment of Dragoons at his disposal. Remaining aboard the man o'war, Burrard left Sir Arthur in command, but, even as that decision was taken, a strong French force with General Junot at its head was hurrying along the road from Lisbon.

A German serving with the 20th Light Dragoons was the first to bring news concerning movement of the French. Sergeant Norberton Landsheit had returned in haste from a patrol in the early hours of the 21st with a positive sighting of Junot's columns advancing from the direction of Torres Vedras and was shown at once to Wellesley's headquarters near the village of Vimiero. On entering the room Landsheit was amused to find the General seated upon a table swinging his legs to and fro, "seemingly for all the world as a man upon whose mind not the shadow of doubt rested".

After being closely questioned on what he had seen, the German Dragoon rejoined his comrades, but not before he heard Sir Arthur give his orders "in a calm cheerful voice". "Now gentlemen, go to your stations, but let there be no noise made – no sounding of bugles or beating of drums. Get your men quickly under arms and desire all outposts to be on the alert."

Shortly after 8.00am a moving cloud of dust along the Lourinha road signalled the approach of the enemy to the waiting British infantry which, standing two ranks deep, betrayed few signs of apprehension or misgiving as to the outcome of this imminent clash with the French. "I felt my mind waver," confessed 18-year-old Thomas Pococke of the 71st, "such a breathless sensation came over me. The silence was appalling. I looked along the line – it was enough to assure me. The steady determined scowl of my companions assured my heart, and gave me determination."

Young Benjamin Harris was also impressed by the resolute features of his comrades. The sun glinting from the musket barrels, the regimental colours streaming in the breeze and the reassuring presence of the cannon sited on a piece of rising ground contributed to a feeling of invincibility that Harris accepted without reservation.

From his vantage point on a hill Wellesley quickly established the likely pattern of Junot's attack and moved his brigades to cover his weakest points before the French could test their strength. Because of the nature of the ground, only a part of the enemy's three columns was visible to the redcoats and with mounting excitement Harris watched the figures in white linen frock coats and light blue trousers picking their way up the slope towards him, "the brass eagle on the front of their shakos sparkling in the sun".

The artillerymen serving the "squat venomous looking cannon" which had so impressed the young rifleman went through the customary drill for loading shot. The range of these weapons, depending on whether roundshot or grape was being used, was about 800 yards. Grapeshot, being a concentration of musket balls, tended to spread out from the cannon's mouth, but, whatever the charge, since there existed no method for absorbing the gun's recoil, the piece had to be levered into position after each round. Muzzle-loading was an operation which could not be hurried, for if the barrel had not been adequately swabbed out to extinguish every last particle of burnt powder or smouldering wadding there was a grave danger of a premature explosion should a fresh charge be rammed home.

Methodically, and with an efficiency born of long practice, the artillerymen completed the drill for loading and stood by with the potfire until the enemy should come within range. Confident that his dense columns would overwhelm the double British line, Junot advanced against Wellesley's centre with four battalions in close order, preceded by a screen of voltigeurs. "The French were very saucy, and firing upon us uncommon sharp," remarked Benjamin Harris. "They greatly outnumbered us, and shewed so much ambition that they appeared inclined to drive us off the face of the earth."

To cries of "Vive l'Empereur!" and with drums beating a sharp tattoo, the massed battalions moved steadily towards an isolated hill south of the village where an extended line of Riflemen and the brigades of Anstruther and Fane stood with ordered arms silently watching their approach. As the French drew near, their columns began to hurry covered by the fire of seven light field guns. An 18-year-old's baptism of fire was about to begin. "I myself was very soon hotly engaged, loading and firing away, enveloped in the smoke I created, and the cloud which hung about me from the continued fire of my comrades," remembered Harris, "that I could see nothing for a few minutes but the red flash of my own piece amongst the white vapour clinging to my very clothes."

The thin screen of British skirmishers could not hope to stem the advancing tide of French infantry and as the white-coated figures emerged wraithlike from the drifting clouds of powder smoke the Riflemen of the 95th were forced to give ground.

Although hard-pressed, Harris nevertheless found time to admire the martial bearing of the French Grenadiers, noting "their red shoulder knots and tremendous moustaches". The Riflemen retiring in the face of a rain of musket balls were still able to make their presence felt and whenever a Frenchman was struck down "the men on each side of me," reported Harris, "would call out, "There goes another of Boney's invincibles!" Such was the growing pressure on the 95th, however, that Anstruther found it necessary to order several companies of the 40th and 71st to cover the skirmishers as they retired. On an adjacent hill the 36th and 40th Regiments of Foot remained passively awaiting the approach of the Grenadiers. Then, when the enemy was less than a hundred yards from the double line of redcoats, the quiet calm was shattered in a blaze of musketry that exploded in flame and smoke along its entire length. The nine hundred muskets and the men vanished in a pall of white smoke which hung in the air and reduced visibility to less than fifty yards. The French officers could see nothing of their adversaries' deployment and as Junot's troops neared the summit roundshot and grape from the batteries on the hill tore bloody swathes through the tightly packed ranks. Shells filled with musket balls and scraps of metal burst above their heads, timed from a short fuse.

Although this new weapon invented by Major Shrapnel caused many casualties, it was roundshot which did most to spread terror and confusion among the raw French conscripts. These heavy balls of iron, rising from their initial point of contact, ricocheted across the ground for up to half a mile, wreaking a dreadful slaughter in their passage.

Junot's troops reeled beneath the weight of artillery and musket fire and, from the swirling clouds of smoke, cries and screams arose on every side. Years later Rifleman Harris noted: "Methinks I can hear at this moment the clatter of the Frenchmen's accoutrements, when they turned in an instant to the right about, and went off as hard as men could run for it." The rumble of artillery carried plainly to the transports moving slowly along the coast towards Peniche. Among the men lining the deck a 19-year-old Irishman, Ensign Robert Blakeney, heard the noise of battle and "felt a compelling urge to join the fray".

By noon Wellesley's victory was almost complete. The leading files of Brennier's brigade had been annihilated and when an unbroken line of redcoats emerged from the fog of battle with bayonets glittering in the sun it was a sight to chill the blood of the bravest young Frenchman. The gun crews of three teams abandoned in the wake of the retreating French infantry cut the horses' traces and galloped hastily away leaving the cannon to the redcoats. A half mile away, Junot, desperate to retrieve the situation, launched 2,000 of his elite Guards against the village, whose defenders were soon hard pressed. One company of the 50th occupied the churchyard and another held some houses lining the road along which the French were advancing. For a time both were in danger of being overwhelmed, but, with the arrival of the 43rd and a battery of

Horse Artillery from the northern ridge, Kellerman's Grenadiers were thrown back in a rare bayonet charge so vigorous that the bodies of a sergeant of the 43rd and a Grenadier were afterwards discovered lying in a narrow lane still grasping their bayonets. The long three-sided blades had been driven through each body from breast to backbone. It was a sight so rare that Harris was led to remark, "Our Riflemen looked at these bodies with much curiosity, and remarked the circumstance as well as myself."

Four separate French attacks had now been broken, thirteen cannon taken and upwards of 2,000 casualties inflicted on Junot's troops, in addition to the prisoners, which included a General captured by a corporal of the 71st. The battle had raged for three hours and everywhere the French were in retreat. The way was open to Wellesley's redcoats to the gates of Lisbon, but it was not to be.

Sir Arthur, knowing that the day was his, nudged his horse to where Sir Harry Burrard stood watching the retreating French army. Doffing his low-crowned cocked hat, Wellesley observed, "Sir Harry, now is the time to advance. The French are completely beaten, we have a large body of troops who have not yet been in action. We can be in Lisbon in three days."

Burrard, however, was having none of it. In keeping with his cautious nature he was convinced that Junot's reserves were far from being exhausted and that his cavalry was greatly superior to Sir Arthur Wellesley's. Despite argument to the contrary, the elderly General would not be moved and an irate Wellesley pulled his horse away with a contemptuous aside to his aide-de-camp: "Well then, you may think about dinner for there's nothing for us soldiers to do but to go and shoot red-legged partridges!"

By early afternoon the entire French army, gathering their shattered divisions together, had retired from the field.

Captain Ross-Lewin of the 32nd, at his post to the rear of the village, had seen little of the fighting, but as he walked over that part of the ground where the action had been most severe, he was made painfully aware of the dreadful consequences. Outside the church now serving as a dressing station, he found "a large wooden dish filled with hands that had just been amputated", whilst between the tables piles of severed limbs lay strewn about to sicken the senses of those awaiting treatment. Ross-Lewin found it hard to accept that the mutilated figures he saw propped up against the wall or lying on blood-soaked straw had earlier that morning "rushed to the combat, full of ardour and enthusiasm, and now they were stretched, pale, bloody and mangled, on the cold flags, some writhing in agony, others fainting with loss of blood, and the spirits of many poor fellows among them making a last struggle to depart from their mutilated tenements."

Further up the hill a great many of the 43rd, who had that morning passed by Ross-Lewin with bands playing and regimental colours streaming in the wind, now lay motionless among the vines. Their new uniforms and accoutrements were so clean and bright that to the Captain "they more resembled men resting after a parade rather than corpses on a hillside".

As the light faded, others with a more sinister interest in the fallen arrived to inspect the battlefield. At Montevideo Private Thomas Plunket had thought nothing of vultures settling upon the dead, but now, for the first time, he witnessed a scene which was to become all too familiar in the Peninsula. With a callous savagery which reminded Plunket of those birds of prey, Portuguese peasants searched the corpses for anything of value.

"When light failed them, they kindled a great fire and remained around it all night, shouting like as many savages," noted the Rifleman. "My sickened fancy felt the same as if it were witnessing a feast of cannibals."

The majority of Plunket's comrades, exhausted by the day's events, bivouacked for the night, untroubled by such ghoulish behaviour.

"Although the air was cold, and our situation comfortless," wrote Captain John Patterson of the 50th, "yet, from extreme fatigue, we rested perhaps more soundly than the pampered alderman on his downy couch."

The next day saw the arrival of Sir Hew Dalrymple whose last experience of battle had been as long ago as 1793 and he was visibly moved by the sight of endless rows of carts laden with the wounded suffering greatly under a fierce August sun. After conferring with Burrard, Dalrymple invited Wellesley to offer an opinion on future tactics. Sir Arthur immediately renewed his plea to be allowed to continue the advance on Lisbon. His request was just as firmly rejected and, commented Adam Neale, a physician with the army, "Every eye seemed to express regret as the gallant Sir Arthur Wellesley rode along the ranks, and publicly resigned the command of his victorious troops to the Lieutenant-Governor of Gibraltar."

Meanwhile a despairing Junot, knowing that he could no longer remain in Portugal now that the British were there in strength, sought the most favourable terms for his beaten army. Before nightfall General Kellerman had presented a proposal to a delighted Sir Hew who could have wished for nothing better than an end to the campaign without further bloodshed and which promised to free Lisbon from the French and give Britain a substantial footing in the Peninsula. At the talks, which afterwards became infamous as the Convention of Cintra, Junot agreed to surrender his magazines, stores, and artillery, providing his men were allowed to return to France. Because Junot had no ships, Dalrymple agreed that the Royal Navy should convey his troops, together with their small arms, baggage, personal effects and regimental accessories, to any French port between Rochefort and L'Orient.

"The Portuguese foamed with rage," commented an indignant Schaumann, "and rightly so. The stupidest owl in the army saw how badly Sir Hew Dalrymple had allowed himself to be diddled by the French Generals."

The far-reaching consequences of returning 25,000 experienced soldiers to Bonaparte's service was not lost upon an astonished William Warre. "Disastrous," he wrote, "for I never can imagine that the struggle is more than begun."

The one notable dissenting voice was that of Wellesley himself who only added his signature to the document at the express wish of Sir Hew Dalrymple.

The clause allowing the French to take whatever personal effects they considered desirable was interpreted by many of Junot's soldiers in the widest possible sense. Their baggage on inspection at the quayside disgorged all manner of loot, including church plate, jewels and expensive dresses. General Jean Androche Junot was not above sharing in the plunder including a mediaeval Bible from the Royal Library for which he eventually received 85.000 francs. Commented Doctor Neale in his memoirs: "You will allow that this piece of Gallic finesse has rarely been surpassed."

The evacuation began on 13 September, when, with bands playing, the French marched through the streets to the harbour and the British transports anchored there. A hostile crowd lined the route, but as the soldiers were escorted by British troops the furious citizens of Lisbon could only hurl abuse, while the bemused British officers did their best to explain to their Portuguese friends that the foolishness which allowed a beaten foe to depart with all its weapons intact was not of their making. Could they have foreseen that within a few short months sixteen of those departing French battalions would play a prominent part in the pursuit of a demoralized British army across Spain to Corunna they too would have shed tears of rage.

When the terms of the treaty became known in England, newspapers carried the official announcement enclosed in a black border, while London magazines lampooned the three Generals in fanciful cartoons. George Canning, the Foreign Secretary, announced with telling sarcasm that from this day, "humiliation" should be spelt with a "Hew". A parliamentary enquiry was convened and the three Generals were summoned to attend a Court Martial from which only Wellesley emerged without a stain on his character.

Now that the three had been removed from the theatre of operations, Sir John Moore, who had landed three days after the battle of Vimiero, remained as the only candidate for overall command of the expeditionary force. Despite some opposition from Lord Castlereagh and Canning, Moore, with an army already experienced in battle, confidently awaited orders from the Horse Guards confirming his appointment and authorizing him to support the Spanish armies against the French with the ultimate aim of restoring independence to the whole of the Iberian Peninsula.

Chapter 3

'FOR THIS COUNTRY WE CAN DO NOTHING'

On 6 October 1808 a Royal Navy frigate dropped anchor in the Tagus Roads and the anticipated despatch from the Secretary of State for War confirming Sir John Moore's appointment as Commander-in-Chief of the British expeditionary force was taken to the General's headquarters with instructions for him to collaborate with the Spanish Generals Blake and Castanos.

News of the Spanish people's spirited resistance to Bonaparte had encouraged the Cabinet to throw the whole weight of Britain's military resources into the north of the country where the French occupied only a relatively small area in the north-east. The fate of Europe was very much in the mind of the Minister when he sanctioned Britain's intervention in Spain, but parliament had the full support of the public who were convinced that 30,000 British troops fighting at the side of the gallant Spaniards would be more than a match for the 60,000 Frenchmen who remained behind the Ebro in Navarre.

A commissary of the King's German Legion, however, had serious doubts about Spanish co-operation with the British after several conversations with the tradesmen of Lisbon. Almost every Portuguese with whom Schaumann came into contact told him: "Do not trust the Spaniards and their promises; for all they tell you about ample stores and large armies are lies. . . . if things go wrong, they will vanish in a twinkling . . . and leave you to your fate in the heart of Spain, surrounded by your enemies, and exposed to every possible privation." It was advice which, unhappily for Moore, was to prove remarkably accurate in the months ahead.

News that they were shortly to cross the border and march to the aid of the Spanish armies in their fight against the French invader was welcomed by the troops, many of whom were becoming indifferent to the attractions of Lisbon.

"The streets were narrow and winding," complained Lawrence, "and indeed, after the French had left, the whole city was in a most desperate state."

Thomas Pococke was even more forthright in his criticism of the Portuguese capital. In his memoirs he pointed out that "The town is a dunghill from end to end."

Certainly the streets, when baking under a fierce summer sun, presented a potent health hazard, for every kind of waste was emptied from the windows and balconies of the lofty houses to fall "like the bursting of water spouts", as a captain of the 43rd graphically described night soils falling into the street below. "It is true, the warning note of 'Guarda!' is sometimes given," he admitted, "but alas! before you are aware from what quarter the evil threatens, it is upon you."

In the summer months swarms of flies were an ever-present torment to the promenader, for the ordure often lay rotting on the cobbles for weeks until washed away by a rainstorm or was scavenged by the packs of wild dogs which roamed the streets.

Fever at this time of the year was endemic and Captain Jonathan Leach, confined to a sick bed for many weeks, began to think it probable that he would find an early grave in Lisbon rather than on some future battlefield.

Following their success at Vimiero, British redcoats had been greeted everywhere as liberators and a generous hospitality was the reward of all who sought it. These friendly overtures cooled appreciably, however, when scenes of drunken brawling became an everyday occurrence in the streets and coffee houses of the Portuguese capital.

Loutish behaviour was not confined to scuffles in the street, for the customs and religious observance of the people became targets for ribald comments even by Irish Catholics who, apart from making the sign of the Cross, seemed to have shown little concern for religious matters. At Portalegre a wardrobe of priestly garments was discovered in an Ensign's billet. The find prompted a number of junior officers, whose high spirits were perhaps fuelled by an excess of wine, to march through the street suitably robed bearing candles held aloft, their gibberish chanting constantly interrupted by peals of youthful laughter. Fortunately few townsfolk were abroad at that hour, but any protest on their behalf would have been to no avail, for, like most Englishmen of their generation, those junior officers shared a common belief that swarthy foreigners were an inferior breed. It was an attitude of mind that Auguste Schaumann found difficult to understand. "The English are admired . . . but they cannot make themselves beloved," he wrote. "They will not bend good humour to the custom of other nations . . . nor will they condescend to smooth the harmless self love of friendly foreigners."

Certainly, with the notable exception of the Irish, most of Moore's army considered the population to be priest-ridden. Corporal John Cooper, one of few men in the regiment who understood Portuguese, had his own opinion of the Catholic clergy confirmed as he sat conversing with his host. There came a rap at the door and a "corpulent figure, slipshod and clad in a coarse grey robe loosely tied with a rope girdle" entered the room. After a few words, the visitor gave a blessing and with a suspicious glance at the Fusilier, left with a basket of provisions given him by the patron's wife. Cooper asked his host, "What sort of man was the padre?" "*Elle gosto muleses mouto!*" (He likes the women much) came the reply.

Sir John Moore prepared for the long march into Spain with his customary thoroughness. He had already ruled out the north as being the principal theatre of operations for that would have entailed a coastal voyage to Corunna or Vigo in the teeth of the autumn gales. After conferring with his Staff, Moore decided to ignore the instructions from Whitehall in favour of operations much further south in the region of Almeida and Ciudad Rodrigo, and, after drawing up a strategical plan, he issued a general order for the expeditionary force to be held in readiness for a march on Salamanca.

The army was to be split into three columns with the first taking a route due north to Coimbra on the Mondego, and then north-east to Almeida, the second leaving Lisbon on a path parallel to the Tagus before turning north through Abrantes, Castello Branco and Guarda, while the third was to proceed by way of Elvas and Alcantara.

To enhance Moore's prospect of success, Parliament had agreed to strengthen his army with an additional 12,000 troops under the command of Sir David Baird who was expected to disembark at Corunna on 19 October with orders to rendezvous with Moore at Valladolid.

The march towards the Spanish border began on 11 October 1808, accompanied by the rattle of kettle drums and the shrill notes of the fife. Sir John Moore, having sent his artillery on a long detour via Badajoz in the mistaken belief that the roads between Lisbon and Almeida were unsuitable for heavy wheeled ordnance, left Lisbon on the 27th with his Staff in the wake of the second column marching to Abrantes.

Meanwhile, Baird's corps had reached Corunna several days earlier than planned, but with a depleted cavalry strength, for, due to an administrative blunder, Lord Paget's three brigades had not sailed until the beginning of November. In that flotilla of thirty-five ships which left Falmouth on the 2nd was the 300-ton transporter *Rodney*, fitted out to accommodate 40 men and 36 horses. It proved to be an uncomfortable week's sailing for Captain Alexander Gordon and his troop of the 15th

Hussars. The pens constructed for the horses left only the barest living space for the men and, to add to their misery, the woefully small vessel pitched and rolled in the Atlantic swell to such an extent that almost everyone was wretchedly seasick.

Gordon, who, as senior officer, had first choice of accommodation, discovered his quarters to be so unpleasant that he was obliged to berth with his fellow officers in the one cabin "free from the poisonous smell of bilge water".

While the ships of that Corunna-bound convoy made little headway in the Bay of Biscay, Moore's troops, with the pleasant scenery of the Tagus Valley to compensate for the fatigue of marching, set off on the first stage of the journey to Abrantes. Olive groves and fig trees were plentiful and the hedges fringing the rough country tracks were thick with blackberries, much to the delight of the children who, happily gathering wild fruit and flowers, were oblivious of each passing mile that brought them closer to the Spanish border.

A despatch which reached Sir John during the early period of the march was both puzzling and disconcerting. Sir David Baird had been prevented from disembarking at Corunna, pending permission from the Supreme Junta in Madrid. The few commissariat officers who were allowed ashore discovered that, far from being welcomed as brothers in arms, the Spaniards resented their presence and only by the use of the most blatant flattery was it possible for Q.M.S William Surtees to obtain the minimum number of mules and wagons necessary for Baird's advance on Valladolid.

This delay at Corunna cost Baird two precious weeks and it was not until 28 October that his Corps was able to begin its march towards the rendezvous with Moore. By then the winter rains, which threatened to turn the atrocious roads into mud slides, had begun in earnest.

Now that Abrantes and the Tagus Valley were behind them, Moore's troops discovered that the autumn tints of brown and gold were giving way to the less attractive prospect of stretches of granite-strewn heath. The bright masses of cumulus were gradually yielding to a leaden sky and the beginning of November saw the long winding columns trudging miserably along mountain tracks through a chilling drizzle which soaked everyone to the skin.

Gazing around during one of the rare bright intervals, Captain Boothby marvelled at the extensive view afforded him of a vast wooded vale whose distant hills were marked by the sparkling lines of numerous waterfalls. Later, after climbing higher, he became enveloped in cloud and could see nothing beyond a circle of three or four yards. The stony path over which he rode was difficult to follow in the swirling mist and the restricted area, covered as it was with burnt patches of heather, led Boothby to imagine

25

that he was "travelling on the bare outside of the world bordered by the chaotic beginning of things".

Charles Boothby was not the only officer to appreciate the grandeur of the mountain scenery. "Everything has the most wild and romantic appearance," wrote Lieutenant Peter Hawker to a friend, "and amidst the awful roar of surrounding cascades, you may conceive yourself deserted by every earthly creature."

While Moore's columns pursued a winding path through the mountains, 200 miles to the north-east upwards of 200,000 French troops were crossing the Pyrenees in preparation for a major offensive against Spain. On 5 November Napoleon rode into the French camp to take charge of operations in central and southern Spain, leaving Soult to take care of the Spanish forces in the north.

Blissfully unconscious of this grave new threat, the British troops made reasonable progress in spite of the abominable roads pitted with ruts flooded by the heavy rains. By 8 November. Generals Beresford and Fane had reached the frontier fortress of Almeida where their brigades joined that of Anstruther before crossing the border at Ciudad Rodrigo. The main column led by Moore arrived a few days later, but, for both early and later arrivals, the change in environment was immediately noticeable in the cleaner houses and improved appearance of the villagers.

Cooke was astonished by the difference in appearance between the Portuguese and Spaniards: "that it could be possible for people living so near to one another to be so dissimilar in complexion, costume, and manners," he wrote, "even when inhabiting respectively the banks of a narrow stream."

The pretty faces and dark eyes of the young women had a predictable effect upon the redcoats, but when they attempted to fraternize, employing a number of stratagems to overcome the handicap of language, they experienced a marked lack of success.

"The soldiers used a most extraordinary dialect compounded of Irish, Gaelic, and the mother tongue, interloaded with a goodly supply of oaths," recalled Captain Patterson. "As to signs and gestures, they were as varied as the movements of a posture master."

It was all in vain. The villagers, wrapped in the ubiquitous brown blanket, lounged against the stone-walled cottages and regarded the redcoats with studied indifference.

While Moore's columns maintained a slow but purposeful advance towards Salamanca, Napoleon, determined to put an end to both Spanish and Portuguese defiance, launched a massive offensive which smashed through Spanish opposition with ease. Soult occupied Bayonne after slaughtering 2,500 of its defenders, Lefebvre captured Valladolid and Victor fell upon Blake at Espinosa where the panic-stricken

Spaniards were routed with heavy loss. As yet unaware of these reverses, Sir John Moore continued along the route which would take him towards Baird and his column marching from Corunna. At length the welcome sight of the church spires and domed roofs of Salamanca quickened the pace of his weary footsore soldiers and on 13 November the vanguard rode across the ancient stone bridge into the city.

It was then that the General received his first intimation of just how grave the military situation had become. Napoleon had occupied Burgos, Valladolid had been abandoned by the Spaniards and it appeared that Moore's planned rendezvous with Baird was in jeopardy. Worsening weather conditions had slowed Baird's progress to such an extent that in the three weeks since leaving Corunna he had advanced no further than Astorga.

In that town Captain Alexander Gordon saw units of the Spanish army for the first time when 2,000 men of General Romana's command entered the town. The soldiers, half of whom seemed to be ill-armed peasants, marched in double quick time to the beat of a drummer who headed each regiment, but their wretched appearance did little to impress the Hussar officer with any reasonable opinion of their military skills.

William Surtees, who was also a witness, was quick to endorse Gordon's opinion of the Spanish regiments: "in their best days . . . more like an armed mob than regularly organized soldiers," he wrote.

There was still no positive intelligence regarding the movement of the French, but there was no doubt in Moore's mind that the enemy could not be far from Salamanca. Just how close Charles Boothby learned from a frightened Spaniard who admitted to conducting a squadron of thirty dragoons to a village just a few miles distant.

Most illuminating were the papers in the guide's possession: a requisition for 50,000 rations of bread and 10,000 of forage, together with a bulletin from Marshal Bessières announcing the defeat of the Spanish General Castanos at Tudela. The French dragoons, the peasant told Boothby, were seeking information and upon learning that Moore had 24,000 troops in Salamanca, had told him, "that it was nothing. They had 40,000 and would soon settle accounts with the English."

From this and other reports it was clear to Moore that he must retire upon Ciudad Rodrigo before the three widely separated columns were overwhelmed. He had no artillery and, without the support of the armies of Blake and Belvedere, any further advance would only court disaster.

A disillusioned Staff officer did not hesitate to blame the Spaniards for the predicament the expeditionary force now found itself. Wrote Captain William Warre to his father, "For this country we can do nothing. They will do nothing for themselves. Never has a nation been more infamously deceived than the English about this country."

As Moore prepared to leave Salamanca Napoleon's cavalry squadrons were already pursuing the remnants of Castanos's broken regiments along the road to Madrid, where the city's hastily formed defences were quickly overcome by the Emperor's Polish Lancers. Madrid surrendered on 4 December and, although news of its fall dismayed Moore, it made little difference to his revised plans. Later intelligence indicated that the French were as yet uncertain of the whereabouts of the British but assumed that they were retiring from Salamanca. They themselves were moving south towards Andalusia.

This French move south lifted the immediate threat to Moore's columns and presented him with an opportunity for striking north-east towards the Douro and harassing the enemy's lines of communication. It would be a calculated risk, for Moore was unaware of the strength of enemy opposition, but, nevertheless, as he made preparations to vacate Salamanca, he was reasonably optimistic that, strengthened by Baird's column, he would be able to draw the enemy away from the Spaniards and give their armies a vital breathing space. If the venture failed, Moore would have to run for the sea and he was astute enough to ensure that sufficient stores were collected along the route to Corunna and stock-piled in the towns of Benevente, Astorga and Lugo.

On 12 and 13 December, almost a month after Moore's troops had entered the city, an unfamiliar noise brought the curious to their doors and windows. The cobbled streets and squares echoed to the rumble of bullock carts and the tramp of boots as the departing redcoats streamed away, with the women and children bringing up the rear. Finally, all that marked their progress was a rising cloud of dust as the troops and baggage train passed into the great plain of Castile.

The first snow of winter was drifting down from a leaden sky when Sir John Moore was put in possession of information which, if correct, would have a vital bearing on his future plans. An intercepted despatch from the French General Berthier to Marshal Soult – the courier had been murdered near Segovia – was purchased from a peasant for 20 Spanish dollars. It indicated that, should Moore's present line of march be continued, he would find both Junot and Mortier at Burgos, having Soult on his left flank and Napoleon's Army of Madrid closing rapidly on his rear. The captured documents also revealed that Soult, at the head of a relatively weak force, was set to cross the British line of march less than 80 miles distant. It seemed that here was an opportunity for Moore to fall upon Soult and by defeating him grant the Spanish General Romana time to reorganize his army in Galicia and afford Moore's own troops an easier passage to the coast than might otherwise be the case.

Moore urged his column along the altered line of march in the teeth of a biting wind at such a pace that, after a few miles, many of his redcoats were reeling with exhaustion. Nevertheless, with every prospect of a fight with Soult, most disregarded the weight of their packs and the numbness of their frozen limbs, and morale remained high.

Five days before Christmas Baird and Moore met at Margay and the Light Brigade, together with Paget's cavalry, were ordered ahead of the main body to reconnoitre the approach to Sahagun where enemy patrols were known to be active.

It was a march made difficult for the Hussars by the state of the frost-bound roads. The horses, unsure of their footing, had to be led forward by troopers whose oaths were occasionally punctuated by the clatter of a stumbling horse and its luckless rider.

Sahagun was reached on the morning of 21 December as a thin veil of mist lifted to disclose the enemy's pickets. As Paget's 10th and 15th Hussars advanced along the road, the French could be seen hastily deploying into close column, while their flanking squadrons trotted forward to engage the Hussars.

Captain Gordon, riding with the 15th, was impressed by their martial appearance: "The heavy dragoons with their shining brass helmets from which the long black horsehair streamed from the crest, excited my admiration," he confessed. The distance between the two bodies of horse was no greater than 400 yards and as Paget's Hussars responded to the shrill notes of a bugle, breaking from a trot into a canter, the intervening ground was covered before the French dragoons could draw their carbines.

Spurring his mount into the charge, Alexander Gordon led his troop against the enemy with numbed hands scarcely able to feel the reins or grasp his sabre. In the uncertain light it was far from easy to distinguish friend from foe and Gordon was very nearly cut down by a trooper of the 15th who in the act of raising his sword, recognized his officer in time. The shock of collision had overthrown several of the lighter-horsed dragoons and, in a running fight which lasted no more than ten minutes, Paget's troopers swept through the enemy horse and put them to flight at the expense of six killed and twenty wounded.

As usual with cavalry, it was difficult to keep order and Gordon wrote of the trouble he had in curbing the men's enthusiastic pursuit: "Having rode together nearly a mile, pell-mell, cutting and slashing, the men were quite wild and the horses blown. Seeing no superior officer near I pressed through the throng until I overtook and halted those who were farthest advanced in pursuit." His action undoubtedly prevented his troop from becoming scattered and attacked piecemeal.

The success of the Hussars was due in some measure to their superior mounts, for the French had been better armed, as a few of Paget's men found to their cost. The large fur caps of the Hussars were no protection against cuts from the heavy swords wielded by the dragoons and a number of frightful head wounds had been the result. A score of dragoons had been killed and one of the few unwounded prisoners admitted to Gordon that he had at first taken the Hussars for Spaniards. The Frenchman readily acknowledged that never before had he encountered such determined charging and confessed to the Hussar Captain that "it was some consolation to have been beaten by English cavalry". Following the engagement at Sahagun, Moore realized that his presence must now be known to Soult and when, later in the day, with snow falling thickly, a message was brought to the British General from the Spaniard Pedro Caro Romana, it confirmed his worst fears. Napoleon was bearing down from the Guadarramas in the teeth of a raging blizzard, in order to cut the British army's line of retreat. It seemed that Moore's optimistic venture into Spain was likely to end in disaster.

Chapter 4

AN INFAMOUS RETREAT

Following the successful action by Paget's Hussars at Sahagun, the Light Brigade had reached that town without incident, but as they were passing through its narrow streets early on Christmas morning a Staff Officer, spurring his horse along the line of Green Jackets, reined in beside General Robert Craufurd and handed him a message. The General, after a quick glance at the despatch, turned in his saddle and raised his arm to halt the column. The long arduous retreat to Corunna was about to begin.

As the rumour spread through the ranks, the mood of the green-jacketed riflemen changed from an anticipation of an early skirmish with the French to one of bitter disillusionment. No less resentful were the redcoats led by Sir John Hope. "Won't we be allowed to fight?" complained one Irish firebrand to his officer. "By Saint Patrick, we'd bate 'em aisy!" The thought of running away from an enemy he had helped to defeat at Vimiero was especially irritating to Private Pococke of the 71st. After the discomfort of the recent forced marches, he felt that any short struggle, no matter what the outcome, was preferable to retiring without a shot being fired.

For the main body of troops under Sir John Moore the journey back to Astorga began on Christmas Eve in pouring rain which did nothing to improve their tempers. These men, most of whom were untried troops from England, faced the immediate prospect of an 80-mile march to be followed by a further 150 miles over barren uplands before reaching the coast and the protection of the English fleet.

A sudden thaw had turned the frost-hardened ground into something approaching a quagmire, which added to the discomfort of the cursing redcoats, who, in an ugly mood, vented their spite on the Spaniards. Each village suffered from the ill humour of the troops, varying from petty pilfering to vandalism and bodily assault. The furious villagers, not daring to remonstrate with any but a handful of the rearguard, retaliated

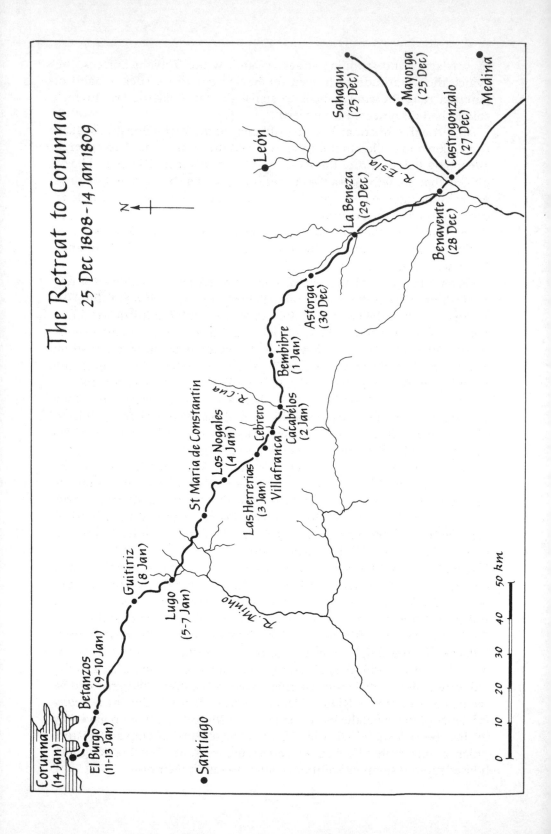

The Retreat to Corunna
25 Dec 1808 – 14 Jan 1809

N

Coruña
(14 Jan)
Betanzos
(9–10 Jan)
El Burgo
(11–13 Jan)
Santiago
Lugo
(5–7 Jan)
Guitiriz
(8 Jan)
St Maria de Constantin
Los Nogales
(4 Jan)
Cebrero
(3 Jan)
Las Herrerias
(3 Jan)
Villafranca
Cacabelos
(2 Jan)
Bembibre
(1 Jan)
Astorga
(30 Dec)
La Beneza
(29 Dec)
Benavente
(28 Dec)
León
Castrogonzalo
(27 Dec)
Sahagun
(25 Dec)
Mayorga
(25 Dec)
Medina

R. Minho
R. Cua
R. Esla

0   10   20   30   40   50 km

by waylaying and stripping stragglers and, wrote William Surtees, "to evince their gratitude to heaven for having got rid of such a band of heretics, rang the church bells to signal the fact that the last English soldier had disappeared from view".

All through Christmas Day the riflemen of the Light Brigade, soaked to the skin and chilled to the bone, retraced the ground they had covered a few days before. From the scowl on Craufurd's face, Rifleman Harris judged that something had gone seriously wrong, but it was not until many hours later, when a puzzled Green Jacket raised his voice, that an explanation was forthcoming.

"Be Jasus! Musther Hill, where the devil is this you're takin' us to?"

The reply left many of his comrades speechless. "To England, M'Lauchlan. If we can get there."

Despite the pace of the retreat being slowed by the action of a few Spanish drivers deserting their bullock carts, by the evening of the 27th the major part of the army with the exception of the Light Brigade and a few stragglers, was across the swollen River Esla with its guns and wagons intact. When the last infantryman had hurried over the ancient stone bridge, its destruction was effected to such an extent that it took the pursuing French more than a day to complete the necessary repairs.

The delay gave Moore's weary soldiers a welcome respite which they gratefully accepted in the old walled town of Benevente where, thanks to Moore's foresight in establishing a stockpile, every officer and man was issued with a blanket and a pair of shoes.

The recent night march over frost-hardened roads had taxed the patience of even the best disciplined of Moore's soldiers. Food supplies had proved almost impossible to obtain, despite the desperate efforts of the Commissariat and an exhausted Schaumann felt justified in complaining, "I am on my legs night and day, and am utterly sick and tired of this constant state of commotion."

In such circumstances it was perhaps not surprising that morale should plunge to its lowest level and when it became known that a large stock of wine was maturing in the cellars of a warehouse what little discipline that still existed collapsed altogether. There was no lack of willing hands to roll the heavy wooden casks up the slope into the square where they were broached by the simple expedient of firing a musket ball into the woodwork. The stone cobbles and gutters were soon overflowing with a frothy red torrent and excited groups of men, women and even children could be seen filling canteens or lying full length to drink their fill. Under the heady influence of the wine, the loose characters in Moore's army soon gave way to their baser instincts. Brushing aside their officers' attempts to restore order, groups roamed the streets terrorizing the townsfolk, breaking into houses and not stopping short of violence to satisfy their lusts.

As the day wore on, the rabble grew in number and scenes of destruction became ever more widespread. The castle of Ossuna, "surpassing anything I have ever seen," noted Thomas Pococke, was an especial target for vandalism. Rich tapestries with exquisite renderings of religious themes were torn from their hangings and used as bedclothes, blasphemy which, confessed Pococke, caused him to "blush for the men". "I would blame them too," he added. "Alas! How can I, when I think upon their dreadful situation, fatigued and wet, shivering, perishing with the cold? – no fuel to be got, not even straw to lie upon. Can men in such a situation admire the beauties of art?"

The German commissary, August Schaumann, was not so forgiving: "What the English soldier cannot see any purpose in does not interest him," he complained. "Everywhere bayonets and nails were stuck into the crevices of precious columns, or into the beautifully decorated walls, and the knapsacks or cartridge boxes hung upon them. Poor castle of Benevente! How quickly thy splendour vanished."

In another incident a Convent in which several hundred redcoats had sought shelter from the biting wind was looted of its sacrificial wine and the empty barrels, together with anything else combustible, including century-old paintings, were fed to the fires which blazed in every hearth. These soon flared out of control and a major conflagration was only averted by an officer of the 43rd who, seeing that a wooden shutter was ablaze and in danger of igniting the bales of straw in the stables below, reached up from the back of a tethered horse to wrench away the smouldering wood and cast it onto the cobbles below.

Fortunately for the army the Reserve and the Light Brigade was still a disciplined force, for frequent rearguard actions had kept the soldiers fully occupied and away from the temptations of the liquor stores. The cavalry in particular had been engaged almost continuously in skirmishes with the French which served to reinforce Alexander Gordon in his belief that they were the equal of any horsemen Napoleon might choose to send against them.

Five days before Moore had reached Benevente the Emperor had dismounted and, at the head of his Imperial Guard, had crossed a range of steep hills known as the Guadaramas in the teeth of a raging blizzard. Now, as Moore's army prepared to leave the old walled town, two regiments of cavalry led by 35-year-old General Comte Charles Lefebvre-Desnouettes, gorgeously attired in a uniform of scarlet and gold, crossed the Esla at a ford above the bridge with orders from the watching Napoleon "to bring those English cavalry prisoners".

The Chasseurs and the horsemen of the Emperor's Guard were immediately engaged by a troop of the 10th and 15th Hussars, but, in the face of superior numbers, it was obliged to retire towards the town, drawing the two French regiments in pursuit.

Before Lefebvre-Desnouettes realized his error, he was attacked by the entire British brigade. The leading squadrons of the 18th Hussars, their Irish blood raised to a white heat, charged with such fury that the French were driven back across the river where several, losing their footing, were swept away by the strong current and drowned.

The French General, who had been cut across the head in the mêlée and was made prisoner by a sergeant of the 10th Hussars, was treated courteously by Moore even to the extent of sending for the General's baggage from across the river. Later, in a conversation, Lefebvre-Desnouettes was said to have remarked that Bonaparte would find it impossible to forgive him, as the Chasseurs of the Guard had never before been beaten. He was to spend nearly four years in captivity before breaking his parole at Cheltenham and crossing the Channel in a smuggler's boat.

Following this defeat, the French cavalry remained at a respectful distance and Captain Boothby's party of engineers were able to destroy the bridge and give themselves and the rest of Moore's army a well-earned rest from the fatigue and stress of a hurried retreat. Later, to a backdrop of raging fires, through streets filled with acrid smoke and littered with the detritus of an all but beaten army, the Reserve left Benevente for Astorga, two days ahead of the French who had delayed in order to reorganize.

The biting cold of the last few days had now turned to a mixture of rain and sleet, adding to the misery of the women and children bringing up the rear, many of whom must have bitterly regretted an earlier decision not to return to Lisbon. Exhausted oxen sank to their knees in mud and, as the carts slowed to a halt, the women handed down their children and struggled along on foot in a desperate attempt to keep pace with the retiring column.

On 31 December Astorga was reached. The town was crowded with refugees and the dispirited redcoats of Hope's and Fraser's brigades, who were joined in the last hours of 1808 by the tattered remnants of Romana's Spanish rearguard. Private Plunet, who saw them hobble past, described the Spaniards as having "the appearance of a large body of peasants driven from their homes, famished and in want of everything". Indeed, many of Romana's wretched troops had not eaten for several days and, being barefoot and half-naked, were shivering with the cold. Alexander Gordon, gazing from the window of a room he shared with five other Hussar officers, was struck with pity, but, having neither the room or any food to spare, he could do no more than invite them to crowd round a fire built by his troopers in the yard.

Further down the street, Lieutenant Blakeney, like Gordon, felt sympathy for the plight of the Spaniards. He discovered that Romana's sick were completely without medicines or medical assistance of any kind and for these unfortunates he was able to issue a ration of rum. Shortly after Blakeney's hospitable action orders were given for the rum casks to be stove in as a measure to curb drunkenness. This action by the Provost succeeded in achieving the opposite effect for it enabled the incorrigible to take full advantage of the sticky brown stream which flooded the gutters and left dozens of redcoats sprawled senseless in a drunken stupor. Drink was more readily available than bread and, with food stocks sufficient only for two more days, the commissariat officers did their best to replenish the military storehouse, but every demand made of the townspeople was met by the same response, wrote August Schaumann: "What do you English think? You are retreating and yet we are expected to supply you with provisions. Tomorrow the French will come and we shall have to scrape something together for them unless we want to be hanged." Commented the German Commissary: "This was certainly an argumentum ad hominem!" Nevertheless, many officers shared Schaumann's disgust at the apathy and hostility with which the Spaniards witnessed the misery of the English troops. "Not only did those puffed-up patriots give us no assistance," argued the German, "but they also took good care to remove all cattle and foodstuffs out of our way, emptied and locked their houses, vanished, and in addition, murdered and plundered our own men who fell out left and right along the road."

With the arrival of the New Year the retreat continued, but on widely differing paths, for Moore had learned from the Chasseur prisoners of the Emperor's plan to drive him back from Villafranca into the arms of Soult. In the light of this information and to safeguard against being outflanked, General Craufurd, with 3,000 of the Light Brigade, was sent along the road to Vigo, whilst Moore, with the bulk of the army, continued to use the mountain paths which led to Villafranca 50 miles to the west. It had already become a route traversed by many hundreds as was readily apparent from the wrecked caissons and dead horses, while here and there a shapeless form, huddled in a blanket, sat staring with unseeing eyes at the bent figures trudging past.

Throughout the hours of darkness the men of the Reserve picked their way along a winding mountain track, many regretting an impulse which earlier had led them to jettison a rain-soaked greatcoat or blanket. To add to their discomfort, much of the exposed rock was coated with a film of ice and not a few redcoats, losing their footing and too tired to attempt to rise, were quickly covered with a mantle of snow.

Lieutenant Blakeney, bringing up the rear of the column, stumbled across a number of shapes half-covered with snow and apparently asleep. As he approached the group with the intention of rousing them, a scene unfolded which was to remain fresh in his memory for many months to come. Three men, a woman and a small child all lay dead, their bodies forming a rough half circle with their heads facing inwards. "At the centre," related Blakeney, "the remains of a pool of rum surrounding a broken cask pointed to the fact that in their misery the poor wretches had fallen asleep in a drunken stupor and had frozen to death."

On that same snow-covered track another officer was witness to an event which in any other circumstance would have been an occasion for celebration. "On this mountain," recorded Ensign Gavin, "Mrs Cahill, our Colonel's servant, was delivered of a fine boy, her bed the snow."

Lieutenants Blakeney and Cadell reached Bembibre – "a wretched filthy little hole," thought Cadell – on the night of 2 January after a long uncomfortable march over steep mountain tracks. In common with the rest of the 28th Foot they had hoped for a few hours' rest before following on in the wake of Sir David Baird's division, but in this they were to be disappointed. Bembibre was the hub of the Spanish wine trade and as such contained immense vaults full of the finest quality.

"The scene of drunkenness that presented itself was truly shameful," confessed Lieutenant Cadell. "The stragglers from the preceding division so crowded every house, that there was hardly a place to be had."

The vats had been broached by earlier arrivals and Blakeney's Company was saddled with the task of clearing the houses of the drunkards and sending as many of the stragglers forward as could be moved. Walking the streets, Blakeney was appalled at the extent of the degradation left by the earlier regiments. "Bembibre exhibited all the appearance of a place lately stormed and pillaged," he noted. "Every door and window was broken, every lock and fastening forced."

Groups of men and women lay sprawled on the cobbles, while others, Spaniards included, reeled past him in an alcoholic haze, oblivious of the action of Blakeney's party in dragging besotted and exhausted stragglers out into the open. The few who could still march were put into the charge of an escort to Villafranca, but all too often kicks and blows had no effect. Even jabs from a bayonet failed to rouse the comatose figures and, warned of the approach of the enemy, Blakeney and his men reluctantly abandoned the sleepers to their fate. Within the hour a patrol of French dragoons were freely using their sword arms and sparing no one. Women pleaded frantically for their honour and bemused redcoats dropped to their knees begging for mercy, but to no avail. Their entreaties fell on deaf ears and the dragoons rode up and down the street indiscriminately cutting down all who came within reach of their sword arm.

A few survivors were left to crawl through the slush to seek whatever shelter they could find among the trees. One such victim was brought into the lines by a patrol of Hussars who at first, had mistaken the figure beside the hedge for a wild pig. The man had wrapped his shirt around his face in an attempt to protect his wounds from the frost and, when this was removed, his terrible injuries were revealed. The flesh of his cheeks and lips were hanging in collops and one of his ears had been cut off. The poor wretch was able to swallow a little wine, remembered Gordon, and as he cowered before the fire, "raking the glowing embers nearer his body with frost-bitten fingers," he spoke with difficulty of the barbarous treatment meted out by the French. "I believe the poor sufferer was himself left behind a day or two after," commented Captain Steevens, "as we had not the means to carry him on."

Later that day a Chasseur who had been wounded in a skirmish with the 15th Hussars was brought in for questioning. From him it was learned that a division of cavalry commanded by General Auguste Colbert, at thirty-two one of Napoleon's youngest and ablest Generals, was within striking distance and that Soult was hourly expected with two divisions of infantry. The Frenchman begged his captors to treat him kindly, adding that all who fell into the hands of his countrymen were shown every consideration. Alexander Gordon thought of the pitiful wretch who had warmed himself at the bivouac fire. His appearance just then would have had been far more effective in nailing the lie than any protestation Gordon might have submitted.

Moore's army was shortly to lose its most illustrious pursuer, for on New Year's Day Napoleon had learned of political intrigues in Paris and warlike preparations by Austria. Realizing that too great a part of his army was being drawn into the Galician mountains, the Emperor decided to leave the pursuit of Sir John Moore to Marshal Soult and return to Madrid with the Imperial Guard.

For the many hundreds of Scottish troops who had struggled into Villafranca that same day there was a marked absence of the festive spirit. "This was truly the most disagreeable New Year's Day that I ever spent," lamented Sergeant Robertson of the 92nd Foot. "Our clothes were falling off our backs, and our shoes were worn to the welts. From the officer down to the private, we were overrun with vermin."

It had been confidently expected that Moore would make a stand at this small town lying at the foot of the mountain. Certainly his officers were of the opinion that, providing the heights were entrenched and supported by artillery, a force of resolute defenders would be able to hold the enemy at bay for several days, giving the army a chance of retiring at a more leisurely pace. Sir John Moore, however, conscious of the need for haste if he was to succeed in saving Britain's only army, ordered an early departure for the morning. When it became known that there was to be no slackening in the rigorous pace of these forced marches morale plummeted.

"The idea of running away without firing a shot, from the enemy we had beaten so easily at Vimiero was so galling for their feelings," explained Thomas Pococke, that "rage flashed out on the most trifling occasion."

The soldiers' vexation soon erupted in scenes of riotous behaviour as witnessed by Alexander Gordon. "Parties of drunken soldiers were committing all kinds of enormities," he wrote. "Several houses were in flames . . . and a promiscuous rabble were drinking and filling bottles and canteens from the stream" (of rum).

Commissariat stocks of biscuit, salt beef, bread and rum, which had been painstakingly accumulated over the weeks, were looted by troops at the cost of leaving later arrivals without any provisions at all, and the familiar scenes of drunkenness were soon in evidence from the broken casks and discarded equipment which littered every street.

Among the later arrivals, only one officer of the 28th was fortunate enough to obtain anything to satisfy his hunger, a Major who tied a piece of salt pork to his saddle holster with the intention of having it for his supper. "But," observed Charles Cadell, "it was very soon cut away, for we were marching in the dark."

With the army's discipline fast melting away, Sir John Moore was determined that an example must be made and when it came to his notice that three soldiers had been apprehended in the very act of looting a commissariat store he dispensed with the formality of a drumhead court martial and the guilty three were made to draw lots for their lives. The luckless trooper, Private Day of the 15th Dragoons, was tied to a tree and then a volley of shots from the firing squad "was followed by a sound as if every man in the division had been stifled for the last five minutes, and now at length drew in his breath," remarked George Gleig. "It was not a groan, nor a sigh, but a sob."

Later that day a soldier was hanged for striking an officer and another given 100 lashes for robbing a householder. While these severe measures were being taken, Moore rode to where the Reserve was drawn up in a field beside the road. After admonishing them and reminding them of the dangers resulting from a total breakdown in discipline, he began his address by saying, "The Commander of the forces has observed, with concern, the extreme bad conduct of the troops of late. . . . It is disgraceful to their officers, as it strongly marks their negligence and in-attention," and ended with the words, "If the enemy are in possession of Bembibre, they have got a rare prize. They have taken or cut to pieces many hundreds of drunken British cowards – for none but unprincipled cowards would get drunk in the presence, nay in the very sight of the enemies of their country and sooner than survive the disgrace of such infamous conduct . . . I would much rather be dead than command such an army."

"This," confirmed Charles Napier, "seemed to produce some effect, and I do think their conduct improved after that day."

Most certainly there were troops capable of putting up a spirited resistance and for the rearguard there were frequent opportunities for a clash with the French. Typical of one such skirmish was an action during the crossing of a small but flooded stream of the Coa at Cacabelos on 3 January. General Auguste de Colbert had been observing the movement of Moore's troops, many of whom were wearing Spanish garments snatched from carts to wear over their own threadbare uniforms. The redcoats' odd attire may have misled the French General into thinking that here was a column of Romana's battered army and he launched his dragoons in a headlong charge against them.

The British rearguard, comprising several Companies of the 95th, had already crossed the bridge when the French cavalry came upon them. Charging down the slope, the dragoons drove the Riflemen and a mixed body of horsemen to the very edge of the village where Captain Gordon and his troop rallied to dispute every yard of the narrow street as the Rifles took up a position on the brow of a hill. Whilst the 15th Hussars were engaged with Colbert's dragoons, two light field guns had been galloped to a spot overlooking the bridge and, as the enemy regrouped for a second attack, they opened with grape, supported by musketry from the 95th. The fusillade, directed from the cover of a walled vineyard, toppled many of the French troopers, but General Colbert, conspicuous on a white charger, seemed to bear a charmed life as he rode about directing operations from the river bank. As the action intensified, competition arose between the men of the two Light infantry regiments for the distinction of bringing him down. Rifleman Thomas Plunket, a noted sharpshooter of the 95th, ran forward and, rolling over on his back and looping the rifle sling over his right foot, took careful aim with his Baker rifle. A spurt of flame, a puff of smoke accompanied by a loud report and the French General was seen to throw up his arms and fall into the muddy waters of the stream. The French, enraged by the death of their General, rushed towards Plunket, but, covered by the fire of his comrades, the Rifleman ran for the cover of the stone wall pursued by several furious dragoons. The impetus of their charge carried them over the bridge and into the ranks of the 95th, where for a few frantic minutes British bayonets parried French sabres in a savage mêlée.

John Green, having been tumbled full length by a collision with a French horse, lay gasping for breath in the long grass beside the wall. Seeing several dragoons bearing down upon him, he had visions of at best a prison in Verdun, but happily grass and brambles provided an effective cover and, once the enemy horse had passed him, Private Green was able to rise to his feet and rejoin his comrades of the 68th Regiment.

Using the shelter of the low stone walls to good effect, the light infantry kept up a telling fire which forced the French to retire, leaving the road to the bridge strewn with their dead and wounded. A later attempt to outflank the defenders fared no better and, when the light faded, the action was broken off leaving the men of the Reserve free to resume the retreat untroubled by further enemy activity.

As Moore's columns left Villafranca silhouetted against a lurid glow from abandoned stores burning in the Plaza, the refusal of their General to stand and fight still rankled with many of Moore's junior officers. Whilst it was generally recognized that it was his responsibility to ensure that the army arrived safely in Corunna, "The idea of running away, without firing a shot, from the enemy we had beaten so easily at Vimerio," protested one Highlander, "was so galling to their feelings."

With Villafranca several miles behind them, the lengthening columns laboriously threaded their way up the long snow-covered hill of Nogales in the teeth of a freezing wind. Looking back, Rifleman Harris could not help remarking to a comrade on the extraordinary sight of thousands of redcoats "creeping like snails, and toiling up the ascent before us, their muskets slung around their necks, and clambering with both hands as they hauled themselves up. Many of the men were entirely barefooted, with knapsacks and accoutrements altogether in a dilapidated state. The officers were also, for the most part, in a miserable plight. They were pallid, wayworn, their feet bleeding and their faces overgrown with beards of many days' growth."

Small snow-covered heaps could be seen at intervals along the route where individuals, overcome with fatigue, waited patiently for death or the French to overtake them. "The road was one long line of bloody foot-marks from the sore feet of the men," wrote Thomas Pococke, "and on its sides lay the dead and the dying. Human nature could do no more." "We waded through snow and mud over the bodies of dead men and horses," remembered Schaumann. "The howling wind as it whistled past the ledges of rock and through the bare trees sounded to the ear like the groaning of the damned."

It was at this stage that many of the women, some of whom had shown remarkable courage and fortitude, found the bitter weather too great an obstacle. Singly and in groups, with frost-bitten feet and legs raw with the cold, they begged for help from the redcoats staggering past, usually without response. The soldiers, heads down against the driving sleet, were too conscious of their own misery to throw more than a cursory glance at the occupants of the broken wagons at the side of the road.

Confessed a shocked Adam Neale, "Never have I conceived, much less witnessed, so awful a scene."

"The enemy did not need to enquire the way we had gone," lamented Schaumann; "our remains marked the route."

Adding to the concern of his Commanding General, the prospect of a major battle was looming ever nearer, while Corunna and the waiting British fleet was still a week's march away.

Chapter 5

THE WELCOME SIGHT OF VIGO

By 5 January Moore's troops were less than fifty miles from Corunna, in the high sierras of Galicia, an area desolate and barren with just a few scattered peasant huts to afford shelter from the inclement weather, huts so utterly wretched that in the opinion of John Harris, "It appeared quite a wonder how human beings could live in so desolate a home". Miserable though they were, the approach of Moore's ragged army, regarded by all Spanish Catholics as '*maldetos hereticos*', had driven many of the inhabitants to abandon their homes in spite of the bitter weather. The barred doors and shutters were not resistant to the repeated blows from the butt end of a musket, however, and no matter how primitive the resources, a good many redcoats had reason to be grateful for the shelter provided and the chance of a few hours' sleep.

The route from Villafranca to Lugo had been a severe test of stamina, for the roads had deteriorated to such an extent that the straggling column of men and women often found themselves ankle-deep in mud. "Hundreds of men lost their shoes and were obliged to walk barefoot for the remainder of the retreat," wrote Private Green. "I had a strap buckled tight over each instep and under each shoe, so that I did not lose mine; but I frequently stuck fast in the road."

Indeed, the regulation shoes issued to the redcoat were heavy and of very dubious quality. Between the thin inner and outer soles was a filling of clay which in adverse conditions was quickly reduced to a glutinous mess. The officers suffered no less than the men and it was not uncommon to see officers with aristocratic connections trudging barefoot save for an odd piece of blanket wrapped around their feet and legs.

"Many were so tired and lame from sore feet," wrote Major Charles Cadell of the 28th, "that they did not care if the French sabres and bayonets were at their breast, so completely did most of them give themselves up to despair."

The French harassed the rearguard for most of the day and towards sunset a determined attack was launched by Soult. For several hours the issue hung in the balance as the Light regiments fell back, but just when all order and discipline seemed to be lost, Sir John Moore rallied his men to such good effect that, following a ragged volley, they surged forward with wild shouts to fling the French back at the point of the bayonet.

This ability of Moore's redcoats to respond immediately to any military threat, no matter what the state of morale, puzzled the French. "When all order and discipline appeared to be lost in the British ranks," confessed a French officer, "the slightest prospect of an engagement produced, as if by magic, the immediate restoration of both; the officers, who the moment before appeared wholly without the slightest authority, or control, being obeyed upon the instant, as if on parade."

Despite the occasional successful rearguard action, the British army was hourly becoming less effective, reduced both in numbers and material possessions. Weapons and accoutrements littered the length of the road which frequently followed a winding path along the edge of precipices several hundred feet deep. At one stage of the journey bullock carts containing the Military Chest with Spanish dollars to the value of £25,000 were toppled into a ravine to be swept away by a mountain torrent. "The casks were soon broken by the rugged rocks," observed Major Cadell, "and the dollars falling out, rolled over the heights in a sparkling cascade of silver."

At length the troops reached the summit to find that the road dropped steeply towards a bridge and the small village of Constantino. Moore was aware that, should the enemy, who were in close pursuit, be allowed to dispute the crossing of the river the consequence could be disastrous, and this he was determined to avoid. His dispositions to safeguard the crossing were quickly carried out. The 28th Foot and the Rifles were drawn up on the river bank, while three other regiments were positioned on an adjacent hill, supported by a troop of Horse Artillery. The French, as expected, attacked with their cavalry and light skirmishing troops, making a dash for the bridge, only to be thrown back by rolling volleys of musketry from the 28th and a storm of grape from the battery on the hill. A second and third attack met a similar fate and when darkness fell, to bring a slackening in the fighting, Soult's dragoons and voltigeurs were forced to withdraw, allowing Moore's troops to cross the river unmolested, leaving bivouac fires burning to deceive the French. This stratagem enabled them to reach Lugo on the 6th and, while the redcoats gathered round the cooking fires to prepare a stew from an issue of salt beef and biscuit, the French vedettes were engaged in similar tasks on the hills to the east of the ancient city, famous for its medicinal springs.

The smoke and noise of battle had brought in stragglers from the surrounding area and orders which only recently had been disregarded or carried out with some reluctance were now obeyed without question. Morale had improved beyond measure with the recent successes over the enemy and there was now a common desire to avenge all the hardship and suffering they had endured at the hands of the French. This feeling was soon to change for their stay in the town was abruptly ended by Moore's decision to resume the march on Corunna with all possible speed. When it became known that a stand was not going to be made against Soult a sense of betrayal swept through the ranks. Groups of soldiers broke away in disgust to resume their search for liquor, whilst others threw down their muskets and refused to join their comrades parading in the square.

Captain George Napier of the 52nd overtook one such group and ordered them to return to their duties. Far from complying with his order, the ringleader presented his musket threateningly at Napier's head. Fortunately it misfired, but, with the memory of the Villafranca executions fresh in his mind, Napier flinched from the prospect of having "a fellow creature put to death" and he refrained from calling the Provost.

In a mixture of rain and sleet the troops moved off late in the night of the 8th, leaving their watchfires burning. Cursing broke out afresh with the redcoats begging their officers to grant them an opportunity to show "them frog-eating fellows what they were made of". The senior officers, although sympathetic to their views, knew that the army was in no condition to fight more than one major battle.

"The British army," wrote a sergeant in the 28th, "had no magazines, no hospitals, no second line, no provisions. . . . there was not bread for another day's consumption in the stores at Lugo." The night march from Lugo gave Moore twelve precious hours gain on his pursuers, for the French, bivouacked above Lugo, did not discover the absence of the redcoats until well after dawn.

A few companies became separated in the darkness and wandered, soaked to the skin, over a featureless terrain until daylight revealed the route taken by the main body. Few of those who spent an anxious and uncomfortable night searching for their regiment were lucky enough to stumble across one of the miserable hovels to be found in the hills. One who did was the German commissary Auguste Schaumann. Upon entering, he found it occupied by an old woman and three children, two of whom were suffering from a fever. "The woman crouched over a fire of moist peat, shaking with cold and misery," he wrote. "Everything was extremely dirty, the children's hair was matted together and they seemed never to have washed since the day of their birth." The whole scene presented the appalled Schaumann with an example of the wretchedness common to these unfortunate hill dwellers. The full light of day also

45

exposed to view the pitiable state of Moore's infantry. Dirty and unkempt, many limped along with frost-bitten feet wrapped in filthy rags and what was left of their uniform was so encrusted with mud that it was difficult to distinguish the Rifleman's green from the red of the Line regiments.

"Our clothes were worn to rags, and for shoes," wrote John Patterson, "they were something like an Irishman's brogues, that were happily supplied with holes to let the water out."

The continual marching had taken its toll, for between 5,000 and 6,000 men had been lost in the retreat so far, a number which would have been greater but for the heroic behaviour and strict discipline of Paget's rear-guard.

Far behind, among those struggling to keep pace with the main body, was Private Pococke. Barefoot and lame, the 19-year-old's strength was all but spent and he found himself unable to resist the urge to sink down upon a snow-covered rock and abandon himself to fate. The only sound above the moaning of the wind was the groaning and curses of men in a similar situation. After sitting listlessly for more than an hour he tried to pray, but his mind was so confused that he found it impossible to collect his thoughts. Sleep was beginning to overtake him when he became aware of a commotion around him. "Sleep was stealing upon me, when I perceived a bustle around me," he recalled many years later. "It was an advance party of the French; unconscious of the action, I started upon my feet, levelled my musket, which I had still retained, fired and formed with the other stragglers." The Frenchmen were few in number and soon turned from the British bayonets, but the incident was enough to rouse Pococke from his lethargy and he was later reunited with his Company of the 71st Regiment at Castro.

Moore had signalled to Admiral Hood from Villafranca on the 3rd and from Lugo on the 7th that transports must be waiting at Corunna to embark the troops. Now, with that city less than 12 miles away, he could only pray that he had made sufficient ground on the French to enable the embarkation to be completed in safety. Several hours later his weary columns reached Betanzos, and Moore called a halt out of sheer necessity. In pouring rain his troops sank gratefully on the damp earth and remained there until early evening when the retreat was resumed.

"When we assembled all hands," wrote Sergeant James Hale, "our regiment did not exceed sixty men, neither did any regiment in the brigade."

There had been no meat or bread available in Betanzos but there was an abundance of salt fish, and as it happened, several casks of rum. It was the matter of moments to knock in the heads of the barrels, with the most unexpected results. "As we had neither fires nor kettles," related Auguste

46

Schaumann, "the salt fish was eagerly swallowed raw, while the rum was poured down afterwards. The combination of the two in empty stomachs resulted in the death of many of the men on the spot, while several others went mad." One soldier under the heady influence of the rum stood swaying in the middle of the road with his musket presented, shouting that the first man to ignore his order to halt and give battle would be shot. In the event, troopers of the 15th Hussars rode over him and his corpse was left in the mud.

Once Betanzos was behind them, the bleak mountain scenery soon gave way to a pleasant green landscape and when the vanguard reached the summit of yet another hill a burst of cheering announced the welcome sight of sunlight glinting on the distant sea. "I felt all my former despondency drop from my mind," remembered Thomas Pococke, "my galled feet trod lighter on the icy road. Every face near me seemed to brighten up." There was one major disappointment to be faced, however. While they gazed with expectation, there was not the sails or rigging of a single transport vessel to be seen.

Back with the rearguard, although much time had been gained, there were frequent clashes with the French. A Company of the 28th had barely succeeded in crossing the Minho before they were followed by a squadron of dragoons in close pursuit. Lieutenant Blakeney immediately gave the order to form square: "Right about turn. Prepare to receive cavalry." With a shout of "*Vive l'Empereur!*" the enemy horse spurred rapidly towards the redcoats and for a moment Robert Blakeney, five or six yards in advance of his men, looked death in the face as a huge Frenchman bore down upon him with a raised sabre poised to strike. Blakeney, kneeling with his own flimsy infantry sword held above his head to parry the expected blow, was aware of a deafening report and the cry of "Mr Blakeney, we've spun him." The dragoon, in the very act of wielding his sabre, toppled from his horse with a musket ball lodged in his forehead.

Not caring to face the square formed by the men of the 28th, the enemy retired, leaving Blakeney to take possession of the dragoon's green cape which, as he later confessed, "served both as a trophy and as protection against the inclement weather".

A hundred miles to the north 3,500 men of the Light Brigade, led by General Robert Craufurd, struggled on towards Vigo. Detached from the Reserve when a day's march beyond Astorga, their route to the sea had proved every bit as arduous as that taken by the Reserve. Craufurd, a short thick-set 44-year-old Scot, possessed a sharp tongue and a temper to match. Determined to maintain discipline on the march no matter what the conditions, he lost no time in imposing his authority.

"You think because you are Riflemen you may do whatever you think

47

proper," he bellowed, "but I'll teach you the difference before I have done with you."

The first lesson was not long in coming, for, when two of his men were apprehended leaving the column, he immediately sentenced the culprits to one hundred lashes. Even though the French were close on their heels, the Green Jackets were ordered to form a square and witness the punishment being carried out, some, wrote John Harris, "with tears falling down their cheeks from the agony of their bleeding feet".

Later, Craufurd felled a man whom he had overheard muttering "Damn his eyes" with the butt of a musket.

Despite his reputation as a disciplinarian, which earned him the sobriquet of 'Black Bob', Robert Craufurd was not unpopular with the men and officers who served under him. That he had earned their respect was confirmed by Harris when he wrote: "No man but one formed of stuff like General Craufurd could have saved the Brigade from perishing altogether."

Certainly his firm leadership was never absent when the situation required it, from offering a canteen of rum to an exhausted soldier to admonishing anyone he considered was not pulling his weight. Marshalling his brigade across a river, he was quick to notice an officer being carried over on the back of one of the men.

"Put him down sir! Put him down. I desire you to put that officer down instantly."

Much to the amusement of Harris and his companions, the soldier dropped his burden into the icy stream and the General turned to the unfortunate officer. "Go back sir, go back and come through the water like the others. I will not allow my officers to ride upon the men's backs through the rivers. All must take their share alike here."

As with the Reserve, the pace of the march began to tell and with each passing day an increasing number of soldiers and camp followers, many suffering from dysentery contracted from drinking rain water out of ditches, were left crouching by the side of the road or stretched groaning beneath a shelf of overhanging rock.

John Harris, his feet a mass of suppurating sores, forced himself to keep pace with the rest of his Company. Once an anguished cry caused him to pause and turn to where a woman was staggering after the column, dragging a small child in her wake. Lacking the strength to afford assistance, he could only watch in anguish as the boy, his legs failing him and too exhausted to cry, stumbled on open-mouthed until both he and the woman sank to their knees in the snow. "The poor woman had for some time looked like a moving corpse," wrote the Rifleman in his memoirs, "and when the shades of evening came down, they were far behind among the dead and dying in the road."

The column led by Craufurd struggled on over hills and narrow mountain tracks made hazardous by ice where men, weighed down by knapsack and musket, sometimes lost their footing and rolled helplessly to the bottom of the slope, bruised and bleeding. Always Craufurd was there to offer advice or to bully stragglers and drive them on. At night the rearguard was ordered to carry long branches topped with flaming bundles of tarred straw or bracken to act as a beacon to the stragglers in the column. John Harris was one who had reason to thank the General's foresight. Hopelessly lost and with every step taking him and a companion further into a morass, the flickering points of light served to guide them back to firmer ground and the route taken by the main body.

At the end of the second week, as the weary and dispirited Green Jackets reached the summit of a particularly steep incline, they saw to their relief the heartening spectacle of English ships riding at anchor in the bay at Vigo. "The glow of delight which every individual seemed to feel as the blue bosom of the distant ocean met the eye," enthused a relieved Adam Neale, "is not to be surpassed." "There never was a sight," acknowledged Sergeant William Surtees, "which inspired me with greater pleasure than the shipping and the sea did on this occasion."

The realization that an end to this fearful march was now in sight acted as a tonic to men's flagging spirits. Those hardly able to put one foot in front of the other redoubled their efforts to reach the beach. John Harris, his sight clouding from illness and fatigue, forced himself along and was among the last of the stragglers to reach the waiting boats. Unable to call out, he waded mechanically through the shallows where the willing hands of sailors hauled him unceremoniously into a small craft crowded with exhausted men on the first stage of their repatriation to England.

Later arrivals were not so fortunate. Shortly after Harris was rescued the French entered the town where shots from their cannon obliged the few remaining vessels to weigh anchor and abandon the many hundreds still struggling across country to reach the harbour and the safety of the fleet.

Chapter 6

CORUNNA

Midday of 11 January saw the last of Moore's soldiers hobbling painfully along the cobbled streets of Corunna, whilst their General and his Staff anxiously scanned the horizon for a sight of the transports which had been delayed by contrary winds in the Bay of Biscay. The few ships which had arrived the previous afternoon were barely adequate to accommodate the sick and the probability of Moore having to fight a major battle with his back to the sea increased with each passing hour.

A brief survey of the area showed him that Corunna possessed only two advantageous positions from which to fight a defensive action, Monte Mero and Penasquedo, the first hill being slightly overlooked by the other. Moore did not possess sufficient numbers to occupy both hills and, after a close examination, he chose the Monte Mero where a scattering of boulders and a tangle of scrub afforded a measure of cover for his skirmishers. Thus Monte Mero became Moore's right flank, the valley and the village of Elvina, three miles from the city, his centre, while his left flank extended to the deep and fast-flowing estuary of the River Mero.

Two days after Sir John's arrival the first of the delayed naval transports dropped anchor in the Bay and the embarkation began with the sick and the cavalrymen, who, now that they were dismounted, were of questionable value, and the bulk of the artillery. Most of the boarders discovered that a wooden vessel wallowing in the Atlantic swell was a far from comfortable berth and Captain Alexander Gordon was not alone in being quickly driven below into what he called "my floating dungeon" by a violent attack of sea sickness.

A painful duty was now imposed upon the cavalrymen of the Hussar and Light Cavalry. Because of the shortage of suitable accommodation, orders were given that only the best of the surviving horses were to be shipped home. It was therefore decided that it was the responsibility of the riders of the less fit to put down their own mounst. Many troopers who had seemed indifferent to suffering during that dreadful retreat "had

50

tears in their eyes", wrote Schaumann, "and more than one begged the infantry to carry out the sorry business." The quayside soon began to echo to the sound of musket shots and, noted Private Pococke, "The animals, as if warned by the dead bodies of their fellows, appeared frantic, neighed and screamed in the most frightful manner. Many broke loose and galloped along the beach with their manes erect and their mouths wide open."

Later that morning of the 13th, during a time of relative quiet, the peace was abruptly shattered by a massive explosion. An arsenal containing 4,000 barrels of gunpowder, originally intended for use by the Spaniards, was destroyed in an eruption that shattered almost every window in the city, although three miles away. As Spaniards and Britons alike gazed in astonishment at the twisting mushroom of black smoke and ash climbing into a cloudless blue sky, further explosions were heard as the bridge over the Mero was destroyed by Moore's engineers. The demolition party, unsure of the amount of powder necessary, ensured success by packing enough to have blown up a structure twice its size. The bridge disintegrated in a pall of smoke and dust, hurling slabs of masonry several hundred yards, to the consternation of a Company of the 28th, who had one man killed and several others injured by flying stones.

The destruction of the bridge at El Burgo prevented the French from crossing the flooded river in strength, but by 14 January they were in possession of Penasquedo and had successfully hauled several of their cannon into position on the heights. From the summit Soult and his Staff could plainly see groups of redcoats deployed along the slopes of the Monte Mero and, beyond them, the red roofs of Corunna and the rigging of scores of ships in the Bay.

In the city, as the sun rose to disperse the early morning mist, Sir John Moore issued his final instructions for the embarkation of the main body of troops. Company officers were notified of the names of the various vessels allocated to their regiments and orders were given for the troops to retire under the cover of darkness with everything being done to ensure an orderly evacuation of the town. A few senior officers had mooted the suggestion that, like Dalrymple at Cintra, Moore should arrange a truce with Marshal Soult to discuss the possibility of an uncontested embarkation, but this Moore dismissed with contempt, confident in his ability to evacuate all of his troops that evening. As to the reference to what had happened at Cintra, commented Captain Hodge, "I fear if we come to a convention Bonaparte will not give us such terms as we gave Junot."

Later that morning, the details for boarding the scores of transports riding at anchor in the Bay being completed to his satisfaction, Sir John Moore turned to his Military Secretary and confided, "Now at last, if there is no bungling, I hope we shall get away in a few hours."

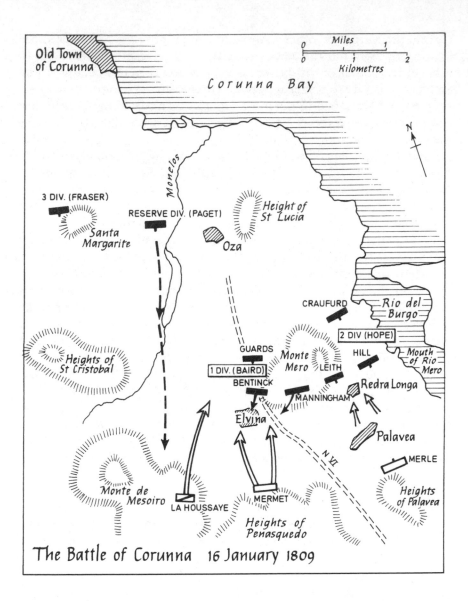

The Battle of Corunna 16 January 1809

On the summit of the Monte Mero the men gazing expectantly towards the enemy were all at once astonished to see a woman carrying a baby coming directly towards them. An Irish woman, the wife of a soldier in the 50th Regiment, she had been attended in her confinement by a French surgeon at Soult's expense. Seeing that her husband's regiment was within cannon shot of the French Lines, she had been sent across with the Marshal's compliments and his assurance that he would be visiting the regiment before the day was out. Later that morning the long-awaited orders were given for the divisions which had not been deployed

1. The Battle of Talavera, 28 July 1809. From the painting by R. Simkin.

2. The Battle of Busaco, 27 September 1810. From a watercolour by R. Simkin.

3. Ramsay's Troop at Fuentes de Onoro, 3 May 1811. From a coloured print after W. B. Wollen.

4. Ensign Latham defending the Colours at Albuera, 16 May 1811. From a painting by W. B. Wollen.

in the defence of the city to march down to the quay and the waiting ships. The Reserve, because of its good behaviour during the retreat, had been granted the privilege of being among the first to embark, but the troops had marched less than a hundred yards before the sound of three gun shots – an arranged signal from the hills – brought the column to a halt. The redcoats were not left in suspense. A perspiring aide, galloping furiously along the line of march, stopped for a brief word with the officer in charge and a few minutes later the men were about-faced and countermarching through the village of Los Ayres towards the Monte Mero.

At the city walls Captain Charles Boothby, busily supervising the erection of a battery, found that nothing he could say or do would persuade the working party to abandon its air of extreme fatigue. "Each shovel of earth approached the top of the bank with aggravated slowness," he wrote. Boothby was therefore pleasantly surprised by the change in behaviour when, early in the afternoon, orders came for the working party to rejoin their regiment. "All thoughts of tiredness was forgotten in an instant," wrote the Captain, "as the redcoats seized their muskets and capered about like boys unexpectedly loosed from school." He, too, was not sorry to abandon the task, for Boothby had never been present at a general action and he was resolved to offer his services to the first senior officer willing to find him employment.

As the Reserve hurried back to Monte Mero the Green Jackets were retiring from the village of Elvina before the dark blue masses of the enemy. Four French columns were advancing, two directed against the right wing of the British line, one against the centre, whilst the fourth threatened Moore's left flank. Major Charles Napier, anxiously watching his men disputing the ground with the enemy skirmishers, turned as a horseman reined in beside him. Looking up, Napier saw "a cream coloured horse with streaming mane, wildly rolling eyes and expanded nostrils." Thrown back upon its haunches, it seemed to Napier that the animal "would soon be away like the wind", but Sir John Moore, bent along the animal's neck, held it in check whilst he studied the oncoming French column "with searching intentness and anticipation".

The French advanced with their usual drummers and skirmishers preceding the main column while roundshot from their batteries on the hill rushed through the air with the noise of an express train, to fall on and around the British positions on the Monte Mero. Moore steadied his glass to look beyond the enemy column to where, half-hidden in the rolling clouds of smoke, French and Polish cavalry were moving along the lower slopes of Penasquedo in a bid to cut the British troops' line of retreat to Corunna. In order to counter this threat, a galloper was sent to Los Ayres with orders for General Fraser to despatch the 3rd Division to the heights of Santa Margarita and for Henry Paget to advance through the valley in a bid to turn the enemy's flank and capture his guns.

The infantry on the Monte Mero were undergoing a punishing bombardment from Soult's artillery. Solid iron shot weighing 12 lbs skimmed the crest of the ridge to rebound off the turf and hurtle on to cut bloody swathes through the assembled companies of the 4th, 42nd and 50th Foot. The noise from the artillery had increased to such an extent that Napier could scarcely make himself heard and he was on the point of pulling his exposed troops back when he was again joined by Sir John Moore. At that moment a roundshot struck the ground between them and, rising from its point of impact, tore the leg off a soldier of the 42nd. The luckless Highlander rolled across the ground, clawing at his wound and screaming, causing those about him to shrink back in dismay. The fear that was written on their faces did not go unnoticed by Moore and he spoke to calm them: "This is nothing my lads; keep your ranks," and then, his voice rising above the noise of battle, he turned to the stricken Highlander. "My good fellow," he said. "Don't make such a noise. We must bear these things better."

Colonel Wynch of the 4th Regiment of Foot was the next to receive a visit. His regiment, being on the flank, was in danger of encirclement and a quick appraisal of the situation was sufficient for Moore to restore the situation. Colonel Wynch was to draw back his right wing at right angles to his front so that at least half his men had a clear field of fire down the slope to the west, whilst the remainder kept watch on their front. This manoeuvre was executed almost if it had been carried out on the parade ground and drew from Moore the rare compliment: "That is exactly how it should be done".

Supported by a fierce cannonade, the French, led by General Jardon, a veteran of the revolution whose foul language was renowned throughout the army, were advancing in a two-prong attack against the troops on the Monte Mero. The right-hand column was climbing the slope towards the 42nd, whilst the left, believing the British could be outflanked, streamed into the valley around the foot of the hill in the direction of the city. To meet this threat, the Reserve, commanded by Lord Paget, who by now had reached the valley in strength, was sent by Moore to oppose the troops of General Merle's command. Meanwhile the rattle of musketry from the centre increased in volume and, judging that the village of Elvina was likely to become the scene of the fiercest fighting, Moore ordered the 50th and 42nd Regiments to throw back the French who had gained a foothold in the village. The 50th, led by George Napier's brother Charles, welcomed the chance of exacting vengeance for the miseries they had suffered during the retreat, and in a bitter bout of hand-to-hand fighting, the French were driven out of the village. The 50th, following up their success, dashed through the smoke-filled streets in pursuit, driving them to the boulder-strewn fields beyond. Here the advance was brought to an unexpected halt by a rain of shells and small arms fire so accurate that the Highlanders and the men from Kent were unable to leave the shelter of the rocks. In a sudden counter-attack by the French, Major Charles Napier was bayoneted as he lay wounded and, but for the intervention of a French drummer who shouldered the man aside, might well have been murdered. Napier was subsequently attended by Marshal Soult's personal surgeon and well treated even to the extent of being released before an exchange of prisoners had been agreed. Commented his brother George: "To treat your enemy when in your power with every respect and kindness is the true characteristic of a brave man . . . the French officers are as brave as any men upon earth, so their conduct was humane and generous."

Meanwhile Soult had discovered the true strength of the British line and the fighting had spread to all areas. Lord Paget, with five battalions, had succeeded in halting Merle's advance and his troops were now deployed behind the walled enclosures which dotted the lower slopes of the Monte Mero. The French dragoons had been thrown into confusion. Unable to gallop *en masse* over the obstructions, the troopers were forced to dismount and fight on the same terms as the infantry. Without the mobility of their horses, the dragoons were no match for Paget's troops, who quickly turned a retreat into a rout, driving the Frenchmen back to their original position on the slopes of Penasquedo.

At Elvina, the village had once again changed hands. General Baird had been gravely wounded and the survivors of the 42nd and 50th Regiments, having exhausted their powder, began to fall back in small groups. "Where is the General?" was the cry which echoed along the ranks. He was soon upon the scene on a lathered horse and once again Moore sought to encourage his men.

"My brave 42nd, join your comrades, ammunition is coming, and you still have your bayonets," he called. "Recollect Egypt, think on Scotland. Come on my gallant countrymen!" Inspired by the example of their General, the Highlanders lowered their bayonets and, with a cheer, charged back through the smoke.

The French began to give ground and Moore was seen to rise in his stirrups and shout encouragement before the sickening thud of a ball striking flesh and bone hurled him from the saddle. General Sir Thomas Graham immediately dismounted and, with the help of Captain Hardinge, raised the stricken Moore to a sitting position against the grass bank. Only then was the seriousness of the wound appreciated. Moore's collar bone had been shattered, the ball driving in a piece of his uniform jacket with two buttons attached. His left arm appeared to be retained only by a few thin strips of skin and his ribs had been stove in. The surgeon who examined Moore after his jacket had been removed was heard to mutter the one word, "Hopeless".

As Moore was being assisted to a more comfortable position his sword hilt became entangled in the wound and Hardinge made to entangle the sword belt. "Leave it," gasped the General. "It is better as it is. I had rather it should go out of the field with me."

Auguste Schaumann was a witness without knowing at the time just who the victim was. "Among many wounded men who were borne past us into the town, there appeared at about 4 o'clock a party of several aides-de-camp and officers," he reported, "marching very slowly and sadly behind six soldiers bearing a wounded man in a blood-soaked blanket slung upon two poles."

Moore was carried back to Corunna just as the responsibility of command was being transferred to another Scot, Sir John Hope, for Baird had also left the field, his right arm mangled by grapeshot and shortly to be amputated at the shoulder.

In the valley below the Monte Mero, the fighting had flared to a new pitch of ferocity as the Highlanders, inflamed by news that their beloved Commander had received a mortal wound, battled to clear a path through the streets of Elvina to the fields beyond. In a fierce counter-attack the French troops strove to re-take the positions they had lost, with the support of General Reynaud's brigade of Swiss attacking from the south. There followed a desperate struggle at close quarters with dirk and bayonet and the butt end of muskets, as the Highlanders met them on the gorse-covered slopes.

The bleak January day was moving to a close when the French, whose ammunition was running low, began to give ground and in the fading light they were at length recalled by their drums beating to retire. The Swiss troops had also halted and Sir John Hope, conscious of his duty in bringing back the only army Britain possessed, dismissed the temptation to continue with the advance and rode straight from the smoke of battle to supervise the embarkation before Soult should decide to resume hostilities. So ended the battle of Corunna and, as General Hope rode past a small white house near the quay, Sir John Moore died peacefully in a darkened room just before the first of the British regiments began to leave the field to take its place in the queue waiting to be rowed out to the transports. By 9.00pm long files of weary troops, hollow-eyed, faces black with powder and in tattered uniforms stained with blood, marched through the lamp-lit streets past appalled spectators, many of whom made the sign of the cross, down to the harbour and the safety of the fleet. Marching with them was Private Thomas Pococke who, like many of his companions transferred to the suffocating heat below decks, soon began to suffer torment from the lice infesting his filthy clothing. Others aboard the crowded vessel had fallen into the deep sleep of total exhaustion, but a few may have noticed in the dawn light of 17 January a small burial party from the 9th Foot making its way slowly along the ramparts of the citadel. Their late Commanding General was quietly and without pomp or ceremony being conducted to his resting place.

At midday, with the embarkation almost complete, Captain Boothby accompanied Colonel Fletcher on an inspection of Corunna's defence works. The two engineer officers found little to engage their expertise, for Spaniards of both sexes manned the batteries and, inspired by a patriotic zeal, they were resentful of foreign interference and it was made clear to them that advice of any kind was far from welcome.

Early the next morning, the ships in the Bay weighed anchor, harassed by a string of parting shots from the artillery sited on the hills. Fortunately for the unwieldy transport vessels, the range was too great for accuracy, but it did cause a few nervous captains to cut their cables with the risk of running aground. Sergeant Robertson, in a contemptuous reference to the manning of his own ship, recorded that, as a consequence of the enemy fire, the sailors refused to man the rigging and it was left to the soldiers to work the vessel. "The French," he wrote, "maintained their bombardment till the *Victory* of 98 guns brought her broadside to bear upon them and quickly silenced their noise."

Two days after the last vessel had sailed for England, Corunna fell to Soult's troops, leaving the stragglers of the late Sir John Moore's army to return to the Portuguese capital as best they could. At Abrantes Ensign Thomas Bunbury, who had been left behind suffering front dysentery, was given charge of one such group and ordered to conduct it to Lisbon. He found it almost impossible to keep the redcoats sober. A store of brandy was discovered in Villa Velho and the entire party, with the exception of a sergeant, became so drunk that a day was lost before the march could be resumed. Discipline crumbled and the soldiers began to quarrel among themselves, leaving the 17-year-old Ensign at times powerless to exercise his authority. On these occasions Bunbury introduced a novel solution to the problem by urging the belligerents to settle their differences in the time-honoured fashion of bare-knuckle fighting.

"I told them not to stand scolding like women," explained Bunbury, "but to fight it out like Englishmen."

After several fights had taken place, order was usually restored.

Bunbury's party was fortunate in having a relatively trouble-free journey, for, although it was made over atrocious roads in poor weather, they were the first redcoats to pass through the Tras dos Montes and, because of this, received greater hospitality from the mountain villages than might otherwise have been the case.

Meanwhile the homeward bound transports, their passage speeded by gale-force winds, had disgorged their human cargoes at almost every port between Falmouth and Dover. For five days from 23 January large crowds had gathered to witness the return of Britain's first expeditionary force to Spain. At Portsmouth they gazed in astonishment, shocked by the fearful appearance of the ragged, grime-encrusted redcoats. Tired men leaning heavily upon the sailors guiding them ashore, many were shoeless with feet swathed in blood-stained filthy rags, caked in mud and carrying weapons dulled with rust.

"In our present dirty, ragged, verminous condition," admitted Sergeant James Hale of the 9th Foot, "we were not fit to march through clean Christian country."

The disturbing spectacle of weary soldiers dragging lacerated feet over sharp cobbles led one of the spectators to consider whether something could be done to improve the quality of military footwear. He applied his considerable skills to such good effect that by 1812 Marc Isambard Brunel had secured a contract to satisfy all of the Army's specifications, leading even the august personage of Lord Castlereagh to sing the praises of Brunel boots.

The ill-fated expedition into Spain had proved disappointing in what it had achieved and expensive in terms of manpower. More than 6,000 soldiers had been lost and, of those who had returned from the Peninsula, so many were suffering from typhus and other illnesses that the hospitals in the coastal towns were unable to cope, leaving an overflow of sick and wounded to the basic facilities of the prison hulks. In these foetid and vermin-infested confines deaths reached a peak of fifteen a day and it soon became apparent to George Canning and members of the Cabinet that it would be many weeks before Britain's army was sufficiently recovered to resume the Peninsula campaign.

In marked contrast to the enthusiasm which had accompanied the news of Britain's decision to come to the aid of the Spaniards, there was now little sympathy for their cause. The soldiers' descriptions of bleak windswept heaths, freezing mountains and vermin-infested hovels, to say nothing of the indifference of the Spanish people, was more than enough to confound earlier romantic notions of sunny Spain.

In the recriminations which followed an investigation into the conduct of the campaign, it was inevitable that a scapegoat should be sought by the politicians. Doubts were cast upon Sir John Moore's qualities of leadership. He was blamed for the widespread breakdown in discipline, and was even criticized for his failure to solve the logistical difficulties when they arose. Many members of the House took the view that, had Sir Arthur Wellesley been in command, events would have turned out differently.

"His memory was assailed alike by those politically opposed to his party and by those who were once his supporters," noted Robert Blakeney. The fact that Moore's venture into Spain had prevented Napoleon from occupying the whole of Portugal was conveniently forgotten, and it was left to Moore's adversary to perpetuate his memory in Spain. Marshal Nicolas Soult, when he learned of Moore's death upon entering Corunna, in recognition of his gallant conduct, caused the body to be re-interred in the garden of San Carlos and an inscription engraved upon a rock near the spot where he fell:

Hic cecidit Johannes Moore, Dux Exercitus,
In pugna Januarii xvi 1809,
Contra Gallos, a Duce Dalmatiae ductes.

Chapter 7

TALAVERA

With the evacuation of the British army from Corunna and Vigo effective opposition to the French in Spain, save that from the various guerrilla bands, had almost ceased. The remnants of Romana's tattered battalions and a few thousand disorganized troops led by General Don Gregorio Cuesta in Estremadura were now all that the Central Junta could call upon.

Portugal, at the beginning of 1809, was in a similar position, for, with the exception of a few thousand British troops in Lisbon, there was no disciplined force in either country capable of offering anything more than the bare minimum of resistance. The French, by exploiting these weaknesses to their best advantage, had overrun Spain and northern Portugal, capturing Almarez, Badajoz, Ciudad Rodrigo and Oporto.

At Oporto Richard Henegan, who, in his capacity as Military Commissary, was responsible for issuing small arms ammunition and muskets to the insurgents, had only narrowly escaped capture when the French entered the city on 29 March. Enraged by the discovery of the mutilated bodies of their comrades – the work of a local guerrilla band – the French indulged in an orgy of violence. From a vantage point on the opposite bank of the Douro, Henegan was a horrified witness to the indiscriminate slaughter of the citizens. The only escape from the marauding French was across the bridge of boats which soon became crowded with panic-stricken men, women and children fleeing from Soult's rampaging troops. Fearful that the enemy would follow them across the river, an officer cut loose the central barge, causing the bridge to collapse, trapping those pushing from behind and precipitating scores into the fast-flowing Douro, where many drowned.

Marshal Soult hesitated to resume his march on Lisbon and, not daring to defy Bonaparte's instructions by returning to Spain, decided to remain in Oporto and declare himself the provincial Governor.

Foreign occupation had quickly led to feelings of bitter resentment in the towns and cities of Spain, but the spirit of patriotism burned even fiercer in the breasts of the fanatical peasantry, who believed that the French were the "instrument of the Devil", a view which the Catholic Church certainly encouraged.

In Spain towards the end of 1808 the Central Junta gave its blessing to the creation of various irregular bands of peasant volunteers, smugglers and former soldiers, which, from their familiarity with the terrain, were able to wage a merciless campaign of harassment against French convoys and couriers. At first their numbers were not great, but, as the efficiency of the Spanish armies declined, so that of the guerrilla bands increased. Theirs was literally a war of extermination. No quarter was given and those unfortunate enough to fall prisoner were subjected to the most horrendous torture before being put to death.

One act of cruelty was invariably answered by another. Several of the followers of 'El Empecinado' were captured by the French and nailed to a tree. Less than a week later a similar number of Frenchmen were also nailed to trees and left to die slowly of hunger and thirst. Brutal activities such as this were not confined to Spain, for in a village outside Lisbon Sergeant Lawrence of the 40th came upon a group of peasants who had surrounded a wounded Frenchman with a heap of blazing straw. Every time the prisoner tried to crawl out of the circle of fire, he was thrust back by the pitchforks of his tormentors. Lawrence and his companions quickly scattered the Portuguese but too late to save the unfortunate Frenchman from the consequences of his maltreatment.

In northern Spain guerrilla activities were so successful that the French were obliged to establish a chain of blockhouses built of wood extending almost to the Pyrenees in order to protect their lines of communication. Every convoy was provided with a military escort from one fort to the next; even so the danger was such that an officer was obliged to settle his gambling debts before embarking on any such journey.

The leaders of these Spanish partisan groups were capable and often colourful individuals. Among the more notorious, was Don Julian Sanchez, formerly a butcher in Ciudad Rodrigo who, with his thick-set build, swarthy complexion, long hair and moustaches, seemed the very personification of a bloodthirsty bandit chief. He was also to become notorious for his gruesome habit of presenting Wellington not only with the contents of a captured despatch pouch, but also with the head of the decapitated courier.

Francis Moreno was another celebrated leader who once boasted of having ambushed a cavalry patrol in a ravine and, by the discharge of a huge blunderbuss loaded to the muzzle, killed or wounded nine Frenchman at the expense of a dislocated shoulder.

Perhaps the most accomplished of these skilful leaders, however, was

Francisco Mina who waged a veritable 'war to the knife' against the French invader in Navarre. As his reputation spread, so the strength of his band increased, eventually reaching the astonishing figure of 10,000 of the best irregulars in Spain.

Whilst the war smouldered on chiefly through the activities of the various guerrilla groups, the Cabinet was busily preparing to launch a second British expeditionary force to be maintained from home ports. The success of the plan depended largely upon the retention of Portugal, with Lisbon being the army's main base of supply. This meant that the Portuguese would be expected to play an active role in co-operation with her British ally.

Sir Arthur Wellesley, from his earlier experience, had quickly recognized that a major defect in the Portuguese army lay in the poor quality of its senior officers, and Castlereagh readily agreed that, financed and placed under the command of British officers, that army could be a valuable addition to the expeditionary force. To this end General William Carr Beresford was invited to accept the Portuguese rank of Marshal and given the task of introducing the British system of drill. This he was to do with such good effect that before the war was ended the Portuguese Cacadore regiments had established an enviable reputation as a fighting force respected by friend and foe alike.

After a heated debate in the Commons, for Wellesley's part in the signing at Cintra had not been excused by the opposition, it was agreed that he should be given the overall command of the new expeditionary force to Portugal. By nature cold and egoistic, Wellesley nevertheless was a born leader and his return to the Peninsula was to have a profound effect on the future course of the war.

Following the evacuation of Moore's army from Spain, a mixed force of British and Portuguese amounting to 10,000 had been left in Lisbon under the command of Sir John Cradock, a man who, "if he had been in any manner successful," Sir Arthur, with recollections of his own embarrassment after Vimiero, would have been reluctant to supersede.

With the collapse of the indigenous armies in Spain, the French were free to invade Portugal, which they meant to do with three separate columns: Soult from Galicia, Lapisse from Salamanca, and Victor by way of the Tagus Valley.

With less than 10,000 men to defend the whole of Portugal, Cradock could be forgiven for believing that a second evacuation of British forces, this time from Lisbon, could not be long delayed. Others disagreed, and General Beresford, with the strong support of Rowland Hill, persuaded the reluctant Cradock to halt the advance of the French by garrisoning troops at Abrantes, Leira and Almeida.

Towards the end of March 1809 a second British expeditionary force set sail for the coast of Portugal. It was not as large as Wellesley's first command, but, with the troops already at Lisbon and its environs, he would have available 30,000 British troops supported by 16,000 Portuguese now trained to acceptable standards by Marshal Beresford. Among those that boarded the transports at Dover on a blustery spring morning were two young Irishmen of the 1/95th Regiment. Twenty-one-year old Edward Costello and Thomas Plunket were returning to the Peninsula after serving with distinction during Moore's fateful march into Spain.

The tedious passage to Lisbon was made more bearable for the three hundred troops crowding the small vessel by the regimental band playing popular airs on the quarter deck. Dancing was a traditional naval pastime in which the soldiers soon joined with enthusiasm. It served as a pleasant diversion for the troops and, in the hornpipe, Costello informs us, "The beating of his feet in the double shuffle" drew loud applause for Tom Plunket not only from the Riflemen but from the entire ship's crew.

After little more than a week the vessels dropped anchor at the mouth of the Tagus and the troops were ferried ashore in small boats. The cavalry followed in flat-bottomed barges adapted to allow the horses to be put over the side in slings before swimming for the beach. Lieutenant William Tomkinson, in company with his brother officers of the 16th Light Dragoons, was billeted in Belem close to the stables of the Royal Palace. Tomkinson, who dreaded returning to his flea-infested quarters at night, and Ross-Lewin of the 32nd, were unanimous in their criticism of the town and its inhabitants: 'Of all residences, a Portuguese house is the worst," complained captain Ross-Lewin. "They do not seem to know what comfort means, and the filthiness of their abodes is insufferable." Such adverse comments were not restricted to Belem. In Lisbon every main street seemed to Private Wheeler to be crowded with "corpulent priests and verminous beggars", whilst Ensign George Bell discovered to his cost that a stroll through the narrow streets was a hazardous under-taking from the slops thrown from the upper balconies into the gutter below. Later arrivals faced similar experiences and, writing to his father in August, Lieutenant William Bragge was scathing in his description of the city's street cleaning methods: "On setting foot on land you are almost overcome with the stench, every filth being thrown into the streets and left there until it pleases God to wash the Town with a shower of rain, a rare occurrence except at particular seasons of the year, when I hear they are deluged with it."

Sir Arthur Wellesley arrived during the third week in April and im-mediately dismissed any lingering notion of abandoning the country to the French, or even waiting to be attacked. Within thirty-six hours of coming ashore he had finalized plans for a march against Marshal Soult at Oporto in the north of the country.

The situation which faced Wellesley could not have been more daunting. The march to Oporto involved an arduous journey of 160 miles over rough country. Marshal Victor, with 25,000 troops, menaced Lisbon from the east, while between Soult and Victor was General Lapisse with another 6,000 men at Ciudad Rodrigo, to say nothing of the 200,000 French troops scattered over the rest of the Peninsula.

After two days, during which time Beresford had pushed far inland to seize the bridge at Amarante, Wellesley entered Coimbra on 1 May – his 40th birthday – beneath a cascade of rose petals from balconies crowded with enthusiastic townsfolk.

Seventy miles further north, four days march for Wellesley's troops, Marshal Soult was enjoying the attractions of the amply provisioned town of Oporto, blissfully unaware of the close proximity of the British, and Wellesley, who had left Coimbra to begin his march on Oporto on 8 May, continued his progress unmolested by French patrols. In the early hours of the 10th his columns were marching along the main highway, preceded by the 16th and 20th Light Dragoons, when the cavalry blundered into a string of enemy vedettes. This clash with General Franceschi's Chasseurs provided William Tomkinson with his first, and very nearly his last, taste of action since arriving in April. Over wooded terrain quite unsuited to cavalry the young Cornet's troop was ambushed in a narrow lane bordered by high hedges. The lane ended in a walled enclosure having a gateway scarcely wide enough for a single horse and there Tomkinson found himself confronted by a line of infantry spread out across a field. He was in the act of firing his carbine at the head of the nearest Frenchman when an agonizing pain in his arm caused him to drop the weapon and collapse across his horse's neck. His next recollection was that of cantering through a large body of the enemy with both arms hanging useless at his side. Fortunately for the young Cornet, his horse, reacting to the jab of a bayonet, turned and galloped wildly to the rear with the nineteen-year-old, whose strength was rapidly failing from loss of blood, just managing to keep his seat until knocked senseless by a low-hanging branch. William Tomkinson's recovery was to be slow and painful. The dried blood was not washed off his arm until a month later when the injury had been probed anew and a jacket button extracted.

The next day General Franceschi's mounted infantry withdrew across the Douro, destroying the bridge of boats behind them.

Almost the first decision made by Wellesley on reaching the south bank of the river at Vila Nova was to set up headquarters in the Convent of Santo Augostinho sited 150 feet above the river. From this vantage point the British commander surveyed the walled city of Oporto through his telescope. He immediately noticed that a large stone building across the river – in fact the Bishop's Seminary – was unguarded and screened from observation by the surrounding trees. Soult had removed all the river craft to the north bank, but, if a crossing could be made, the assault party would have every chance of seizing the building which would give them a foothold on that side of the river.

Fortunately, while he continued to examine the area, a Portuguese barber provided Wellesley with the solution to his problem. The barber, brought to him by an officer on Wellesley's staff, had crossed the river in a skiff which had been concealed from the French, with the news that four empty wine barges lay partly buried in the mud but undamaged and unguarded on the French side of the river, east of the walled city. Wellesley, in high spirits, exclaimed, "By God! Water's has done it," in a reference to the Colonel who had questioned the barber. A salvage party was at once sent to recover the barges and within the hour they had successfully brought all four to the south bank unseen by the French. Each was capable of carrying thirty men and, once they had been made secure, no time was lost in putting Wellesley's instructions into effect and with a gruff word, "Well, let the men cross," three Companies of the 3rd Foot were poled across the three hundred yards of fast-flowing waters hidden from observation by a mass of vegetation on the overhanging cliffs. For an hour the barges crossed and recrossed, each conveying its human cargo without a shot from the enemy to disturb the peace.

In fact Soult, confident that only a large-scale operation by the British could pose a threat, was sitting down to an early lunch, and it was said that, on being notified that British troops were believed to be crossing the river, exclaimed, "Bah! It is just a party of red-coated Swiss going down to bathe."

Ensign Bunbury had been in the second barge and he now led his men up the grass slope to the unoccupied Seminary which was quickly forti-fied with the help of men from the 48th and 66th Foot. When at last the alarm was raised and General Foy rushed his brigade to the scene, six hundred British infantrymen were firmly established on the north bank and howitzers had been placed in position on the high ground across the river from where the very first shell burst among a French gun crew as they manoeuvred their piece into position, killing every man in the team.

As the enemy swarmed towards the Seminary Thomas Bunbury noticed that every Company had a drummer boy at its head, creating as much noise as he could, and it was these poor wretches who fell victim to the musketry directed against Foy's advancing columns. Without their drummers, the three French battalions seemed to lose much of their vigour and, faced with disciplined volleys from 48th and 60th and a plunging fire from the howitzers on Convent Hill, Foy's assault soon broke down. A second attack, led by Delaborde, fared no better over the open ground and the French retired to the city's eastern suburbs, abandoning their wounded.

Now that the remaining boats no longer had guards, dozens of Portuguese were able to ferry them across and return packed to the gunwales with redcoats. Within the hour the 29th Foot and the Guards were busily engaged with the French, fighting their way up the steep, cobbled streets, where, assaulted on every side, the French were driven out of the city and into headlong flight down the road to Beltar.

The rapid advance of Wellesley's troops had not been achieved without a considerable number of casualties on both sides; wrote Lieutenant Hawker, "The streets were strewn with dead horses and men, and the gutters dyed with blood."

So rapid and complete was the British victory that the Guards officers entering the Palacio das Carrancas were able to do justice to a dinner which had been laid out for the consumption of Soult and his staff.

As Soult's broken battalions hastened along the road they were briefly menaced by General Murray's column which had crossed the Douro east of Oporto. That General failed to press his advantage, however, and it was left to Charles Stewart's 14th Light Dragoons to fall upon Soult's rearguard and take three hundred prisoners.

By the following day Beresford and the Portuguese had reached the port of Amarante on the Tamega, to cut Soult's line of retreat and leave him with just one escape route northward across the mountains. Faced with what was going to prove a test of endurance, the Marshal abandoned everything that could not be easily transported, including the sick and wounded, and after a hasty retreat along winding tracks half-buried in vegetation, he emerged in the Ave Valley on 13 May. A further six days' march in pouring rain across the rocky uplands of Galicia brought him and his weary troops across the frontier to the town of Orense.

Defeated and dejected, his men then discovered that the inhabitants had fled, leaving nothing behind and Soult was obliged to continue the withdrawal as far as Lugo, which he reached on the 23rd. There they joined Ney's Corps, little better than a ragged starving mob, many barefoot and the majority without knapsacks or firearms.

The two Marshals met in an atmosphere of mutual antipathy. They quarrelled constantly, on one occasion even to the extent of drawing swords, as a French officer was to inform Captain Boothby many months later. Ney's parsimonious attitude to replenishing Soult's depleted stores was bitterly resented by the Marshal and the officers from both camps were quick to catch the mood of their respective Commanders. Duels were fought and brawling became so widespread that Soult and Ney were forced to recognize that only a combined operation against the insurgents in northern Galicia would improve morale.

Having abandoned the pursuit of Soult and seen that Portugal was free from French occupation, Sir Arthur Wellesley turned south for Abrantes, reaching that town on 7 June, but with his troops in a wretched state. Many were shoeless from the forced marches over muddy roads, provisions were scarce from the failure of the Commissariat to find any means of transport, and officers and troops were alike in arrears of pay. "The army is still three months in arrears and the Commissariat without a farthing and a year in debt," complained John Mills in a letter to an uncle. "So much for the Civil Department . . . grumbling is a true picture of our present state."

Despite the privations it had undergone, the morale of Wellesley's small army was high. Only the fact of an almost empty Military Chest prevented the British Commander from conducting a fresh operation against Victor in New Castile. In a letter to the British Ambassador in Lisbon, Wellesley had made his difficulties plain to see. "I should begin immediately but I cannot venture to stir without money," he wrote. But by the end of the month sufficient finance had been raised to enable him to prepare for a combined operation with the 70-year-old Spanish General Don Gregorio de la Cuesta against Marshal Victor in the Guadiana Valley. Leaving the recently formed Portuguese Militia to guard the Galician frontier, Sir Arthur crossed the border near Zarza la Mayor on 4 July with 23,000 men for his meeting with Cuesta near Talavera

The difference between the two countries was as immediately apparent to Wellesley's troops as it had been to those of an earlier campaign. Leaving behind the dilapidated smoke-blackened hovels whose occupants, from constant exposure to wood smoke, gave every appearance of premature ageing, the redcoats now passed through hamlets of neat whitewashed stone. Lieutenant George Simmons was astonished that such a marked contrast in manners, customs and appearance could occur in the space of a few miles. "The Portuguese peasant wrapped in a large brown cloak with his long uncombed hair hanging loosely about his shoulders," he wrote, "presented a most unfavourable contrast to his neighbour across the border." The Spaniard, he found, unlike the Portuguese, took a pride in his appearance. His costume was neat and his hair combed and plaited. It occurred to Simmons that the Spanish peasant "had a distinct advantage over most others of a similar class". There was one facility for which he was especially grateful. The billets in Spain, even the poorest, afforded a greater degree of comfort than those available in Portugal. At least one room was guaranteed to be free from a leaking roof and an icy draught. Although the floors were usually of baked clay, the simple furnishings of the Spaniards' accommodation were spotlessly clean and the officer of the 95th looked forward with relief to a night's sleep undisturbed by fleas or bedbugs.

Whilst his men enjoyed a few days of pleasant relaxation in their new surroundings, news reached Wellesley of Victor's concentration of troops at Merida on the Guadiana with the possible intent of attacking Cuesta's army before the British could reinforce it. The decision of Wellesley to advance into Spain with a small mixed force of 20,000 Anglo-Portuguese was undoubtedly attended by a high risk factor. Not only did he have the army of Marshal Victor to contend with but Joseph in Madrid could call upon Ney, Soult and Mortier, all with sizeable armies within easy marching distance of the Tagus Valley, whilst General Sebastiani with 20,000 men was just 75 miles to the south east at Madridejos.

As uncertain of the odds ranged against him as Joseph was of Wellesley's movements, Sir Arthur left Abrantes on 27 June to effect a rendezvous with Cuesta before marching on Madrid. It was a march notable for the degree of indifference with which every request made by the Commissariat for supplies was met by the Spanish authorities. The granaries and store houses of Spain were far from empty, but, despite promises from the Junta, Wellesley's troops often went hungry. The Army lacked funds to purchase provisions from local sources, the soldiers had not been paid and, as the situation worsened, discipline broke down completely and looting became widespread. Although the most troublesome group was undoubtedly the Irish, the miserable plight of peasant families standing in silent despair beside the blackened ruins of their homes evoked feelings of pity from at least one Irishman when their plight reminded Costello of the good fortune of his countrymen in not having their land laid waste by a marauding army.

In the weeks since leaving Abrantes for the Alberche Wellesley's troops had covered a distance in excess of 150 miles to reach Oropesa on 21 July, where they joined with Cuesta's force, comprising 27,000 infantry and 6,000 cavalry supported by thirty cannon, for a joint operation. The two leaders had met ten days earlier at Plasencia for a four-hour meeting which had not been without its difficulties. Don Gregorio Cuesta, described by Edward Costello as "that deformed-looking lump of pride, ignorance and treachery," had been badly bruised in a confrontation with the French at Medellin; he could speak neither French or English and was fiercely jealous of his independence. There followed a lengthy discussion about the tactics to be employed against Victor in which Sir Arthur requested that 10,000 Spaniards should be held available to protect the northern flank of Wellesley's proposed march on Madrid. Cuesta could not agree and it was only after an exasperated Wellesley

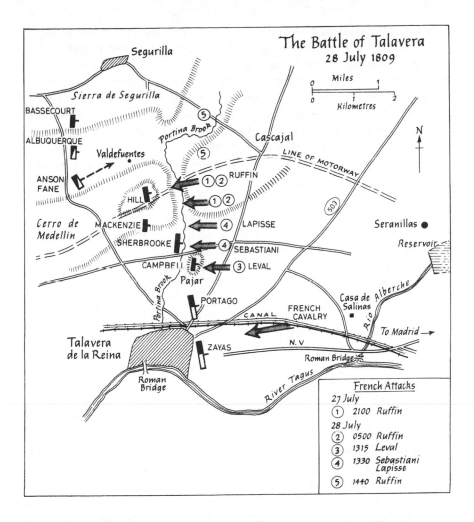

The Battle of Talavera
28 July 1809

Miles
0   1
0   1   2
Kilometres

Segurilla

Sierra de Segurilla

BASSECOURT

ALBUQUERQUE

Valdefuentes

Portina Brook

Cascajal

LINE OF MOTORWAY

ANSON
FANE

HILL

(1)(2) RUFFIN

(1)(2)

503

Seranillas ●

Reservoir

Cerro de
Medellin

MACKENZIE

(4) LAPISSE

SHERBROOKE

(4) SEBASTIANI

CAMPBELL

(3) LEVAL

Pajar

Portina Brook

PORTAGO

CANAL

FRENCH
CAVALRY

Casa de
Salinas

Alberche

Rio

To Madrid →

Talavera
de la Reina

ZAYAS

N. V.

Roman Bridge

Roman
Bridge

River Tagus

French Attacks		
27 July		
(1)	2100	Ruffin
28 July		
(2)	0500	Ruffin
(3)	1315	Leval
(4)	1330	Sebastiani Lapisse
(5)	1440	Ruffin

threatened to withdraw to Portugal that a joint operational plan was at last finalized.

The combined strength of the allies was believed to be greatly superior to any that either Victor or Joseph could bring against them and, with the Spanish General Venegas's 30,000 men in the north available to exert pressure on Sebastiani's brigades near Madrid, the way was open for the allies to strike a damaging blow against Victor at Talavera.

At first all went well and it was not until the two armies were encamped beside the Alberche that enemy pickets were seen for the first time in some strength on the opposite bank. The river at that point was fordable and the opportunity existed for an immediate attack on the French forces, but when the British Commander requested an audience with the Spaniard he was told that Cuesta was asleep and could not be disturbed.

69

At dawn the next day Wellesley brought his troops to a state of readiness in the confident expectation that their combined forces would cross the river, but, it being Sunday, Cuesta declined to march and an incredulous Wellesley was obliged to stifle his anger and order his brigades to stand down. The next day, the 24th, the combined force did advance, but by then it was too late; the French had fallen back ten miles and the allied force had missed a chance to defeat Victor before he could be reinforced by either Joseph or Sebastiani.

Now that the enemy had retired the Spaniards were all for pursuit, despite advice to the contrary, but Cuesta was adamant and, although Wellesley declined to join him, the Spanish General left on the 25th, determined to meet Victor at Toledo.

Anglo-Spanish relations were now at a low ebb and for most of that morning the redcoats watched with ill-concealed contempt as 6,000 Spaniards left in a cloud of dust accompanied, as one British soldier noted, "by various musicians, priests and camp followers".

In the afternoon they were back. Cuesta's dream of destroying Victor's army and liberating Madrid without the assistance of the British had vanished when, instead of finding a comparatively weak army near Toledo, he was charged by the dragoons of Latour-Maubourg and put to flight. The strong force of French cavalry galloped in pursuit but could only inflict a minimum of casualties before the Spaniards were able to rejoin their ally across the Alberche in some disorder.

Sir Arthur Wellesley, meanwhile, had been reconnoitring an area three miles north of Talavera which promised a strong defensive position, placing the Tagus on his right flank and extending over broken ground to the Cerro de Medellin and a deep ravine on his left. The two Commanders had previously agreed that the Spaniards should be deployed in an area around Talavera intersected by olive trees and irrigation ditches, while the British occupied the northern sector which was mainly scrub.

After crossing the Alberche, Victor's troops began the day's operations by surprising Mackenzie's battalions which had been covering Cuesta's crossing of the river, causing them to fall back in some disorder, a reverse in which Sir Arthur and his Staff were fortunate to escape capture, galloping off with the noise of a fusillade of musketry singing about their ears. An even greater embarrassment was to befall the Spaniards when, later that afternoon, French cavalry approached the position held by Cuesta's troops and, although out of range, the French amused themselves by letting loose an occasional shot from their carbines. The reaction from Cuesta's men was singularly odd. Their entire line fired a volley which created so much noise that four battalions threw down their muskets and, with shouts of "Treason!", fled in disorder, only stopping to loot the British baggage train in the rear. Wellesley, who stood a short distance away, stared in amazement as they streamed past him, but restricted himself to a single comment: "Just look at that ugly hole those fellows have left." Cuesta, to his credit, quickly filled the gap and, although many who had deserted their post returned, he ordered the immediate decimation of the guilty battalions. Wellesley managed to dissuade him from committing such an extreme act, but, as an example, the Spanish General ordered the execution of thirty men.

As the light faded Wellesley's troops, satisfied that there was no threat of further action before daybreak, posted their pickets and settled down for a night's rest on the steep hills of the Medellin in the anticipation of a major battle in the morning. In fact three battalions were to be engaged much earlier than expected, for, aware of the importance of the Medellin ridge, Marshal Victor had decided to launch a night attack. It was only partially successful, for, of the three regiments which launched the attack, two lost their way in the darkness and only the 9th Legere managed to scale the slope to surprise a brigade of the King's German Legion. In a bitter exchange of fire the brigade was routed, but General Hill, bringing up three battalions from Stewart's brigade, caught the French as they were reforming and drove them back down the slope at the point of the bayonet.

In the town of Talavera Captain Charles Boothby discovered that the wildest of rumours were circulating. The occasional thunder of cannon and the crackle of musketry had given rise to fears that the French were about to overrun the suburbs. Their fear was such as to cause many of the inhabitants to panic, rushing wildly about, as Boothby colourfully phrased it, "with as much anguish in their faces as if they already felt French bayonets in their bodies."

Tired of refuting the townsfolk's accusations that the British were abandoning Talavera to its fate, Boothby decided to ride towards the position occupied by Major-General Charles Stewart's brigade on the slopes of the Cerro de Medellin, only to spend the hours of darkness among the dead and listening to the groans of the wounded.

Among those whose task it was to defend the heights Ensign Bunbury lay wrapped in a cloak which was of no further use to its owner. Having the regimental colours wrapped around his body as a further insulation against the cold, he drifted into a fitful sleep only to be aroused as dawn was breaking by the thunderous explosions from fifty cannon. King Joseph had reluctantly agreed to Marshal Victor's suggestion that a fresh attempt be made against the Medellin ridge and at 5.00am an avalanche of iron enveloped the British positions along the entire length of the ridge. As roundshot tore great gaps in the ranks of an adjacent battalion and fused shells burst to scatter lead balls in all directions, Ensign Bunbury ensured that his men were lying prone against the rearward slope. Other officers were quick to follow his example and, by so doing, greatly reduced the number of casualties. Shortly afterwards the plunging fire was replaced by roundshot. Bunbury's men could plainly see the heavy iron balls rolling towards them with deceptive slowness from their first impact with the ground, but, although almost spent by the time they reached Bunbury's position, the mass of iron still possessed sufficient momentum to cause terrible injury, as one luckless redcoat discovered to his cost; stretching out to arrest one's progress, his foot was horrifically mangled.

The British six-pounders were not long in replying to the French cannonade and the crest of the ridge soon became enveloped in a pall of black smoke. A light breeze carried it towards the advancing French, effectively masking the Grenadiers of General Pierre Lapisse's division as they led an attack against the redcoats positioned on the heights. The Green Jackets on the forward slope retired before a screen of voltigeurs, pausing occasionally to load and fire their Baker rifles as the two French columns emerged wraithlike from the fog of battle. At the centre of the British position General Stewart had deployed his men in a double line stretching some two hundred yards, which gave him an advantage of 1,500 muskets to bring to bear upon the compacted enemy columns.

As Lapisse 's infantry emerged from the swirling smoke, sixty men wide and forty deep, the waiting lines of redcoats stiffened in anticipation of the command to fire. The distance between them and the French was less than twenty yards when the order came. The volley which crashed out wrought terrible destruction among the closely packed ranks of Grenadiers, which quickly broke apart in confusion. The French soldiers, stumbling and reeling in the smoke, left the ground littered with heaps of their dead and, as they desperately tried to reform, a second volley struck them with equally deadly effect. To shouts of "*Sauve qui peut!*" the dazed grenadiers retired in haste to the bottom of the hill.

In less than five minutes the attack by General Pierre Bellon Lapisse had collapsed in bloody ruins before his men had been able to engage with Stewart's redcoats. When Victor's second column failed to push the British off the hill the intensity of the fighting slackened and, as the sun climbed higher in the sky, groups of sweating and powder-blackened warriors, at first in dozens and then in hundreds, broke ranks to make their way down to where a muddy pool of water known as the Portina Brook wound its way between the antagonists' lines. Blue, red, and green-coated figures mingled on the friendliest terms as French and British soldiers quenched their thirst and filled their canteens. Jocular remarks were exchanged in broken English and fractured French as old campaigners shared a pipe of tobacco or swapped flasks of brandy or skins of wine, until the rattle of drums and calls from a bugle summoned them back to their respective stations.

Shortly after midday a concentrated bombardment from the French artillery preceded a massed attack by Sebastiani's and Lapisse's divisions as, 20 miles away, the Light Brigade hurried towards the sound of gunfire. Craufurd's men were nearing the end of a march remarkable for the distance covered – 42 miles in 26 hours over sandy terrain and beneath a burning sun. Nearing the conflict, the alarming reports that they received from the walking wounded and deserters from Cuesta's army, rumours that Wellesley was dead and that the battle was lost merely served to increase their anxiety to reach the scene of battle.

It was now the turn of the cavalry to make their contribution and early in the afternoon French dragoons spurred furiously towards several hastily formed British squares to be met by a hedge of bayonets and disciplined volleys which brought men and horses crashing to the ground in a tangle of broken limbs and thrashing hooves which broke the impetus of the charge and impeded the oncoming squadrons. The infantry, following in the wake of the cavalry, attacked the centre of Wellesley's position, driving Sherbrooke's skirmishers out of the olive groves to approach within fifty yards of the British line. Orders were rapped out: "Make ready! Present! Fire!" Struck by the devastating impact of 4,000 musket balls, the leading French files were swept away. Lapisse fell mortally wounded and the attack disintegrated in the face of rolling volleys of musketry. Victor's courageous troops were forced back across the bloodstained waters of the brook. Cheering wildly, the Brigade of Guards and the two battalions of the K.G.L rushed in pursuit and were themselves subjected to a fierce counter-attack which inflicted heavy casualties, the Guards alone losing more than six hundred men.

Wellesley's cavalry had as yet played only a small part in the battle but now, as a new threat from General François Ruffin's division took shape to the north of the Cerro, the 23rd Light Dragoons and the 1st Dragoons of the K.G.L were ordered forward to engage them. As Ruffin's infantry, warned of the approach of the horsemen, formed square to meet cavalry, the dragoons broke from a trot into a canter when several hundred yards away and were soon stretched in a wild gallop across the intervening scrub. It was then that disaster struck. A dry watercourse some nine feet wide and six feet deep lay across the path of the charging horsemen, concealed by the tall waving grass. Colonel Elley, several lengths ahead on his superb grey charger, cleared the dry bed in a prodigious leap, but the following cavalrymen were not so fortunate or so skilful. Caught by surprise, the dragoons tumbled headlong in a tangle of screaming horses and cursing troopers. The few who emerged without serious injury remounted and galloped on, but with diminished enthusiasm, until,

73

exhausted, demoralized and outnumbered by more than five to one, they came to a halt before the waters of the Alberche there to be made prisoner.

The suffering of the wounded, and for that matter the horses, lying helpless on the battlefield, was now increased by the long tinder-dry grass being set ablaze by smoking shells and smouldering cartridge papers. By early evening a wall of flame fanned by a strong breeze had swept across that part of the field to engulf the injured of both sides, who, because of their wounds, were unable to crawl away.

With three hours of daylight remaining, six thousand dead and wounded lay across the area and the soldiers of both armies were totally exhausted.

King Joseph, fearful that the Spaniards might be closing on Madrid and realizing that the day belonged to Wellesley, ordered an immediate retreat, much to the disgust of Jourdan who suggested that they wait for Soult to arrive with his division.

Sir Arthur may have toyed with the idea of pursuit, but, faced with the uncertainty of securing the co-operation of Cuesta and short of wagons, was content for his soldiers to bivouac for the night, thankful that the bloody affair was over.

Before daybreak the last of Joseph's forces had crossed the Alberche and were back in their old positions around Toledo.

The two days' fighting had cost them 7,270 officers and men, several field commanders and seventeen guns. Wellesley had not escaped lightly, for in the savage fighting the British had suffered 6,700 casualties – almost a quarter of their strength – and Wellesley himself was fortunate to escape serious injury when he was struck on the chest by a spent musket ball.

The total butcher's bill surprised even the veterans of previous hard-fought campaigns. "I never saw a field of battle," confessed George Napier, "which struck me with such horror as Talavera."

On the morning of the 29th General Robert Craufurd arrived with the Light Brigade, after accomplishing a prodigious feat of marching to reach the battlefield only in time to witness the stripping and looting of the dead by the people of Talavera. The plain was strewn with hundreds of muskets, wrecked caissons and blood-stained clothing. Here and there a few poor wretches with shattered limbs dragged themselves with cries and groans from smouldering patches of grass and, certainly in the view of George Simmons, the scene was as horrific as any he had witnessed. As he gazed at horses with swollen bellies and stiffened legs, and corpses whose distorted faces had been blackened by the sun, he wished for a moment that "he had not embraced the trade of a soldier with so much enthusiasm".

Since there were no burial parties available the 1/95th was given the task of collecting the bodies and building them up into large heaps mixed with faggots for burning. The first few cremations created such an unpleasant stench that Costello's Company rebelled against the duty and this method of disposal was soon abandoned.

No longer sustained by the excitement of battle, Corporal John Cooper became aware of the fact that he had not tasted food for almost 48 hours. It was not the fault of the Commissariat, who had arranged for the distribution of a large number of loaves, but of Cuesta's men who in the early stage of the battle had broken open the store house to leave nothing for their British ally. The Spaniards, by robbing the peasants of the bread and vegetables they were offering for sale, had made the shortage even worse and prices rose so sharply that George Bell was obliged to pay six dollars for a loaf of bread. These inflated prices were beyond the reach of most redcoats who in many cases discovered that their appetite anyway was no match for the awful smell rising from the hundreds of swollen bodies scattered across the sun-baked battlefield.

Chapter 8

BUSACO RIDGE

The first day of August brought the disturbing news that Soult, with 15,000 men, having brushed aside the feeble force of Spaniards led by the Marquis del Reino at Banos, had reached Plasencia with the aim of seizing and destroying the bridges over the Tagus at Almarez and Arzobispo. These crossing points were vital to the British army's line of communication with Lisbon and, after a heated exchange with the Spanish General Cuesta, who still entertained thoughts of a march on Madrid, Wellesley gave orders for an immediate withdrawal. Since there was no possibility of obtaining transport for the 1,500 wounded – British and Spanish – they were to be left in the care of the Convent nuns.

Two days after Wellesley had first learned of Soult's movements, the remaining 1,800 men of his command, including the Light Brigade, left at daybreak in full marching order for Oropesa. It spelt the end of both his and Cuesta's hopes of taking Madrid, and was a melancholy occasion for many of those leaving, for the redcoats could hear, rising above the jingle of equipment, the pleas of the wounded begging their comrades not to desert them. "Wounded and sick men who one would have thought incapable of moving suddenly recovered the power of their limbs," recalled Schaumann, "and staggered, limped and hobbled away, so that they might escape falling into the enemy's hands."

Among those left behind was Lieutenant Peter Hawker, his hip shattered by a ball during one of the last engagements. For reasons unknown to him, Hawker was refused entry to the Convent by the Spanish custodian, despite his urgent pleading. "Thus I was left bleeding in the street," he later wrote, "surrounded by the most pitiable and horrid objects that can be imagined, who were lying on the pavement, screaming and groaning, without the soothing of compassion or succour of any kind." Fortunately, his plight was seen by an officer of the hospital guard and Hawker was eventually given a comfortable billet.

The army had moved westward towards the mountains, their route marked by a trail of the wounded who had succumbed to freshly opened wounds or had collapsed from exhaustion. In the event the fears of those left behind proved groundless, for the French, impressed by the care given to their own wounded by the British surgeons, showed great compassion towards their redcoat prisoners, treating their wounds with sympathetic consideration. One captive in their care was Charles Boothby, whose leg had been badly mangled in the night attack against the Cerro de Medellin. For several days Boothby had lain recovering from an amputation awaiting the arrival of the French with some trepidation. He need not have worried for the French even allowed their British prisoners to keep the specie they had plundered from the battlefield.

Later during the march word reached Sir Arthur of just how outnumbered his small force was, for Soult's army had been sadly underestimated and was double the strength Wellesley's staff had estimated. Even this knowledge paled into insignificance when a captured despatch was sent some hours later by General O'Donaju, Cuesta's Chief of Staff. From its contents Wellesley learned that three French Corps, to the number of 50,000, were advancing through the Pass of Banos from northern Spain and would shortly be in a position to occupy most of the country.

It was obvious to the British Commander from his recent experience with Cuesta that the Spanish army was in no position to meet this threat and was in grave danger of annihilation. Therefore his main consideration had to be that of a continued British presence in the Peninsula, even if this meant an immediate retreat to the Portuguese frontier.

The war was becoming one of manoeuvre rather than confrontation and this new phase was likely to prove as dangerous and far more demanding to his exhausted and hungry troops than a pitched battle.

"We are starving," Wellesley wrote to Beresford on the 19th, "our men falling sick, and we have nothing to give them in the way of comforts; and our horses are dying by hundreds in the week. . . . We have no means of transport, and I shall be obliged to leave my ammunition on the ground on quitting this place."

Fortunately, not a moment too soon, the Government agreed with Wellesley that the future of Europe would most likely be settled in the Peninsula and reinforcements were quickly raised from the Militia and put under sailing orders. Portuguese troops in the pay of the British were increased to 30,000 and as many battalions as could be spared from the disastrous Walcheren expedition were redirected to Portugal.

Meanwhile, the retreating army found the long march back to Lisbon by way of Badajoz tedious in the extreme. The rough country roads had to be widened in many places to allow the passage of artillery and, because of the acute shortage of commissariat wagons, the hungry soldiers could only assuage the gnawing pangs of hunger with wheat which they boiled into a thick paste, complemented with honey when they could obtain it.

It was hunger and not the close pursuit by the French cavalry which caused the men of John Green's Company the greatest anxiety. After a hard day's march each man of the 68th Foot was grateful for an issue of four ounces of flour, which, after being dampened and rolled into balls, was then boiled in a kettle. John Green, as he finished the last of the 'doughboys', remembered that it was his village's 'feast day' and he thought with envious longing of his friends at Lutterworth in Leicestershire sitting down to roast beef and plum pudding.

Now that high summer had reduced the river level to little more than a few pools, the banks of the Guadiana were covered with copious masses of green slime and decaying vegetation over which clouds of gnats and mosquitoes hovered. The nauseating stench rising from these stagnant pools, together with the absence of a healthy diet, had its effect and the health of the troops suffered accordingly. An increasing number began to fall ill and a frustrated Wellesley was obliged to notify the Secretary of State for War: "With the army which a fortnight ago beat double their numbers, I should now hesitate to meet a French Corps of half their strength."

Some indication of the sorry condition of Wellesley's troops is indicated in the poor performance of Craufurd's Light Brigade, celebrated throughout the army for its marching ability. On 20 August it left Almarez and the Riflemen, who only three weeks previously had covered more than 40 miles in record time, were able to hobble no further than a few miles in suffocating heat before they were forced to halt. Some regiments were particularly badly affected and the hospital at Villa Vicosa soon began to fill with the victims of dysentery, fever and scorpion and snake bites. Among the invalids was a Fusilier from the 1/7th Foot. Although only half-conscious, John Cooper suffered tortures from the jolting of a bullock cart and it came as a great relief when he was deposited upon the cold flagstones of the hospital corridor. Since he was just one of hundreds of sick and dying, the Fusilier received little sympathy and, with his hearing impaired, the suppurating blisters on his feet and back undressed, Cooper felt that "no one on the hospital staff cared a straw whether I lived or died".

Faced with such indifference to their welfare, many soldiers sought the relief and comfort of alcohol, Corporal Plunket among them. Found the worse for drink while on picket duty Thomas Plunket was placed under arrest and confined to the guard house. There, still under the heady influence of the wine, he seized a musket and attempted to prime it before being overpowered. His offence was too grave to be overlooked and Plunket was sentenced to 300 lashes. Such was his popularity and standing in the Company, however, that, after witnessing the drummers administer 35 strokes of the cat, his Colonel brought the punishment to an end and Plunket was cut down and had his wounds dressed.

On 4 September Sir Arthur Wellesley was elevated to the peerage as Viscount Wellington of Talavera, although not until the 16th would the news reach him. Pressed to keep the army in Spain, the newly created Lord Wellington steadfastly refused to enter into any joint venture with the Spaniards. He was content for the moment to remain just inside the Spanish border at Badajoz.

It was now that Wellington took the opportunity of visiting Lisbon where he spent the next few weeks examining the terrain around Torres Vedras with a view to ensuring the security of this vital port. He had noticed the formidable barrier of steep and broken hills to the north of the Tagus, natural features of the country that were particularly suited to defence and, if supplemented with manmade redoubts, would become an impassable barrier to an enemy advancing towards the city from north of the Tagus.

By mid-November, Wellington had returned to Badajoz, leaving the construction of a double line of fortifications in the capable hands of his chief engineer, Lt. Colonel Richard Fletcher of the Royal Engineers. On his instructions work began on 20 October with a labour force of 7,000 Portuguese peasants who, over the next eleven months, were to complete a network of natural and artificial obstacles to become famous as the Lines of Torres Vedras. The cost was less than £100,000.

Two parallel chains of masonry redoubts with parapets twelve feet thick enfiladed all approach roads and defiles. Spaced some five miles apart, the Lines stretched from the Atlantic coast eastwards to Torres Vedras before turning south-east to the right bank of the Tagus, a distance of 28 miles. Colonel Fletcher was at pains to ensure that every natural obstacle was used to its best advantage. Rivers and streams were dammed in order to turn them into broad areas of marsh, bridges were mined and forward slopes treated to give a clear field of fire. A system of roads was built to ensure the rapid transfer of troops to any threatened sector, and a number of semaphore stations set up at strategic points to be manned by seamen from the British frigates in the Bay.

The construction of these complicated defence works had begun not a moment too soon, for by the end of 1809 the long-expected reinforcements to the French armies in Spain began to cross the Pyrenees. Long columns of wagons, artillery trains and blue-clad infantry wound their way through the passes, to follow a route already taken by many regiments of cavalry now spread out across the plain. By mid-January

French strength in Spain would reach the staggering figure of 325,000 men.

Next to crushing Spanish resistance, their principal objective was to drive the British army from the Peninsula and to this end Napoleon sent his most experienced Marshal. André Masséna, Duke of Rivoli, Prince of Essling, was a 52-year-old Genoese Jew, not popular with his immediate subordinates, who had only accepted the assignment with considerable reluctance. After 20 years of rigorous campaigning he did not enjoy the best of health, being troubled with rheumatism. He was certainly appreciative of the problems which faced him.

Masséna was not alone in having misgivings about campaigning in the Peninsula, for the British public, shocked by adverse reports from Spain coming so soon after what had appeared to be a brilliant victory, were growing pessimistic. Newspaper articles encouraged this view and accounts of operations in Spain painted such a picture of gloom that Lieutenant William Tomkinson, now fully recovered from his wounds and returning to Portugal, was surprised to discover that the army was not about to embark from Lisbon.

On 10 May the Army of Portugal, with Masséna at its head, arrived in Vallodolid with orders from the Emperor to lay siege first to Ciudad Rodrigo and then to the Portuguese fortress of Almeida 25 miles to the north-west. The border fortress of Ciudad Rodrigo was garrisoned by 5,000 men and commanded by the Governor of the town, Don Rodrigo Andres Herrasti. It was a formidable strongpoint built on the upper slopes of a steep hill overlooking the Agueda and a road bridge leading to the town.

Wellington's army, just to the west of the town, had not the resources to risk raising the siege and were obliged to adopt a passive role which did nothing to improve Anglo-Spanish relations. The Spaniards in Gallegos, a village just a few miles away, were bitterly critical of the decision and repeatedly asked the Riflemen billeted on them why they did not march to the relief of the garrison. The young women in particular were quick to point out that "if the English fought as well as they drank, they must be fine fellows indeed". These veiled accusations of cowardice were both galling and undeserved, but George Simmons found it useless to explain that his Company of Green Jackets were simply an advance party and too weak in numbers to be of any assistance to the garrison.

Ciudad Rodrigo, after a terrible bombardment lasting sixteen days, during which half the town had been reduced to rubble, fell to the French Marshal on 6 July. General Craufurd's Light Brigade had been engaged in skirmishes with the French almost every day since the beginning of the siege, but, with the surrender of the fortress, he was advised by Wellington to retire across the river in the event of Masséna capturing the town. Craufurd, however, was not the man to shirk a confrontation and he was determined not to retire until his brigade had given a good account of itself. Confident of the ability of his superbly trained Riflemen, he deployed the 4,000 men of the Light Brigade along the exposed bank of the Coa, with the river and its single bridge to the rear of the Brigade. Later that morning Ney's perusal of the area from the vantage of a tower confirmed his suspicion that Craufurd's only escape route lay down a narrow winding lane leading to the stone bridge over the river and he ordered an immediate attack.

Lieutenant Simmons of the 1/95th looked up from his post in a vineyard to where a mass of cavalry and blue-coated infantry were advancing rapidly across the fields towards the river. The attack against the riflemen was headed by a line of voltigeurs, closely followed by infantry, who pressed forward with drums beating and shouts of defiance at the riflemen who kept up a brisk rate of fire. Plunging shot now began to fall among the Green Jackets from the enemy's six pounders and when a strong force of cavalry was seen to be closing rapidly on their right flank the men of Simmons's Company were given the order to retire. They had scarcely set foot in the lane before a troop of Hussars in bearskin caps and light-coloured pelisses swept among the 95th to wreak a bloody execution among the riflemen. As Simmons dashed towards a group of the 43rd who were forming a protective square, several of the horsemen cut at him, but, aided by a timely volley from the redcoats, Simmons reached the protection of the square without so much as a graze.

The torrential rain of the previous night made a crossing of the Coa except by way of the Almeida bridge extremely hazardous and it was towards this that George Simmons and the surviving members of his Company ran with all possible haste. The French kept up a harassing fire from a walled enclosure, which caused considerable annoyance to Craufurd's men who were giving covering fire to the retiring Green Jackets. Directing this fire from the opposite bank, Captain Leach narrowly escaped death when a musket ball ripped through his shako, grazing his head before burying itself in the earth behind him.

Using the opportunity of a slackening in the enemy fire, George Simmons, with others, made a dash from the square in a bid to reach the bridge. He had almost reached it when he was struck by a ball and hurled to the ground. Dazed and suffering from shock, Simmons felt about his body for the wound. All feeling had gone from his legs and, looking down, he saw a stream of blood pulsating from a hole in his trousers. Fortunately for him, he was saved from bleeding to death by William Napier, who had the presence of mind to improvise a tourniquet from a neckerchief and a ramrod. So severe was the firing which had resumed from the hill that, within moments of arresting the bleeding, a sergeant who had been helping fell victim to a ball in the head. Lieutenant Simmons was carried off in a blanket by four of his men, in defiance of an instruction from General Craufurd, who had stipulated that the heat of an action was no time to go to the assistance of an officer.

In the rush towards the bridge Edward Costello narrowly escaped with his life when a dragoon seized his collar, while several others made a cut at him as they passed. A chance shot brought down the horse of his captor and, aided by a fellow rifleman, Costello was able to rejoin his Company at the cost of a painful leg wound.

Marshal Ney, believing that the precipitate flight to the opposite bank had sapped the morale of the riflemen, launched a determined attack on the bridge with a strong force of Grenadiers. But he had clearly misjudged the mood of the 95th, for, as Captain Leach commented, "A few hundred French Grenadiers advancing to the tune of *"Vive l'Empereur"* were not likely to succeed in scaring away three British and two Portuguese regiments supported by artillery."

The bridge was long and narrow and the concentrated fire from the five regiments soon cut a swathe of destruction through the oncoming French columns until the bridge became choked with the dead and wounded almost to the top of the stone parapet.

Jonathan Leach, watching the havoc being wrought by the rolling volleys of musketry, could only admire the bravery of the French and condemn the General responsible for such a foolhardy action. It seemed to Leach an unforgivable piece of butchery.

Lord Wellington, when he learned of "the foolish affair" in which Craufurd had involved his outposts, was furious enough to issue a reprimand. It was certainly justified, although most of the officers on Wellington's Staff acknowledged that no one other than Craufurd could have "fought himself so ably out of a scrape".

The retirement of the Light Brigade to Alverca had left the fortress of Almeida isolated and at the mercy of the French. On 15 August, flushed by his success at Ciudad Rodrigo, Masséna set up his siege train. He was in no great haste and it was not until Ney began a bombardment of the citadel and the town that the French began to make progress. Wellington had hoped that Almeida, strongly constructed and garrisoned by 4,500 Portuguese under the command of an Englishman, Colonel William Cox, would have resisted for many more weeks, but, within 24 hours of the first cannonade, the fortress suffered a signal catastrophe which overwhelmed the garrison. A chance shell ignited a trail of spilt powder back to the magazine and seventy tons of gunpowder erupted in a massive explosion which killed 700 men of the garrison and left only six un-damaged houses in the town. The fortress was rendered virtually defenceless and a demoralized garrison forced Cox to surrender after a siege lasting no more than twelve days.

With the capture of this last obstacle to his advance into Portugal, Masséna, at the head of 50,000 men and 80 guns, crossed the border on 16 September with a promise that no harm would befall the Portuguese people since his avowed intention was to regain their country for them from the English. The Portuguese, however, exhibited a marked lack of confidence in Masséna's promise by abandoning their homes and taking to the road, driving their cattle and poultry before them.

Peasant families, their few possessions piled high on donkeys, were joined by ladies of a more sophisticated class who stepped daintily over patches of mud in silken shoes, resigned to the necessity of sacrificing personal comfort to the interest of escaping the attentions of the rapacious French.

"It looked as though no soul that could move had remained behind," commented Lieutenant Field of the Guards. "The strong, the healthy and the young were on foot in flight." Inevitably there were distressing incidents and, in describing one, Auguste Schaumann wrote: "At one moment an old grandmother riding a donkey, supported by two other old women, could be seen passing through the throng, and a little later she was knocked down by a mule bearing a load of camp kettles, and, amid piteous cries, trampled under foot."

Given that each passing hour was vital to Wellington in his drive to reach the Mondego before the French, it was perhaps fortunate that the maps in the possession of Masséna's Staff were wildly inaccurate, being at least 30 years out of date. Not every road was featured and the French Marshal, by choosing a route through Viseu and the Sierra Alcoba in order to reach Coimbra, had taken the longest and possibly the worst, causing a relieved Wellington to remark, "There are many bad roads in Portugal, but the enemy has taken decidedly the worst in the whole kingdom."

The road taken by Masséna was a narrow twisting track strewn with rocks, in parts low-lying and marshy, making it difficult for the cavalry to move at anything quicker than a walking pace. The Portuguese guides employed by him were in unfamiliar territory; consequently his army made little progress and had constantly to widen the track to permit the passage of the artillery. Their slow and shambolic advance was admirably suited to the operations of the Ordenanza. These Portuguese partisans, with few weapons and no military training, descended from the hills at nightfall to create havoc among the crowded columns of the French infantry. Their tactics may have been crude, but a boulder rolled over a precipice onto carts drawn by slow-moving oxen was nonetheless effective. Under cover of darkness, small groups of men armed with blunderbusses would creep close to the enemy's bivouacs and discharge infuriating volleys of birdshot before melting away into the hills.

After four days of a perilous and uncomfortable journey, Masséna's army eventually reached Viseu on 19 September, where the Marshal was obliged to halt for a week in order to effect repairs to his artillery train.

These delays proved invaluable to Lord Wellington in his race to cross the river before the French and establish a defensive position on the heights of the Busaco Ridge. The site chosen was eight miles long, with Wellington's right flank extending to the river and his left stretching across broken ground to the Sierra de Alcoba and a Carmelite Convent at its northern end. The Busaco Ridge, "a damned long hill", in the opinion of one British officer, rose to almost 500 feet above the surrounding countryside with a slope so precipitous that the old Colonel of the 24th Foot had to be carried up in a blanket borne by four sergeants. A single road crossed the summit in the direction of Coimbra and, apart from one or two goat tracks, the only other path was a narrow lane which wound along the rear slopes through a pine wood to the Convent.

The steep slopes covered with heather presented Masséna with the difficult choice of either risking an attack or skirting the position held by Wellington. Despite his experience, after a brief survey of the ridge, the Marshal opted for a major assault with its attendant risks and issued orders for the following morning: "II Corps will attack the right of the enemy army . . . VI Corps will attack along the two pathways which lead to the Coimbra road . . . VIII Corps will assemble behind . . . and will make dispositions to support at need, the attacking corps, and to march on the enemy itself."

Wellington, as usual, displayed a cool attention to detail by issuing his orders in a crisp and precise fashion but in a way which left nothing open to question. Auguste Schaumann, who heard the orders communicated to the Staff, was impressed by Wellington's calm manner and lack of ostentation: "In his there is nothing of the bombastic pomp of the Commander-in-Chief surrounded by his glittering staff," he wrote. "He wears a feathered hat, a white collar, a grey coat, and a light sword."

The 34th Foot having taken up its allotted position, Lieutenant Joseph Moyle-Sherer climbed up to a position from which he could view the enemy camp and was astonished at the display of military might spread out before him. Immediately below, many hundreds of French soldiers were busily engaged in setting up their bivouac, while,

5. The Battle of Salamanca, 22 July 1812. From a painting by R. Simkin.

6. 'The Triumphal Entrance of the Duke of Wellington into Madrid' 12 August 1812. Mezzotint by John Bromley and J. G. Murray.

7. Wellington crosses the Pyrenees. From a painting by T. J. Barker.

8. The Rifle Brigade at the Battle of the Pyrenees, 25 July 1813. From a painting by R. Simkin.

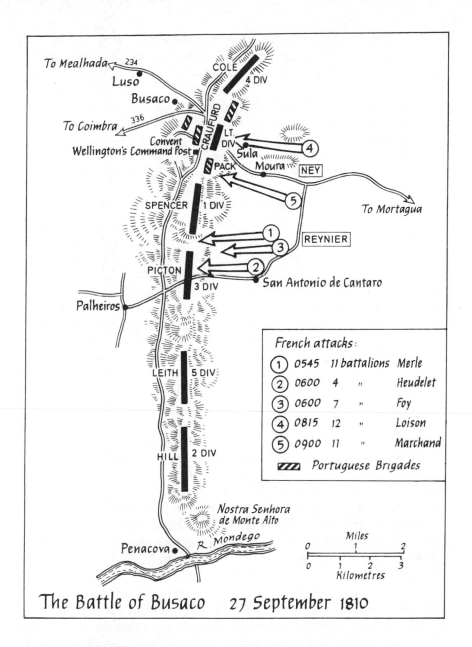

The Battle of Busaco   27 September 1810

French attacks:

①	0545	11 battalions	Merle
②	0600	4 "	Heudelet
③	0600	7 "	Foy
④	0815	12 "	Loison
⑤	0900	11 "	Marchand

▨▨ Portuguese Brigades

stretching far into the distance, the glitter of steel and an occasional flash of polished brass displayed the approach of Masséna's army, some 65,000 strong.

With the onset of darkness came a sharp drop in temperature, but on the heights occupied by the British no camp fires were lit for fear of betraying the deployment of the troops. Captain Leach, huddled for warmth beneath a blanket, stared down at the myriad points of light in the French camp and thought that it "was a sight indescribably grand, and far exceeding the illuminations that were ever exhibited at the Vauxhall or Tivoli Gardens".

At daybreak on 27 September the beating of drums and the notes of a bugle betrayed the fact that the French too were alert and preparing for battle. It began with a screen of tirailleurs leading two divisions of Reynier's II Corps against what was believed to be Wellington's right flank but was actually his centre. As the French climbed laboriously up the heather-coated slope to emerge wraithlike from the early morning mist a double line of redcoats made sure that their muskets were primed and loaded. The British and Portuguese riflemen fell back before Reynier's infantry, scurrying from boulder to boulder and discharging their Baker rifles as the opportunity presented itself. The Portuguese were in high spirits noted one Green Jacket, laughing and shouting encouragement whenever a well-aimed shot brought a Frenchman tumbling down. The undergrowth and the patchy fog affected the cohesion of the enemy columns and their progress was further hampered by the galling fire from a battery of Portuguese six-pounders. Although the mist and swirling clouds of smoke greatly reduced the visibility, the leading French regiment, the 31st Leger, could just be seen inclining across the broken ground to the south, seeking to conceal its deployment in an area of patchy fog. As they passed across the front of General Mackinnon's 74th and 88th Regiments, they were met by rolling volleys of musketry which decimated their leading files and brought the regiment to a stumbling halt. General Merle's division, following in their wake, fared little better, although his troops did gain the crest of the hill. There, however, they were subjected to a flanking fire from Picton's 88th and 45th Regiments and a pounding from a battery of field artillery which had galloped into action. The closely packed columns of Merle's division, each 40 men wide and 50 ranks deep, suffered severely from grapeshot before the 36th Leger broke ranks and fled the escarpment in confusion.

Meanwhile Ney had committed Loison's and Marchand's twelve battalions to a difficult climb against Craufurd's defence line on the crest of a hill near the Convent. Advancing from a wood which masked the Convent from their view, the Frenchmen slowly picked their way up an ever-steepening slope to where, concealed in a sunken road, Craufurd waited with the 43rd and 52nd Regiments. Seeing nothing but a battery pulling away from the crest, Loison's troops surged forward with triumphant shouts only to come to an astonished halt as 1,800 redcoats rose from cover in a double line to loose a tremendous volley from less than ten yards.

"Now! Fifty-second, revenge the death of Sir John Moore," roared General Craufurd. George Napier, dashing forward at the head of his Company, quickly became embroiled with a Grenadier who lunged at him with his bayonet. The thrust was partly parried by Napier's sword but, in deflecting the blow, Napier received the contents of the Frenchman's musket just below his hip. As the Captain fell, a blast of musketry swept over his head to bring down several of those behind him. Napier ever afterwards maintained that the flesh wound he received that day, although leaving him with a permanently stiffened leg, very probably saved his life.

Stunned by the sudden appearance of Craufurd's brigade and the carnage from that first volley, the French were quickly driven to the foot of the hill. Even there the unfortunate Grenadiers did not escape further punishment, for Picton's artillery continued to direct a rain of shells and grape upon them as they struggled through the narrow streets of San Antonio.

The battle over, each side set about the grim task of recovering the wounded and burying the dead. Men who had earlier fought each other with the utmost ferocity now exchanged good-humoured banter until they were called away by their bugles. "For all the world," commented George Napier, "like a parcel of schoolboys called in from play by their master."

By mid-afternoon Masséna, recognizing that his bid to take the Busaco Ridge had failed, abandoned the attempt and withdrew the various brigades. When darkness fell he left his camp fires burning and marched off along the Malhada road near Sardao and on 1 October entered Coimbra.

French casualties had been severe. A captured Grenadier, in conversation with John Leach, told the rifleman that his Company, which had numbered more than one hundred in the morning, could barely muster twenty at its roll call in the evening. Sixteen-year-old Ensign William Hay was new to campaigning, having joined his regiment just two days after the battle, and his first impressions of a soldier's life fell far short of his expectations. "The weather was wet and cold and the roads in a most dreadful state," he wrote, "and I shall never forget the shock to my nervous system on seeing the careless way the bodies of dead men were trodden on as we passed them lying in the muddy roads." Later, with experience, he was to become quite familiar with such sights.

The misfortunes of the French did not diminish after Busaco, for the battle had exposed a serious shortage of provisions among Masséna's troops, a scarcity which was not resolved as they progressed towards Lisbon.

"We chiefly lived upon Indian corn and beans," confessed Joseph

Maemphel, "but by degrees these became scarcer, and we suffered severely from want of all kinds."

Unhappily for the young Saxon, his was to be a permanent state of hunger not to be relieved until he was taken prisoner by the British some seven months later.

Chapter 9

'I WILL INSURE YOU ALL NOW, FOR HALF A DOLLAR BY GOD!'

Elated at the successful outcome of their confrontation with Masséna's elite divisions, Wellington's troops resumed their march on Lisbon, but at a leisurely pace now that the French were known to have taken a circuitous route along the coastal plain.

The attempts made by Masséna's troops to take the Busaco Ridge could not have been more gallant and they had suffered accordingly, conservative estimates being in the region of 800 killed and 3,500 wounded. That the allies' casualties of 1,250 were proportionally so much less was no doubt due to Wellington's choice of a defensive position and the superior fire power given by line over column. Even so, the number of allied wounded had been considerable and Private Donaldson, resting at the side of the road, watched the long trail of wagons bearing the wounded on their long journey to the hospital at Cavallos with a sympathetic eye. They were carried in the usual open carts whose rough wooden wheels, described by him as being "more nearly octagonal than round", shook the unfortunate casualty violently at every rut in the road. For a long time afterwards the hideous screeching reminded Joseph Donaldson of "the pallid faces and heart-rending groans" of the poor wretches he saw that day a few miles beyond Busaco.

Coimbra was reached shortly after Lord Wellington's proclamation urging the Portuguese to adopt a scorched earth policy and leave nothing of benefit to the enemy. The inhabitants of that town had obeyed his instructions to the best of their ability, vacating their homes and taking with them those goods which could be easily carried and concealing or destroying the rest. When the 16th Light Dragoons trotted down the main street a few hours later it seemed as though they had entered a ghost town.

Lieutenant Tomkinson, who had dismounted to enter one or two of the houses, discovered, however, that one owner, in his haste to leave before the arrival of the French, had abandoned several fine linen shirts and other personal effects. Geese and chickens grazed freely in his garden and the dragoon officer could not help thinking with envy of the sumptuous meal a Frenchman would enjoy.

Masséna's troops, when they did enter the old University town several hours after the last British soldier had left, proceeded to sack it with their customary efficiency ,even to the extent of removing gold rings from the fingers of corpses in the graveyard. But, while the French stayed to plunder, Wellington's redcoats had increased the pace of their retreat, covering some twenty miles a day with Craufurd's brigade, now reconstituted as the Light Division, bringing up the rear. There were frequent clashes with the enemy's vedettes and, in retiring with the rearguard after one such skirmish, Tomkinson narrowly avoided being made prisoner after his bridoon rein caught in the webbing of a French Hussar he had unhorsed. In a frantic attempt to break free, Lieutenant Tomkinson set spurs to his horse, but the rein held firm and, finally, with the enemy almost upon him, he managed to cut through the leather with his sword. As he galloped thankfully away, Tomkinson vowed that never again would he ride into action with a loose rein.

The last few days of September saw Wellington's army marching among an ever-increasing number of fugitives and their emaciated livestock. George Napier, bringing up the rear of this tide of human misery, could still find a pang of remorse, despite the pain of his wound. That he and his companions should be instrumental in inflicting such distress, however indirectly, troubled his conscience and he "heartily cursed the war and all its dreadful consequences".

An officer who had earlier condemned the Spaniards for their show of indifference to the suffering of the British troops during their retreat to Corunna could sympathize with the plight of these refugees. In a letter to his mother Captain William Warre described the effect of the scorched earth policy adopted by the Portuguese acting on Wellington's advice: "It was impossible to pass through a country so completely devastated without feelings of horror and pity for suffering humanity. . . . It is quite impossible to give people in England an adequate idea of the sufferings of these unhappy people."

Little more than a week's march away lay the ingenious series of defence works known as the Lines of Torres Vedras. They had been kept such a closely guarded secret that many of the troops, until the Lines were reached on 8 October, believed that Lisbon and another shameful evacuation lay in front of them.

On 6 October the French marched into Villafranca in a rainstorm and, from prisoners taken in a skirmish with Anson's cavalry, Masséna learned that Wellington had halted behind "some sort of defence line" around Lisbon.

The French Marshal had been expecting Wellington to offer battle and, when, on 14 October, he saw the Lines for the first time, he was astonished at their complexity. It was plainly impossible to force Torres Vedras and he turned angrily to his Portuguese guides to demand why he had not been informed of the full extent of these works.

Nervous explanations that the Lines were but of a recent construction and therefore not shown on any map were brushed aside by Masséna with the angry retort, "*Que diable! Wellington n'a pas construit ces montagnes.*"

Although any attempt to storm the defence works would be certain to end in disaster, the Marshal was nevertheless reluctant to leave the area. There was always the chance that Wellington might be tempted to leave the entrenchments, but the British Commander was far too experienced to commit any such folly and for the next few weeks the respective armies remained passively awaiting developments, although the British did not relax their vigilance.

Towards the end of the month the weather worsened and, although the redcoats enjoyed a greater share of provisions, they could do little to mitigate the discomfort brought on by the pouring rain. The picket huts, for the most part simple constructions of bracken and turf, soon fell apart and blankets hastily draped over a wooden support afforded poor protection against violent gusts of wind and rain. Huddled miserably together in their bivouac, Grattan and his friends could do little more than wrap their cloaks tightly about themselves and, wrote the Ensign philosophically, "seek solace from good cigars, brandy punch and convivial conversation."

A surprisingly friendly relationship was quickly established between the French and British outposts, and it was not uncommon for the soldiers of each army to be seen fraternizing and drinking wine from each others' canteen. Indeed, it was rare for any feeling of hatred to be expressed and, as George Napier commented after an officer of the opposing picket had been entertained to supper, "I should hate to fight out of personal malice or revenge, but have no objection to fight for fun and glory."

On another occasion General Beresford, as Commander-in-Chief of the Portuguese Army, was invested with the Order of the Bath at Mafra before a glittering assembly of allied officers and prominent members of the Civil Authority, while, less than a quarter mile away, the French looked on as interested spectators. It said much for the spirit then prevailing that guests who had celebrated a little too freely and strayed into the French lines after dark were all returned safely the following morning.

As the days passed a shortage of provisions and the persistent rain, which was turning the French camp into a mud pit, were making

Masséna's position almost untenable and his soldiers were forced to scour an increasingly wide area for food with diminishing success under leaden skies.

"The army was in a miserable condition," confessed Joseph Maemphel, "without clothes, without shoes, without provisions, and reduced half in numbers . . . no one could assist his comrade, because no one possessed anything."

Every day deserters streamed into the British lines, many in a pitiful state after having existed on a diet of undigested maize collected from the dung of horses and washed and fried. Having known acute hunger himself, Sergeant Lawrence could sympathize with the wretched condition of the French.

"They were far away from all supplies," he wrote, "and there were guerrillas always on the watch to intercept such as were sent."

Cut off from Almeida and Ciudad Rodrigo by guerrilla bands in the north, his soldiers facing starvation and their numbers continually being reduced by sickness, Masséna at last decided to withdraw to Santarem on the night of 14 November. Under the cover afforded by a dense fog, he began a retreat through a denuded countryside over roads made almost impassable by cloying mud. In order to deceive the English patrols, figures of straw, dressed in old uniforms complete with shakos and sticks to represent muskets, were set up in positions usually occupied by sentries. So successful was this ruse that it was not until the 16th that Masséna's withdrawal was discovered and the pursuit taken up.

The nature of the waterlogged ground prevented any operation on a large scale, however, and Wellington had to be content with the rounding up of marauding parties and the occasional straggler. Lieutenant William Tomkinson found himself actively engaged in this work, for Masséna's orders had been carried out so promptly that many in his foraging parties, unaware of the decision to retire, were left straggling all over the province. For the most part Tomkinson found that his prisoners were glad to be taken, thankful that an English patrol had saved them from the vengeance of the Portuguese.

Four days after leaving Torres Vedras Masséna's army of 50,000 reached Santarem where it was dispersed behind the region's wide expanse of marshes to spend the winter under less trying conditions. Here the Army of Portugal remained for the next three months, barely sustained by roots, acorns and whatever produce the Portuguese had failed to destroy. The French foraging parties became adept at locating hidden caches of grain. One favoured method was to flood the area adjacent to a building and then dig wherever the water drained away more easily. Usually it was the spot chosen by the farmer to bury his corn. Another practice was to measure the outside of a cottage and, if the inside did not roughly correspond, then it was reasonable to assume that it contained a secret hide, not unusual among the homesteads in that part of Portugal.

During this period of relative inactivity, a supply of rockets developed by Sir William Congreve was sent out from England in order that Lord Wellington might witness a demonstration under field conditions. The rocket, usually with a 12pdr explosive head together with the propellent charge, was contained in a pipe made of stout leather mounted on a tripod and stabilized by means of a wooden stick up to 24 feet long. The rocket's hollow head, usually an explosive shell, contained a fuse to ignite a charge at a range of 800 yards, but was notoriously erratic, as this particular trial was to demonstrate.

A strong wind was blowing from the heights and Lieutenant Field, who was present among the observers, wrote, "The wind carried them perpendicularly up and brought two of them back among us; this made a scurry, and we galloped off in different directions, to give room for the shells to explode harmlessly."

As the last days of December brought Wellington's campaign of 1810 to a close, 200 miles to the south a Spanish garrison in Cadiz waited in the anticipation of a rescue by a Spanish army with the assistance of a British force from Gibraltar.

Earlier in the year, desperate for funds with which to maintain his armies in Spain, King Joseph had turned his attention to the rich province of Andalusia. French troops had not set foot in the region since mid-July 1808 and the Spaniards, taken by surprise, were thrown into disarray. With the fall of Seville on 1 February, the Supreme Junta had transferred its headquarters to Cadiz, with Marshal Victor's V Corps hard upon its heels. The Spaniards fell back before Victor to the Isle de Leon, a vast triangular marsh two sides of which were washed by the Atlantic and the third separated from the land by a stretch of water known as the Canal of Santi Petri. Without boats, Victor's progress towards Cadiz was effectively brought to a halt and the Marshal had to be content merely with the erection of batteries with which to enforce a blockade.

Now, almost a year later, an Anglo-Spanish army of 11,000 had disembarked at Tarifa to operate against the enemy's rear at Chiclana. The Spaniards were commanded by General la Pena and the British by General Sir Thomas Graham, who had agreed to place his force of 4,500 under the command of the Spanish aristocrat.

The 60-mile march along the coast towards Cadiz was beset with difficulties from the very beginning. La Pena insisted upon marching at night despite advice to the contrary from General Graham. It was, as the Englishman had predicted, a time-wasting exercise, for the troops became separated in the dark and the British column, led astray by its

Spanish guide, spent the greater part of the night searching for the main body.

On 2 March the allied soldiers surprised a picket and from the prisoners Graham learned that 3,000 of Victor's Corps had been sent to occupy Medina Sidonia some 12 miles to the east of Chiclana. It was therefore only necessary to make a feint against this weak force to oblige Victor to come to its assistance, argued Graham, and perhaps bring matters to a speedier conclusion. Despite the allies' superior strength, La Pena refused to act and, leaving a few hundred of his men to observe the movements of the French, he continued westward along the coastal road, requesting Graham to follow at his leisure.

So laggardly was the Spanish advance that Graham's leading battalions became entangled with the rear of the Spanish columns before more than a few miles had been covered. The redcoats waited patiently for the Spanish troops to resume their march, but when Q.M.S. William Surtees and several others of the 2nd/95th rode ahead to seek a reason for the delay, they found La Pena's men taking their ease at the edge of a stream. A few of the Spaniards were removing their shoes and stockings before crossing the stream, others were cautiously feeling their way through the water, carrying the officers on their backs. La Pena's lack of urgency so infuriated Graham that the fiery Scot promptly ordered the Spaniards to stand aside while the Rifles came up, together with a detachment of Horse Artillery. The Green Jackets exhibited their contempt for La Pena's disorderly approach by marching straight through the stream, which at mid-point was waist high, without a pause and in less than an hour Graham's contingent, together with all its equipment, was safely on the other side of the stream and in full marching order.

It was while fording a second stream that a cart came to a sudden halt when its wheels became firmly wedged between two large stones on the stream's bed. General Graham watched with mounting impatience from the opposite bank as an attempt was made to free the obstruction without success. Eventually Sir Thomas, reputed to be one of the strongest men in the British army, waded into the water and, setting his shoulder to the wheel, lifted the wagon clear of the offending boulders by his own efforts.

The slow progress of the Anglo-Spanish force had allowed Marshal Victor to leave Villatte's division outside Cadiz and, although unsure of the precise objective of La Pena's operation, to take up a position on the sandy heights between Chiclana and Barossa with Ruffin's division, whilst sending Leval on a flanking march to the north.

On 2 March La Pena, strengthened by the addition of 1,600 Spaniards and a number of guerrillas, continued his advance towards the forest of Chiclana until he halted on the Cerro de Puerco three days later.

Dominating this stretch of the isthmus now occupied by the allies was a hill rising to 160 feet above the surrounding countryside and crowned by a ruined watch tower known to the local Spaniards as the Vigia de la Barossa. Here a halt was made while a troop of the King's German Legion was sent to reconnoitre the district in a search for French patrols. Meanwhile, elated by a previous success against a French column near the village of Bermeja, La Pena invited Graham to join him in an operation directed against the investing forces around Cadiz. Sir Thomas, irritated by the irregularity and tardiness of the Spanish movements, merely pointed out that to abandon the hill they occupied would be a grave mistake, for the enemy was unlikely to attack La Pena's column while the threat existed of a strong force descending upon his flank. Since the Spaniards bringing up the rear were still straggling all over the country, La Pena could only agree, and he grudgingly agreed to Graham's request that three Portuguese and two Spanish battalions should remain to strengthen the single British battalion commanded by Colonel Browne. Reassured by this arrangement, Sir Thomas Graham resumed the march towards Cadiz through the pine woods on a parallel path to the coastal road taken by La Pena.

An hour after Sir Thomas's departure, the men of Colonel Browne's battalion, tired after their long march, sank gratefully down upon the turf on the reverse side of the hill. Their welcome break was soon interrupted by a trooper of the K.G.L with news concerning the approach of three enemy columns, preceded by cavalry, from the direction of Chiclana. Browne's battalion immediately formed square to meet the expected attack from cavalry and the Colonel, in an attempt to lessen the tension and lift morale, rode nonchalantly round the square issuing instructions and reminding his men "to be sure to fire at their legs and spoil their dancing". He had scarcely dismounted to take his place in the square when a voice from the ranks exclaimed in the thickest of Irish brogues, "Colonel! Sorr. What shall I do wid Commissary O'Meara's baggage sorrr?" "Take it with you to hell!" came the quick reply and the entire square exploded in laughter.

The men, now relaxed and prepared to meet the expected cavalry charge, were not put to the test, for a troop of the K.G.L swept into the Chasseur brigade, broke it apart and scattered the French in confusion before wheeling away in the direction taken by La Pena's column. This engagement, which had put Colonel John Browne's companies on the alert, unsettled the Spaniards, who immediately retired from the hill. Close by Lieutenant Bunbury a Portuguese captain of the 20th Cacadores was addressing his company. "Boys," Bunbury heard him say, "I always told you that these mad Englishmen would get us into some such scrape as this, but let us be off. What are we doing here?"

The withdrawal of the Spaniards and Portuguese from the hill was watched in astonishment not only by General Graham at the edge of the wood but also by the French Marshal who had moved his column up to deliver a flank attack. The fact that the allies were split and stretched across his front presented Victor with a unique opportunity and he was quick to profit by it, sending Ruffin to attack La Pena's rear and Leval to stem Graham's advance on Bermeja.

Realizing what a hopeless position he had been left in, Browne reluctantly gave the order to follow the Portuguese, leaving the hill to the French battalions and a battery of artillery. Sir Thomas Graham, under orders from La Pena to retire, saw at once the perils of a precipitous retreat and resolved to buy time until his British battalions could return from the wood. Galloping up to Colonel Browne, he asked him why he had retired from Barossa Hill. In reply, Browne asked, "You would not have me fight the whole French army with just four hundred and seventy men?"

There was nothing for it, Browne was told; he must attack in close formation.

"That I will do with pleasure," said the Colonel, "for it is more to my way than light bobbing."

Rejoining his six companies, two from each of the 1/9th, 1/28th, and 2/82nd, Browne doffed his hat and announced, "Gentlemen, I am happy to be the bearer of good news. General Graham has done you the honour of being the first to attack those fellows. Now follow me you rascals," and, pointing to the French, he called, "Now, cheer up, my lads, 'tis to glory we steer," finishing with a verse from *Hearts of Oak*.

As his companies began to ascend the hill the entire French force opened with such a storm of musketry and canister from their cannon that more than half of the redcoats were struck down in a matter of seconds. In the words of Robert Blakeney, "We had by this time lost upwards of two hundred and fifty men and fourteen officers . . . the remainder of the battalion now scattered." As the survivors recoiled in dismay, the Guards and the 67th Foot were seen to be emerging from the trees, closely followed by an assortment of Cacadores and British light infantry.

Sir Richard Henegan of the Field Train Department, who was with them, recalled Colonel Browne's voice ringing through the air, "Hurray flankers, here comes Graham and the Guards. I will insure you all now, for half a dollar, by God!"

A volley of musketry met the Guards, felling the front ranks of the leading company, but miraculously Colonel Wheatley, leading the advance up the hill, escaped unscathed. Despite Browne's exhortation, his men were loath to leave the shelter of the rocks and trees and were content merely to return the enemy's fire as and when the opportunity presented itself. Among the casualties of the earlier attack was Captain Robert Blakeney, having been struck on the thigh by a ricocheting musket ball. Fortunately his wound proved to be nothing worse than an ugly spreading bruise, but Blakeney was annoyed to discover that the ball had spent itself by passing through a ration loaf and a roast fowl in his haversack.

To many of the bruised and battered redcoats the oncoming lines of Leval's six battalions advancing to the beat of drums and bugles presented a stirring sight. Thomas Bunbury grudgingly admitted that in similar circumstances his own regiment could not have matched the Frenchmen's "display of plumes and martial music".

To William Surtees, admiring the long waving red plumes in the caps of the Grenadiers and the green and yellow feathers worn by the light infantry, "It appeared that the whole of the French army were wearing their best suits of clothing".

As the brigade of Guards closed with the enemy column a volley was exchanged which, because of their close-order formation, was far more damaging to the blue-clad soldiers of Leval's division. Even so, the musketry of the French caused many casualties among the British. In the hail of lead, Surtees's horse dropped from under him "like a stone", enraging the 30-year-old North Countryman, who promptly picked up a musket and joined the ranks of the attackers in the hope, as he put it, "of taking a few potshots at the fellows with the beautiful green feathers", in revenge for his horse.

Colonel Wheatley, meanwhile, had reformed his broken battalions and brought up ten field guns, the fire from which cut down the leading French battalion and scattered Leval's closely packed column. Faced with regular rolling volleys from the double line of redcoats, the French began to waver. General Graham, advancing on foot with the Coldstream Guards, realized that this was the moment of crisis in the battle and called for a last effort. The Guards and the Irish of the 87th Fusiliers responded with a cheer and, before the enemy could deploy, the Irishmen, with howls like so many banshee, were among them, their long bayonets thrusting a way through the ranks in a mêlée of savage hand-to-hand fighting. "Many of the Englishmen broke their weapons in striking with the butts or bayonets," remembered one captured French officer, "but they never seemed to think of using the swords they wore at their sides. They went on fighting with their fists."

At the height of the encounter Ensign Edward Keogh of the 87th caught sight of a French Crowned Eagle borne aloft by Lieutenant Gazan of the 8th Leger and fought his way towards it, followed by Sergeant Masterton and four private soldiers. Keogh managed to grasp the Eagle's staff but fell dead from multiple wounds before he could wrench it free.

The fight around the Eagle continued for some minutes, during which time seven Frenchmen were killed, before Masterton tore it from the grasp of the severely wounded Gazan and bore it away in triumph.

The remnants of the 8th Leger were thrown into disarray by the loss of their Eagle and, as Graham's men swept forward, the frightening spectacle of 500 yelling, powder-blackened and blood-stained devils rushing towards them from fifty yards was more than the young French conscripts could stand. They broke and fled.

On Barossa Hill the 300 survivors of Browne's battalion, now reinforced by the Guards and the 67th, advanced to ply the enemy's flank with rolling volleys of musketry. The French endeavoured to deploy into line, but, when General Ruffin fell mortally wounded, his demise signalled the end of the battle. It had been a savage fight which had achieved little. The allies had suffered 1,740 casualties, while French losses amounted to 2,400, including Generals Ruffin and Rousseau, together with the loss of four cannon and the coveted Eagle, later to be displayed in London.

The departure of the French left the exhausted and depleted battalions of General Sir Thomas Graham's division in possession of Barossa Hill. Marshal Victor's beaten troops, covered by a screen of cavalry, fell back on Chiclana, while the British, too weary to entertain thoughts of pursuit, fired a few departing shots from their cannon.

Two days after the battle Ensign Bunbury found himself commanding three companies of Portuguese charged with bringing away the wounded, who, for want of transport, had been left by the French where they had fallen.

"The French," complained Bunbury indignantly, "had not removed their wounded from the field, nor had any of their people been sent to them, and the sight was both sickening and appalling."

General Graham, furious with La Pena for remaining aloof from the conflict, retired into Cadiz without even bothering to inform the Spaniard of his intention. An astonished Marshal Victor, who had been on the point of retiring to Seville, renewed his investment of the fortress town with added vigour.

Chapter 10

'NEVER IN THE WORLD WAS SO CRUEL AND DISTRESSING WARFARE WAGED'

At Santarem in the spring of 1811 Marshal André Masséna, Duke of Rivoli, faced the prospect of fighting his way back to Spain with a depleted army. Although the wider area he now occupied had greatly increased the scope of his foraging parties, even their ingenuity had been severely tested in a desperate search for food. With the army close to starvation and suffering crippling losses from sickness and desertion, a decision to strike camp and retire from Portugal could no longer be delayed. By 4 March most of his sick and the few pieces of ordnance he still possessed had left the area and the army was in full retreat along the left bank of the Mondego on a route which would take it through Garda to Almeida.

Despite the low state of morale, the troops bringing up the rear still possessed a sting in their tail as an officer of the 1/95th discovered. In one of the frequent skirmishes with the French Captain John Kincaid certainly had reason to feel grateful for the cover which a Spanish oak afforded his lanky frame when, much to his discomfort, he found that "balls were rapping into it as fast as if a fellow had been hammering a nail on the opposite side".

Following in the wake of Masséna's retreating army, the allies discovered Santarem to be little more than a ghost town. George Simmons was reminded of how much it had changed since he was last there. On that occasion, recalled Simmons, "all had been gaiety and happiness with the shops overflowing with every possible luxury." It was a memory which bore no resemblance to the smoke-blackened ruins, through which, he noted, "the few remaining inhabitants wandered like living skeletons".

"Everything was converted into a wilderness," wrote Auguste Schaumann, "in which soldiers, vultures . . . dogs without masters, wolves and foxes, lived their lives undisturbed."

A shortage of carts had obliged Masséna to leave behind large numbers

99

of his sick and wounded who were to be seen at every street corner. Costello and his fellow Green Jackets were moved to pity at the sight of their pallid faces, and threw them biscuits as they passed, but, wrote the Rifleman, "Abandoned by their own people and without protection, their misery was in all probability quickly brought to an end by the Portuguese who were gradually returning to their homes."

At first, in the face of a vigorous pursuit, the French Marshal conducted his retreat in a skilful fashion, ever ready to turn upon his pursuers and fight a rearguard action. At Redinha on 12 March a 7,000-strong infantry force under the command of Marshal Ney resolutely held its ground against an Anglo-Portuguese army of 25,000 for a whole day, until forced to give way to a determined mass attack which carried the allies to the heights on each side of the river crossing. So close was the chase at times that on one occasion Masséna and his staff were surprised by a troop of Hussars and only by setting spurs to his horse did the Marshal narrowly avoid capture.

As the days passed so the retreat continued, but now on a line between the Mondego and the mountains. The scorched-earth policy of the Portuguese had denuded the countryside and, as the French became ever more desperate for food, the once orderly retreat began to assume all the worst aspects of Moore's infamous withdrawal to Corunna. "Every morning at dawn when we started out," wrote Schaumann, "the burning villages, hamlets and woods, which illuminated the sky, told of the progress of the French."

The evidence of atrocities committed by them on their passage through Portugal appalled Wellington's troops, hardened as they were to scenes of violence and misery. The bodies of men, women and children were left lying in the streets, some without ears and many others with disfigurements which shocked the redcoats.

"Their retreat resembled more that of famished wolves than men," observed Private Pococke. "Murder and devastation marked their way. Our soldiers used to wonder why the French were not swept by Heaven from the earth, when they witnessed their cruelties."

"Marmont and his Goths have behaved with their usual barbarity, having destroyed and sacked most of the unfortunate towns which had previously escaped," a despondent Major Rice informed his brother. "Never in this world was so cruel and distressing warfare waged. It cannot last; the misery is too great to be endured."

In a village near the town of Guarda Lieutenant George Simmons came upon the body of a young woman who he afterwards learned was the wife of the Alcalde. She had been raped and lay pinned to the ground beneath a piece of granite taken from the market cross, a stone so heavy that it took the combined exertions of Simmons and four men from his

Company to remove it. Confessed Sir Richard Henegan, a Military Commissary: "This sad evidence of the atrocities of war oppressed me like a waking nightmare during the remainder of the march."

Regrettably, such incidents were to become ever more numerous as the French pursued a path signposted by rising columns of smoke. When, a few miles further along their route, the men of the 51st Foot entered Leira, they discovered every house to be a blackened ruin. One scene in particular left a lasting impression on Private Wheeler, for it was here that the graves in the churchyard had been desecrated and the corpses dragged out in a search for valuables. This callous irreverence exhibited by the French to the dead was not confined to graveyard corpses, it was even extended to their own men. Young John Cowell-Stepney of the Guards was outraged to discover in a roofless chapel a dead French soldier which the enemy, in a fit of macabre humour, had seated half-clothed in the pulpit with his musket placed in the position of 'Present Arms'.

Masséna's retreat was to become notorious for the degree of savagery meted out to the luckless civilians caught up in the conflict. Almost every village had been put to the torch with not the slightest regard for human life, as a soldier of the 94th was about to discover. After a frustrating search among smoking ruins for a safe corner in which to conceal a sack of biscuit, Private Donaldson entered a church. When his eyes had become accustomed to the gloom, the young Scot recoiled in horror. The floor in front of him was covered in ash, in part still glowing. Lying a few feet away were a dozen bodies half-consumed by the fire; but what made Donaldson's blood run cold was the sight of a figure in a kneeling position which, with its scorched and blackened features and with outstretched arms, seemed to be imploring him to seek vengeance. It was a scene which filled Donaldson with revulsion for an enemy who, "although he fought with courage, could still behave in such a bestial fashion".

Unhappily, as the pursuit continued, such scenes were to become ever more frequent and horrific.

On 21 March Masséna's weary and dispirited columns reached Celerico in the Ceira Valley thirty miles from the Spanish border. Apart from the garrison in Almeida, there were now no French troops in Portugal apart from prisoners, and the hundreds of peasant families who had fled to the mountains began to return to what was left of their homes. Emaciated, and with pinched features, they wandered the countryside begging food from the occasional party of redcoats, having lived a primitive existence for months. The extent of their suffering was brought home to a soldier of the 95th when, in seeking shelter from a sudden rain squall, he entered a hut to be confronted with the spectacle of a woman

101

and three children huddled together in the misery and despair of starvation. Lieutenant George Simmons gave one child the last of his bread ration and left embarrassed, unable to do more, "not having enough to satisfy the cravings of my own empty stomach".

The redcoats did what they could to alleviate the wants of the peasantry by distributing soup and Indian corn once a day and the men of Wheeler's Company willingly emptied their haversacks until the last biscuit was gone, but even this relief, small as it was, ended with the departure of the troops and for those without sustenance no doubt disease and death quickly followed.

Ensign John Mills, on his way through the region to join his regiment, wrote to his mother describing his journey: "You can form no idea of what a ruined country this is; the houses in the towns and villages are most of them unroofed and not a vestige of anything that can be called furniture in them. When we were upon our journey the inhabitants of the different towns were beginning to return to them from the mountains. They appeared nearly famished – such a scene of distress you cannot imagine."

Masséna's 'Army of Portugal', now joined by Marshal Bessières' 'Army of the North', rested for a few days at the Spanish border whilst the two Marshals conferred with their respective Staff. Masséna had yet to recover from the humiliation of being forced to cross the frontier almost at the very point at which he had entered Portugal with such high hopes eight months before and he desperately needed a success in order to retrieve something of his reputation. With this in mind and to the astonishment of his Generals, Masséna suddenly announced his intention of marching for the Tagus Valley in a bid to launch another operation in Portugal. It meant crossing the barren uplands of the Sierra das Mesas into Spanish Estremadura, which for an army without most of its equipment and suffering from the aftermath of an exhausting retreat was a dubious undertaking at best. Marshal Ney, who advocated a withdrawal on Almeida, thought it quite absurd and refused to accept an order to march. After an acrimonious exchange of communications with Masséna he was relieved of his command and replaced by Loison, an action which encouraged the other two Generals, Junot and Reynier, to lend their support, and at daybreak on 24 March Masséna's three Corps set off on the first stage of its long southerly route. After four days of marching across a desolate mountain region over tracks so rough that the artillery could not keep pace with the infantry, Masséna was forced to recognize that further progress could only be achieved at the cost of a depleted army. Reluctantly he abandoned all thoughts of an attack on Lisbon from the south and began a general withdrawal through Ciudad Rodrigo to the line of the Agueda.

Twelve miles to the west three divisions bringing up the rear under General Reynier were about to cross the River Coa near Sabugal when they were attacked on their flank by the Light Division and two brigades of cavalry, while two other divisions of Wellington's army closed on their centre.

Although a thick mist blanketed the entire length of the valley, the fact that he was heavily outnumbered soon became apparent to the French General. To give battle was to risk certain destruction and Reynier wisely ordered an immediate change of direction towards the main body of Masséna's army then on the road to Ciudad Rodrigo. In the face of a violent rainstorm and hampered by a sea of glutinous mud, the British regiments soon lost sight of the enemy, finally giving up the chase and retiring to their quarters in Sabugal.

Masséna, his left flank turned and his men disheartened by their seemingly endless retreats, cancelled his plan of campaign and by 11 April was back in Salamanca. "We have arrived in this town with as much joy as if we had returned to France," wrote a relieved Captain Marcel of the 69th Leger.

Now that Portugal was free of the French Wellington was at liberty to put into practice a scheme he had prepared a month earlier. Before this venture into Spain could be safely undertaken, however, the frontier fortresses of Almeida, Ciudad Rodrigo and Badajoz would have to be overcome in order to safeguard the line of communication with Lisbon. Ciudad Rodrigo was already blockaded by Wellington's troops, but, without siege artillery, there was little more they could do and the Commander rode south to visit Marshal Beresford then investing Badajoz. Here Wellington found the situation similar to that at Ciudad Rodrigo and, after riding round the walled city, he gave the Marshal permission to terminate the siege should Soult make a determined bid to relieve the garrison. By 2 April he was back with the army, having ridden 130 miles to the north, disturbed by the news that Masséna, his deficiencies made good, was on the march towards Almeida.

Rumours of the Marshal's intention to relieve that fortress town had been circulating among Wellington's staff for some weeks and plans had been laid to bar the way by putting a strong force around the village of Fuentes de Onoro where a series of hills overlooked the Duas Casas gorge.

The cluster of granite houses were well known to the Light Division who made it known to the villagers that, unless they abandoned their homes, they would be at grave risk in a battle which was sure to take place. A few of the inhabitants were acquainted with the officers of the 95th and a patron of George Simmons singled him out as the Company marched past. "Oh Sir! I hope God will guard and protect you," called the old man. "If you beat these monsters, I do not care though my house and everything I have left is destroyed."

With his customary flair for choosing the ideal defensive position, Wellington deployed his troops along a stretch of hills between the village of Fuentes de Onoro and Fort Conception east of Almeida, a position which could only be outflanked from the south. Behind and overlooking the village was a gentle slope studded with outcrops of rock which afforded excellent cover for the Green Jackets, most of whom were armed with the latest version of the Baker rifle. On the left General Erskine's 5th Division blocked the road to Ciudad Rodrigo, while further north, where a river gorge dropped to a depth of 150 feet to the Vel de Mula, Wellington stationed Campbell's 6th Division with its right flank protected by Spencer's 1st and Picton's 3rd Divisions. In Reserve were the Light Division and Houston's 7th, giving Wellington a total of 35,000 infantry, 2,000 cavalry and 48 guns.

Masséna possessed a numerical advantage of 4 to 3 in infantry, but it was his overwhelming strength in cavalry which posed the greatest threat to Wellington's mastery of the roads leading to the bridges over the Coa and the Dos Casas.

The morning of 3 May was marked by the return of General Robert Craufurd to the Light Division after an absence of six months on family business. His appearance on the familiar bay cob was greeted by a tumultuous welcome from the 95th bivouacked by the smoke-blackened ruins of Fort Conception. Loud as his welcome had been from John Harris and his fellow riflemen, their huzzas were drowned in the roar of acclaim from the Cacadore regiments in which Craufurd had taken an especial interest.

Ensign William Grattan and his Company of the 88th, exhausted by their morning's work barricading the streets of Fuentes de Onoro and the neighbouring village of Posa Velha, thankfully rolled their blankets about themselves and immediately sank into a well-earned sleep. It was not to last, for early in the afternoon they were awakened by the sound of cannon fire. Joseph Donaldson, from his position on the high ground above the village, watched as three dense columns advanced towards the collection of granite houses that made up the village of Fuentes de Onoro. It seemed to him that "everything I had ever read about feats of arms or the pomp of war" was there to see as, with drums beating the familiar rub-a-dub-dub and with bayonets glinting in the sun, General Ferey's VI Corps advanced across the undulating plain towards him.

This forward movement of the VI Corps culminated in a charge across the shallow water of the Dos Casas and into the walled gardens of the village where the five defending battalions were driven out before Colonel Williams launched a counter-attack with the 24th and 79th Foot.

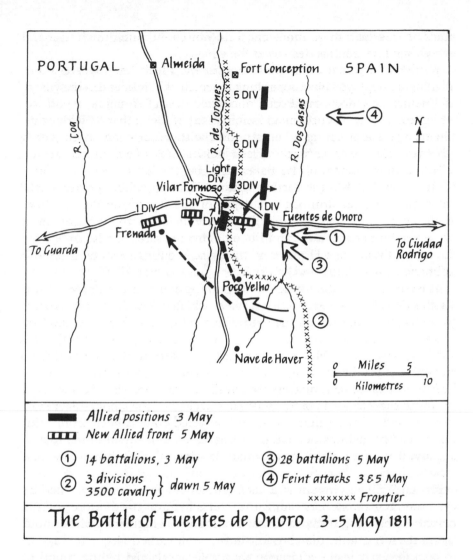

PORTUGAL   ■ Almeida   ⊠ Fort Conception   SPAIN

R. de Torones

5 DIV

6 DIV

R. Dos Casas

Light Div

Vilar Formoso   3DIV

1 DIV — 1DIV   1 DIV

1DIV   DIV   Fuentes de Onoro

Frenada ●

To Guarda

To Ciudad Rodrigo

①

③

Poco Velho

②

R. COA

N

Nave de Haver

| 0 | Miles | 5 |
| 0 | Kilometres | 10 |

▬▬▬ Allied positions 3 May
▭▭▭ New Allied front 5 May

① 14 battalions, 3 May   ③ 28 battalions 5 May

② 3 divisions / 3500 cavalry } dawn 5 May   ④ Feint attacks 3 & 5 May

                xxxxxxxx Frontier

The Battle of Fuentes de Onoro   3-5 May 1811

Prominent in the French attack had been a battalion of the Hanoverian Legion whose uniform, similar to the British redcoats, enabled them to close with their enemy before the danger was recognized. The scarlet coats, however, proved the undoing of the Hanoverians, for Masséna's artillery opened fire upon them and paved the way for a counter-attack by two Highland battalions from Spencer's 1st division.

The men of the 71st and 79th had been without their ration of biscuit for two days and the Colonel of the 71st, conscious of the fact that his men were hungry, led them forward with the invitation, "My lads! You have no provisions. There is plenty in the hollow in front; let us go down and divide it." The Highlanders needed no second bidding and, carrying

105

their muskets at the trail, they headed towards the cottages and gardens which stood at the eastern end of the village.

In the vicious hand-to-hand encounters which ensued a bayonet pierced Thomas Pococke's tunic, grazing his skin and embedding itself in his knapsack. The Frenchman who wielded it fell to a musket ball, but so engrossed was Pococke in the excitement of battle that he felt not the slightest concern even as a ball tore off the shoulder wing on his jacket. "Narrow as the escape was," he later confessed, "I felt no uneasiness, I was become so inured to danger and fatigue."

In a bloody half-hour of street fighting the Scots suffered a number of needless casualties from their reckless disregard of cover. Shouts from their officers to take advantage of the protection afforded by the low stone walls was largely ignored, for, as one Highlander afterwards confided to Lieutenant John Cowell Stepney, "They would rather stand on top of a wall and be shot like men than bide behind it and be killed like dogs."

It was largely thanks to the Scots' fighting spirit that the ground won by the French in the earlier attack on the village was recovered yard by yard and, come evening, the enemy had been driven from all but the lower regions of the village. As the light faded and the smoke of battle drifted away the combatants consolidated their respective gains and bivouacked for the night.

A great deal of ball cartridge had been expended in the short struggle in which the 71st had played no small part. Thomas Pococke estimated that he had fired off more than one hundred rounds and wrote: "My shoulder that day was as black as a coal from the recoil of my musket."

Now that fighting was over for the day, troops of the Imperial Guard passed in review order before Marshals Masséna and Bessières, watched with interest by a crowd of British soldiers. "On our side we had no reviews," commented Ensign Fielde, "the band of the German Legion raised their strains in answer to the French, and gave back note for note, as on the morrow we did shot for shot."

The next day was remarkable for the lack of activity other than the movement of French cavalry reconnoitring the positions taken up by Lord Wellington. In a careful scrutiny, Masséna's dragoons noted that the British right flank was thinly held by just a few horsemen and a single battalion occupying the village of Posa Velha. Masséna quickly revised his battle plan and that evening, under cover of darkness, transferred the whole of his cavalry, together with Junot's Corps, to an open area in front of the village where the river was fordable. Wellington, for his part, was not unaware of the danger and that same night sent Spenser's and Picton's divisions to support the 7th division commanded by Sir William Houston.

Daylight on 5 May brought renewed French attacks against Fuentes as Montbrun's dragoons were ordered into the field against Houston and the exposed right flank. Driven from the village of Posa Velha, Houston's men were forced to seek the shelter of a wood and Craufurd's riflemen, now in extended order through the trees, were sent to their assistance, preceded by a squadron of Light Cavalry.

The dragoons and Chasseurs, reforming at the French end of the wood, wheeled and charged the British squadrons cantering towards them. The respective horsemen met with an impact that was heard by the infantry half a mile away. Men and horses were thrown to the ground by the shock of the collision, while many more saddles were emptied as a result of some fierce sword play. Lieutenant Tomkinson, overtaking a dragoon, brought his sabre down with such force that it severed the half-circle of brass which crowned the top of the Frenchman's helmet. The noise and tremendous jolt made by Tomkinson's sword so close to the dragoon's head was such that, although uninjured, the Frenchman was catapulted from the saddle as if struck by a roundshot.

The riderless horses galloped back through the trees and soon engaged the attention of Rifleman Costello and other skirmishers of the 95th, who, in the excitement of the cavalry charge, had ceased to engage with the enemy. Now they vied with the French skirmishers in their attempts to capture the valuable mounts which each side regarded as its rightful prize. Eventually, outnumbered and under pressure, the 95th were obliged to give way and retire in company with the Light Dragoons, pursued by Montbrun's Chasseurs. Doubling back, the Green Jackets reached the shelter of the low stone walls and, by turning to face their attackers with volleys of musketry, successfully repelled every attempt by the French to break through their ranks.

For the men of the 7th Division it was a different story. Caught on a plateau without cover, they were forced to form square in the face of a determined attack by Montbrun's cavalry. Infantry caught in the open were always vulnerable to cavalry and when first the 85th and then the 2nd Cacadores broke from the square to stream across the plain they paid a fearful price. Small groups of mixed British and Portuguese fought fiercely to defend themselves, while others who had broken away ran for their lives. But even in groups they were no match for the horsemen and almost all were ridden down and cut to pieces.

Wellington now faced the crucial question of whether to abandon the bridge over the Coa and withdraw his right wing in order to form a new line at right angles to his original position. Aides galloped his orders to the survivors of the 7th Division and, with the Light Division to cover their flank, the redcoats began to retire from Posa Velha towards the new position on a hill surmounted by a ruined tower.

The Chasseurs, smarting from their earlier failure to dislodge the riflemen, swept in once again and, to meet this threat, the retiring columns adopted Craufurd's tactic of forming square on the march with the front rank kneeling and the second rank firing over their heads. When the cavalry had been beaten off, the march was resumed, for to remain in square would have invited heavy punishment from the French cannon.

Good marching discipline was not dispensed with even under fire and the 51st came in for a measure of criticism from their Colonel who dismounted and stood facing his men whilst roundshot dropped around him. The standard of marching was not to his liking and, in a voice which was sometimes lost in the noise of an approaching cannon ball, he repeatedly called out the time and instructed the sergeant-major to watch for anyone marching out of step and mark them down for extra drill.

By employing the practice of alternately retiring and halting to form square, which brought admiring comments from the watching Staff, Houston and Craufurd ably resisted the numerous cavalry attacks which on occasion were pressed home so vigorously that the horsemen all but broke through the hedge of bayonets.

That the retiring infantry escaped punishing losses over a distance of two miles was in part due to the action of Stewart's Light Cavalry, who repeatedly charged the enemy, and to Bull's troop of Royal Horse Artillery, who did not hesitate to unlimber in order to bring their field guns into play, which at times exposed them to the risk of being overrun by Montbrun's cavalry. In one instance two guns of Captain Ramsey's troop were surrounded and forced to cut their way out from a mêlée of circling horse. Surrounded by Cuirassiers, the gun crews put up a spirited fight, supported by squadrons of the 1st and 14th Light Dragoons who repeatedly turned and charged the encircling mass of enemy horse. Then, through a rising cloud of dust, Ramsey and his team burst out at full stretch "his horses breathing fire . . . his guns bounding like things of no weight," as Napier so graphically describes the incident, to carry his battery clear of the mêlée, protected by the Light Dragoons.

At noon the battle rose to a new pitch of intensity as Masséna renewed his attack on Fuentes de Onoro with 5,000 troops led by his elite Corps of Grenadiers.

"How different was their appearance to ours," wrote Thomas Pococke, "their hats set round with feathers, their beards long and black, gave them a fierce look, their stature was superior to ours. We looked like boys, they like savages."

A fierce cannonade was directed against the upper part of the village before a determined assault by Masséna on both flanks. The vigour and strength of the French attacks proved too much for the three defending regiments, the 74th, 83rd and 88th and they were soon forced to retire, abandoning the blood-soaked streets to the victorious Grenadiers.

As the redcoats retreated up the slope behind the village, the wounded who had fallen in the earlier engagements begged them to drag them out of the path of the cavalry, but although, as Pococke later confessed, "his heart bled for them," few men had time for anything other than to save themselves, so close were the French.

At one stage of the fight a dragoon spurred his horse to where the young Scot was busily engaged in priming his musket. The stroke of the Frenchman's sword severed the stock of Pococke's musket before a bayonet thrust from a neighbouring Scot brought the dragoon down from his horse. The men of the 71st and 94th, fighting a rearguard action, were at times hard put to effect their escape. A sergeant in Donaldson's company sought refuge in one of the cottages and, with the French close upon his heels, just had time to tumble into a large wooden chest and close the lid before the Grenadiers burst into the room. The sergeant lay sweating and half-smothered by the contents as the Frenchmen searched for plunder. Fortunately for the Highlander, a timely intervention by men of the 88th obliged the Grenadiers to make a hasty exit before they could examine the chest.

The fighting in the streets had now spread to the churchyard on the hill and, in the battle which raged around them, the 85th, fresh from England, were experiencing their baptism of fire. Conspicuous in new scarlet uniforms with yellow facings, they suffered the effects of a punishing fire before reaching the protection afforded by a scattering of tombstones. In Reserve was the 88th, an Irish regiment renowned throughout the Army as notorious pilferers, although no one doubted their fighting spirit. Now, as they ran to engage the enemy, they were cheered to the echo by the hard-pressed 85th, who begged them to give those "frog-eating fellows" no quarter.

As the Irishmen advanced through the churchyard Lieutenant Grattan, at the head of his Company, turned to face his men, but they needed no encouragement. The wild Irishmen from Connaught responded to his call, "Forward ye rascals" with a cheer which, as Grattan later confessed, lived in his memory and left him "in no doubt as to their eagerness to get to grips with the enemy".

The bayonet charge by the 88th helped Picton's other three regiments to recapture the village, for the Grenadiers were sent reeling back through the smoking ruins into a street which had been barricaded the previous day. Trapped in what was virtually a cul-de-sac, one hundred and fifty Frenchmen fought to the last man without thought of surrender. The battle for possession of the village had been desperate and the heaps of corpses, Highlanders, Irishmen and French Grenadiers, bore mute testimony to that most savage of all encounters – street fighting.

As evening approached, a grave shortage of ammunition began to have its effect on Masséna's 6th Division, which had been his main instrument in storming the village. Some Companies were down to four rounds of ball cartridge per man and, as the light faded, it was clear to the Marshal that a withdrawal from Fuentes de Onoro was inevitable. It was a decision greeted by friend and foe alike with a heartfelt sigh of relief.

"The pickets were thrown out, the moon rose, we wrapped our cloaks around us, and slept away the fatigue and heat of the day," wrote Lieutenant Field, "many losing themselves in the happiest of all English soldiers' dreams – that of England, friends, and home."

Private Pococke, despite the pain of his bruised shoulder, slept "as sound as a top" until awakened by the call of a bugle sounding dawn assembly.

The morning of 6 May found the opposing armies in the same position with neither attempting to renew hostilities. Not a shot was fired that day and from the high ground above the village Jonathan Leach watched as cartloads of wounded Frenchmen moved away in the direction of Ciudad Rodrigo. Later that afternoon, arrangements were made to remove the dead and injured who filled the streets and houses of both Fuentes and Posa Velha. Under a flag of truce working parties of French and British soldiers went about their mission of mercy. A few took the opportunity to fraternize and discuss the battle. "I had some conversation yesterday with some French officers who came out to me as I was employed in burying the dead," wrote John Mills to his mother. "They were extremely polite, talked much of their cavalry and lamented their being obliged to leave Salamanca, where they said the women were so beautiful."

Much to the amusement of Captain Leach, a French officer called his attention to where a young man, gorgeously attired in a Hussar uniform, stood talking to a fellow officer. "Do you see that boy?" the Frenchman asked Leach. "He is only twenty, has just arrived from Paris and commands one of our Hussar regiments. But," he added with a shrug, "he is the nephew of the War Minister, which accounts for it."

The battle for Fuentes de Onoro – Fountains of Honour – was over and, although Wellington was prepared for a further day of conflict by building new defence works, the French were seen to be retiring along the road to Ciudad Rodrigo. Masséna had abandoned his attempt to relieve the garrison in Almeida.

In the afternoon Lieutenant Grattan went in search of a wounded comrade. The spacious house of a wealthy hidalgo had been requisitioned to serve as a hospital and in the outer courtyard upwards of 200 wounded lay on straw mattresses, most of them awaiting amputation. William Grattan, as he passed among them, was horrified at the sight.

Many had received their injuries when the fighting had been at its peak three days earlier, and the blood, hardening in the sun, had swollen their limbs to twice their normal size. His search led Grattan into an inner courtyard where the floor was stained with blood and littered with severed arms and legs. A number of doors, wrenched from their hinges, had been laid across barrels to serve as operating tables for the surgeons, who worked at their grim task unmoved by the screams and cries of their patients.

Although the survival rate from the totally unhygienic operation was considerably less than half, a greater risk was from the lack of medical knowledge on the part of the assistant surgeons. Their ignorance sometimes led to an artery being severed and, even as Grattan watched, one poor wretch needing a tourniquet to arrest a flow of blood was left unattended whilst the assistant went in search of a surgeon.

The young Ensign could stomach no more and, conscious of his own good fortune, he left, praying that fate might continue to protect him "from the ministrations of the hospital assistants".

Lord Wellington, now that he was no longer threatened by Masséna, resumed the blockade of Almeida, but in that area events were about to take an unexpected turn. The French Marshal had no thought of leaving the garrison to its fate and, before crossing the Agueda, he asked for volunteers to carry a message to General Brennier instructing him to destroy his arsenal and attempt to rejoin the army with the garrison. Acting on the promise of a rich reward, three of Masséna's soldiers set out on their mission. Two were caught disguised as peasants and shot, but a third, a Chasseur of the 6th Leger by name of Tillet, succeeded in reaching the fortress and, on the night of 10 May, the garrison fought its way past the British pickets after blowing up the ramparts. It was while attempting to cross the picket lines that Joseph Maemphel was made captive. "I was now a prisoner," he wrote, "and, with many others, was driven off like a drove of cattle by the English . . . I must allow that we were excellently well fed; our rations were as good, and often larger than those of their own soldiers."

The escape of most of the garrison from Almeida had been successfully and efficiently carried out and when Wellington's troops entered the town further surprises awaited them. Before destroying the magazine, Brennier's men had been careful to conceal live shells in the baking ovens and fireplaces of the houses in the hope that they would be overlooked by the new occupants. Fortunately the redcoats were more diligent and working parties were soon busy clearing the booby traps, among them a detachment of the 32nd Foot. Captain Ross-Lewin, in charge of one party, found the town a mere heap of rubble. The explosions had destroyed many of the houses and the recent siege had reduced the inhabitants to a state of abject poverty. The sight of the famished and shivering Portuguese moved Ross-Lewin to reflect that "accounts of victories and the storming of cities might read well in the newspapers for the politician sitting at home in comfort, but for the soldier it would always be received with mixed feelings; joy for the success and pity for the sufferers."

While Wellington's men busied themselves in repairing the devastated fortress, General Brennier eventually joined the main body of Masséna's army with three-quarters of his Almeida command intact, only to find that the 'Army of Portugal' had a new Commander. Marshal Marmont, Duke of Ragusa, had replaced Marshal Masséna, who had been ordered back to Paris by a wrathful Napoleon Bonaparte. His disgrace, however, was eased somewhat by the arrival of the Military Chest at Salamanca containing 300,000 francs for the army. After satisfying his own arrears of pay, the Marshal left Ciudad Rodrigo in rather better humour on the final stage of his journey to Paris.

Chapter 11

'WHORE'S AR ARTHUR?
AW WISH HE WOR 'ERE'

At Badajoz Marshal Beresford had done his best to put into effect Lord Wellington's detailed instructions, but every attempt by the troops to dig trenches and parallels in the stony ground proved ineffectual. The working parties engaged in the erection of gabions, necessary for the protection of the gunners, laboured with little shelter from the garrison's musket and cannon fire, and half of Beresford's small band of Engineers were lost in a single day.

The fortress, which had fallen to the French on 11 March through an act of treachery by the Spanish Governor, was commanded by General Phillipon, an able and energetic man who had repaired the fortifications and whose frequent sorties against the working parties had prevented the besiegers from making much progress with the covered approaches to the fortress walls. The massive walls were indeed proof against anything but the heaviest siege gun and these, as Beresford was only too aware, were yet several days away in their slow progress from Elvas.

On 11 May a battery of heavy cannon did get into action, but the French quickly silenced them and, to add to Beresford's anxiety, a report from General Colborne warned him that Marshal Soult with 18,000 men and 40 guns was marching to the relief of the garrison and was expected to arrive from Larena in less than a week.

Mindful of Lord Wellington's instructions, Marshal Beresford began to scale down his operations against the fortress town, sending his heavy siege cannon back to Elvas and destroying whatever material his wagons could not evacuate. The abandonment of the siege and the removal of the artillery came as an unexpected event to the troops in the field. "On the 13th, in the afternoon, while lounging in our camp of ease about four miles from the trenches," recorded Lieutenant Moyle-Sherer, "we were surprised by an order to hold ourselves in readiness to march at the shortest notice."

The die had been cast and the next day William Carr Beresford raised the siege and left Badajoz to unite with the Spanish armies of Blake and Castanas. By early afternoon on the 15th the allies had taken up a position overlooking the ruined village of Albuera, twelve miles to the east of Badajoz. Beresford's strength had increased to 31,000 and 50 cannon with the arrival of 8,000 Spaniards from Cadiz, but, although the allied force was numerically superior to the French, the British contribution was less than 7,000, most of whom had yet to be tested in battle, unlike the French who almost to a man were veterans of many conflicts.

The Spanish soldiers, under General Joachim Blake, had arrived late and it was well after midnight before they were able to take up a position behind the River Albuera on a slope just south of the village. A few miles to the north, the 7th Fusiliers, who for the past 36 hours had been employed on picket duties, received their orders to parade in full marching kit. Bitterly resentful of the order, the weary men of John Cooper's Company took to the road in the early hours, complaining of their need for sleep and refreshment.

"Had we known that in a few short hours we would be taking part in the bloodiest battle of the Peninsula War," commented Cooper, "our tiredness would have been quickly forgotten."

Marshal Soult, meanwhile, had reconnoitred Beresford's dispositions from the cover of a wooded hilltop and had carefully noted the various national uniforms: Portuguese blue on the left, British scarlet in the centre, and Spanish yellow on the right. Now, as Blake's troops rested after their night march, Soult brought up his artillery and Girard's V Corps to the cover of a thick copse immediately in front of the Spanish position on the ridge.

The battle opened at 8.00am on 16 May with a bayonet attack pressed home with vigour against Beresford's centre by 8,000 men led by Generals Werle and Godinot. It was, in fact, a feint which succeeded in drawing off Beresford's Reserve and allowed Soult to deploy a major part of his army against the weaker-held Spanish right wing. Joachim Blake, in the mistaken belief that the attack being directed against the centre was the main French assault, merely re-deployed a quarter of his strength to meet the mass of blue-clad infantry to be seen closing upon him from four hundred yards.

Two full divisions struck the four Spanish battalions, who, to their credit, withstood the shock of Girard's attack with admirable courage, the three-deep line of troops holding their ground for more than an hour before giving way. The continuous crackle of musketry was heard by the 7th Fusiliers as they marched through the valley, although Corporal John Cooper, in common with the rest of his Company, was completely ignorant of the close proximity of the French. Puzzled by the noise of gunfire

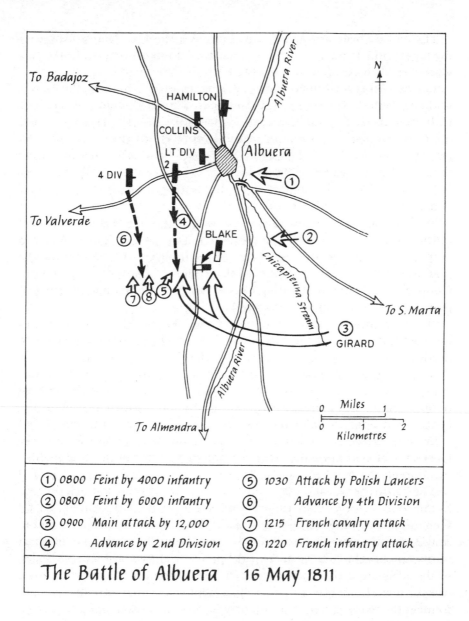

①	0800	Feint by 4000 infantry	⑤ 1030	Attack by Polish Lancers
②	0800	Feint by 6000 infantry	⑥	Advance by 4th Division
③	0900	Main attack by 12,000	⑦ 1215	French cavalry attack
④		Advance by 2nd Division	⑧ 1220	French infantry attack

The Battle of Albuera   16 May 1811

from an unexpected source, he was at a loss to explain it, but when the fusiliers breasted the hill drifting smoke and bright flashes betrayed the fact of a major confrontation taking place in the valley below.

The prospect of a battle quickened the pace of the 1/7th and Cooper noted that the men "were now wide awake and roused in earnest". Few of them regarded the darkening sky with any sense of foreboding, however, but as the battalion halted to await further orders, a heavy rainstorm, preceded by a roll of thunder, swept across the hill. It was to have a profound effect on the ability of the 48th Foot to defend itself as it advanced to the support of the Spaniards.

Marshal Beresford, who now appreciated that Soult's real objective was to turn his right flank, responded to the threat by sending aides galloping furiously southward with orders for General Blake to change his front by drawing his men back at an angle to the main position and form a new line of defence. The hard-pressed Spaniards did their best to comply with this difficult manoeuvre as the voltigeurs, skirmishing ahead of Girard's main columns, harassed the Spanish line to great effect.

Meanwhile, screened by cavalry on each flank, a concentrated mass 8,000 strong, directed by General Jean Baptiste Girard, advanced resolutely against Beresford's right wing. Against this onslaught the Spaniards began to waver and, to assist them, Colborne's brigade from General Stewart's 2nd Division was sent to outflank the French column and shatter it with rolling volleys of lateral fire.

"Just as our line had entirely cleared the Spaniards," wrote Moyle-Sherer, "the smoky shroud of battle was, by the slackening of the fire, for one minute blown aside, and gave to our view the French Grenadier caps, their arms, and the whole aspect of their frowning masses." Even at this stressful moment as a further blaze of musketry erupted, Sherer found time to admire the martial bearing of his enemy. "It was a momentary, but a grand sight," he added approvingly.

Four of Colborne's battalions wheeled into line, but scarcely had they time to discharge more than one volley before the curtain of rain which had soaked the Fusiliers reached them, rendering paper cartridges and powder virtually useless.

The thick mist and swirling clouds of smoke had allowed the 2nd Hussars and a strong contingent of the 1st Lancers of the Vistula to sweep round the right wing of Colborne's brigade unobserved, and now, as his troops stood for the most part defenceless, they heard a noise which infantrymen dreaded above all others – a drumming sound from hundreds of charging horsemen. The alarmed redcoats had little time to form a defensive square, the one formation in which they stood any chance of resisting a cavalry charge, and, because most of the muskets had been rendered useless by the rainstorm, three brigades were cut to pieces in less than five minutes.

"There was nothing left for it but to run," confessed Ensign Edward Close of the 48th Foot. "In my flight I was knocked down by some fugitive like myself, who, I suppose, was struck by a shot. Whilst on the ground I was ridden over by a number of Lancers, one of whom passing close to me was about to save me the trouble of recording this event, when a Spanish dragoon rode up to him with his sabre, which brought him over his horse's head."

Groups of redcoats ran to form a circle, but in a very short time three out of four battalions had lost two-thirds of their complement, hacked down or trampled upon. No quarter was given by the Polish Lancers who trotted backwards and forwards sticking their victims at will, even the helpless wounded, who were speared where they lay. Ensign Thomas of the 2/48th, not yet sixteen, refused to yield the Regimental Colours and was cut down still gripping its staff. The Colours were retrieved later, whilst Lieutenant Latham, with the King's Colour, was surrounded by cavalry, but like Thomas, defended it. A sabre slash destroyed part of his face, another severed an arm and he was knocked down and trampled on. In the search for wounded at the end of the day, he was found with the Colour hidden beneath his body. Happily, Matthew Latham made an astonishing recovery, despite his appalling injuries, and continued to serve the 3rd Buffs, having received treatment at the Prince Regent's expense.

General Godinot's cavalry now swept round Beresford's right flank towards the Spaniards' rear, scattering Marshal Beresford and his Staff, who barely had time to draw their swords. In the mêlée the Marshal was attacked by a Polish Lancer, but Beresford, whose physical strength was second only to that of Sir Thomas Graham, grasped the Lancer's spear and threw him from the saddle where he was quickly despatched by Beresford's orderly dragoon.

During the slaughter of Colborne's brigade French cavalry had captured six of his guns, but now, when all seemed lost and Beresford was seriously thinking of disengaging, Colonel Harding took it upon himself to suggest that General Sir Lowry Cole should advance with Colonel Abercrombie who commanded the remaining brigade of the 2nd Division.

A little over a mile away, John Cooper, from his hilltop position, had viewed with horror the decimation of Colborne's brigade and had been convinced that the day was lost. The order "Fall in Fusiliers" quickly dispelled all such gloomy thoughts and, forgetting his weariness with the promise of action, Cooper eagerly joined the others in forming line. The order to advance followed and, with General Cole leading the 7th and 23rd Fusiliers in person, the column moved off.

The Spaniards had lost thirty per cent of their original strength and Beresford undoubtedly faced a crisis when General Cole began his advance. Beresford's was a decision not without risk, involving, as it did, the movement of a large body of troops across an open plain in the face of two regiments of Latour-Maubourg's cavalry. Nevertheless, flanked by three squadrons from the 4th Dragoons and supported by two

Cacadore regiments, three Fusilier battalions, the 1/7th, 2/7th, and 1/23rd, advanced to meet the combined brigades of Generals Gazan and Giraud, now reinforced by a section of Marshal Soult's Reserve.

Beresford's hesitancy of command had not gone unnoticed and a belief that there was only one man who could be relied upon to get them out of a perilous situation was made clear by an observation by Private Horsefall. Turning to the Fusilier corporal, he remarked, "Whore's ar Arthur? aw wish he wor 'ere!" So too did Corporal Wheeler.

In parade ground order, the 4,000 men of Cole's command, together with Abercrombie's brigade, advanced up the corpse-strewn slope past the survivors of Hoghton's brigade, to emerge from the swirling clouds of grey-white smoke. When Cole's 9-pdr field guns were hauled laboriously to the summit, deadly discharges of grape were added to the havoc wreaked by the musketry of the infantry on the densely packed columns of General Gazan's command.

In the exchange of fire, General Sir Lowry Cole and three Colonels were hit and carried to the rear, but, although more than a thousand men had fallen, nothing could check the remorseless pressure being applied to the blue-clad masses by the Fusilier battalions. Cooper's Company greeted a confused body of Spanish infantry intermixed with French and Polish Lancers with a volley which cleared their path, bringing down friend and foe in equal measure. Scattering the Lancers, Cole's troops recovered the six cannon lost to the French and, joined by the survivors of Hoghton's brigade, advanced to meet the three columns of General Werle, amounting to some 7,800 men.

It soon became apparent to Soult that, if Gazan and Girard were to be saved and their columns given time to reform, he would have to throw the entire weight of his Reserve into the battle. The rain had ceased as suddenly as it had begun and the three Fusilier battalions each engaged an enemy column at close range in a furious exchange of musketry. In their column formation, the French could only bring to bear a fraction of their available fire power, but the British troops were being raked by grape and canister from the French artillery with telling effect. The two sides closed in what was to develop into the most ferocious battle of the Peninsular War.

At such close range the carnage suffered by each army was severe. The French were reeling from the devastating, disciplined volleys of musketry which was the hallmark of British firepower, whilst the extended line of Fusiliers were being knocked over like so many ninepins in a skittle alley. Despite this punishing fire, the British remained firm, methodically loading, priming and firing into the blue-clad masses now little more than thirty yards distant.

Commented Lieutenant Joseph Moyle-Sherer, "A heavy atmosphere of smoke again enveloped us, and few objects could be discerned at all, none distinctly. The coolest and bravest soldier, if he be in the heat of it, can make no calculation of time during an engagement. . . . We were the whole time advancing upon and shaking the enemy."

To Sherer the whole dreadful scene seemed divorced from reality: "To describe my feelings throughout this wild scene with fidelity, would be impossible," he added. "At intervals a shriek or groan told that men were falling all around me; but it was not always that the tumult of the contest suffered me to catch these sounds." Rather it was the shouted commands of "Close up! Close up! and the ever-shrinking line of redcoats that more truly betrayed the frightful losses his regiment was sustaining.

For an hour the murderous conflict continued over what was barely two acres of blood-soaked ground. Frenzied men climbed over the dead bodies of their comrades to club each other with the butts of muskets, stab down with bayonets, or simply use their fists. Although visibility was restricted to a few yards in the billowing, choking clouds of smoke, the Fusiliers fought on until they could hardly raise muskets against shoulders bruised and blackened from the recoil.

Hoghton's brigade had virtually ceased to exist and its commander lay among the dead. Command of the brigade now passed to Colonel Inglis of the 57th, who, after his horse had been killed beneath him, shook his feet clear of the stirrups and calmly strolled up and down the line encouraging his men until he too fell mortally wounded. An Ensign and two Privates of the 57th made as though to carry him to a less exposed position, but he waved them away with an exhortation which was to win a glorious sobriquet for the regiment when he asked his men to "Die hard 57th! Die hard."

Marshal Soult had also braved the sustained volleys of musketry to encourage his men, but, in the face of withering fire from the Fusiliers, he could do little to prevent the gradual falling back of his shattered columns towards the reverse side of the hill. "At the distance of about twenty yards from them, we received orders to charge," wrote Moyle-Sherer. "We had ceased firing, cheered, and had our bayonets in the charging position. Already, however, had the French infantry, alarmed by our preparatory cheers . . . broke and fled." The Veteran Guard, coming to the support of their comrades who had been forced to the edge of the plateau, could do nothing to check the British regiments and merely added to the carnage, the shattered remnants trampling each other in their haste to reach the bottom of the hill. Sir William Napier, in his *History of the War in the Peninsula and the South of France*, describes the inexorable advance of the 4th Division in lyrical fashion: "Nothing could stop that indomitable infantry. No sudden burst of undisciplined valour, no nervous enthusiasm weakened the stability of their order; their

119

flashing eyes were bent on the dark columns in their front; their measured tread shook the ground; their dreadful volleys swept away the head of every formation; their dreadful shouts overpowered the distant cries that broke from all parts of the tumultuous crowd, as foot by foot and with a horrid carnage, it was driven by the incessant vigour of the attack to the furthest verge of the hill."

For a short time the fighting continued as isolated groups persevered in their efforts to dispute possession of the village, but, four hours after the opening skirmish, the murderous conflict ended with the exhausted and battered French columns retiring eastward as another deluge of rain blanketed the battlefield.

Marshal Beresford had won the day, but at a terrible cost. Of the 7,500 British troops engaged, 4,158 had fallen, and of the allied forces 1,400 Spaniards and 400 Portuguese. Total French losses were estimated at some 7,000 officers and men.

"Our muster on coming out of the field," wrote Ensign Close, "was, including non-commissioned officers and drummers, just twenty-five and six officers, and I was one of that number."

"It is impossible," wrote Marshal Beresford in his report, "by any description to do justice to the distinguished gallantry of the troops; but every individual nobly did his duty; and it is observed that our dead, particularly the 57th Regiment, were lying as they fought, in ranks, and every wound was in the front."

It was many weeks before news of the battle reached the London papers, where it was greeted enthusiastically as a victory, albeit one bought at a heavy price. The wildest rumours circulated in the capital and Lieutenant Robert Knowles, who was awaiting orders to join the depleted 2nd battalion of the Fusiliers, heard with more than a measure of scepticism that Marshal Beresford had been killed and that Lord Wellington had lost a leg.

Two days after the battle Lieutenant Joseph Moyle-Sherer wandered across the field where Polish Lancers and French artillery had decimated Colborne's brigade. Stripped naked by the local people, the bodies "lay ghastly and unburied, the paths cut by the cannon shot clearly marked by headless trunks and shattered limbs." A few of the corpses, he noted, were in attitudes of seemingly peaceful repose, but others, the victims of lance thrusts, lay with "contorted bodies and with agonized features". Inspecting the scene with a growing feeling of dismay, he was gratified to find that the British dead had received touching tokens of esteem from their Spanish ally. "The hands of many of the redcoats," wrote Sherer, "had been clasped together in an attitude of prayer and their bodies arranged in a way that the Spaniards usually accorded their own dead awaiting burial."

Fifteen months later, when all traces of that savage event had long since disappeared, Lieutenant Sherer had occasion to return to the site. On the walls of a ruined chapel, which at one time had housed several hundred French prisoners, an inscription scratched on a wall with charcoal, caught his eye: *"La Guerre en Espagne est la Fortune des Generaux, L'Ennui des officiers et le Tombeau des Soldats"*.

Major Samuel Rice of the 51st was even more scathing in his condemnation of the field commanders. "I have just been reconnoitring the ground of the battle of Albuera," he wrote to a friend, "and have been conceited enough to think that even I could have managed it better. The blundering was great, and terrible the sacrifice . . . in short it is the richest 'bed of honour' I have seen for a long while."

For several days after the battle small groups, previously listed as missing, returned to their units, some having lost their way in the dark in pursuit of the French, earning for themselves the sobriquet of 'The Resurrection Men'. After nonchalantly sitting down to clean and inspect their flintlocks, many enquired after yesterday's rations. "Being very hungry after hunting them frog-eaters through the woods – bad luck to 'em."

A few had escaped after being taken prisoner and one, who had been questioned by Marshal Soult, was asked by Lord Wellington what it was that the French Marshal had said to him. 'Sir!' the escaped prisoner replied. "He only wanted to know if the English General who commanded the day of battle was hanged yet!"

Although Beresford's personal courage was never in question, his battlefield tactics certainly were, as instanced in an encounter Wellington had with the wounded in hospital at Valverde. "Men of the 29th," he remarked, "I am sorry to see so many of you here." "If you had commanded us, my Lord," replied a veteran sergeant, "there wouldn't have been so many of us here."

Beresford's army had all but been shattered and, as Wellington is said to have remarked, "Another such victory would ruin them".

Chapter 12

'SOLDIERS! THE EYES OF YOUR COUNTRY ARE UPON YOU'

Once Soult had retired on Llerena in the face of superior numbers, the investment of Badajoz was resumed by the Portuguese on 19 May. Two days later Lord Wellington arrived, having marched south from Elvas to make good the losses suffered at Albuera and to take over control from Marshal Beresford.

The wall around the fortress was immensely strong, possessing eight bastions thirty feet high with the curtain wall between them rising to twenty-six feet and encircling the town. To the north across the Guadiana River lay the heights of San Cristobal, while to the south and east could be seen the Pardaleras and Picurina forts, both of which were garrisoned under the overall command of the Governor, General Armand Phillipon.

Although there were now more siege guns available to Wellington, many were defective and he was further handicapped by a shortage of artillerymen and military engineers. Nevertheless, operations were commenced on the 30th with parallels being extended in front of San Cristobal and the castle on the south bank of the river. These were circuits of trenches connected by zig-zag saps which were dug ever closer to the outer walls and obviously labour-intensive. Private Wheeler and his comrades of the 51st were soon numbered among the 1,600 workmen employed on this unpopular task, one which was bitterly resented by the redcoats, who considered themselves fighting men and not labourers. The hard rocky soil could only be broken with difficulty and the close proximity of the enemy meant that protection had to be provided for the working parties with bales of wool and sacks filled with earth. As the work progressed, marksmen armed with the Baker rifle stood by and George Simmons of the 95th boasted of having silenced the fire of a French battery by calling upon "forty as prime fellows as ever pulled a trigger".

Cannon fire was always a problem, but an experienced lookout could always distinguish the flat trajectory of a roundshot from the approaching arc of a shell and Kincaid writes of an occasion when a Portuguese was posted to call out "bomba, bomba" or "balla, balla", according to whether a shell or roundshot was approaching the workings. "Sometimes he would see a general discharge from all arms," related the Rifle officer, "when he threw himself down, screaming out, 'Jesus!, todos, todos', meaning, 'everything'."

Water was soon in demand and those who had neglected to fill their canteens suffered torture from thirst, for, although the river was not far off, a soldier had only to put his head above a trench to bring a dozen musket balls singing about his ears.

During the day the working parties were baked by the sun and tormented by flies, while at night, although conditions were less hazardous, the men working above ground were sometimes caught in the glare of potfires thrown over the wall when they became conspicuous targets for the garrison's sharpshooters.

Occasionally a sortie would be made by the garrison, which obliged the working party to vacate the trench in a hurry, after which Phillipon's men would make a triumphant return with as many entrenching tools as they could carry.

A period of heavy rains during the early part of the siege caused considerable discomfort to the soldiers labouring in the trenches, for earth thrown up to act as a rampart turned to liquid mud which ran back into the trench. The parallels rapidly filled with chilling slime which caused a number of men to fall sick with complaints ranging from freezing limbs to ague, and at one stage caused Wellington to seriously consider abandoning the operation. Despite these setbacks, the saps crept slowly forward and, four days after commencement of the earthworks, the siege guns were brought up and a bombardment opened against the curtain wall. Unfortunately the cannon soon developed major defects. Carriages were shaken to pieces and the barrels of many of the heavy pieces became warped from the heat after only a few discharges.

Wellington, knowing that Soult and Marmont would soon be marching to the relief of the garrison, was growing impatient. When, on 6 June, two breaches in the San Cristobal fort were reported by the engineers to be practicable, he ordered that the fort be stormed without delay. After a brief period of artillery fire designed to keep the defenders' heads below the castellated walls, a 'Forlorn Hope' led by Ensign Dyas of the 51st rushed ahead of the main storming party drawn from Houston's 7th Division.

A 'Forlorn Hope' amounted almost to a suicide mission. An ambitious officer would volunteer to lead the party on the understanding that he would be promoted should he survive the assault, but the men stood to gain nothing. Strangely enough, there was never a lack of volunteers. The stormers reached the ditch in front of the breach without casualties, only to discover that the foot of the breach had been cleared by the resourceful Phillipon and a sheer ascent of some seven feet confronted them.

As the storming party struggled to erect their scaling ladders the parapet became crowded with jeering French soldiers, many armed with three muskets apiece. Live shells, grenades, heavy stones and bags of gunpowder were dropped into the ditch, which caused panic among the redcoats struggling to escape, half of whom became casualties in the first few minutes. Near the top of the wall Private Wheeler's ladder was shattered and he crashed to the ground amid a confused mass of bodies and broken masonry. Dazed by the fall, he barely heard Dyas calling his men to retire, but before Wheeler could join them a sortie by the garrison cut off his escape route. Only quick thinking on his part saved Wheeler from being made prisoner. Smearing his tunic with blood from the bodies around him, he feigned unconsciousness even as a Frenchman searched his pockets and removed his boots. When night fell Wheeler made good his escape, arriving in camp to the cheers of his comrades and in time to avoid having his name included among the list of casualties.

On 9 June another attempt was made to escalade the fort, but again, in the face of an alert defence, the attack collapsed with a quarter of the assailants falling victim to the garrison's fire power. This latest failure, and the fact that, without artillery of the required strength, Badajoz was virtually impregnable, decided Wellington in favour of raising the siege. On 19 June the allies retired on the Caya and just as Phillipon's men were on the point of consuming the last of their dwindling food supplies the relief force commanded by Soult marched into the city.

For the greater part of the month Marshals Soult and Marmont remained at Badajoz until, after stripping the countryside of everything edible, they departed from Estramadura, Soult to Seville and Marmont northwards beyond the Guadiana.

There now followed a period of inactivity which Lord Wellington used to reshape and rest his divisions in preparation for a campaign in Leon, where the fortress of Ciudad Rodrigo stood as a barrier to a passage into Spain from the north.

For a short while the redcoats were able to relish their freedom from regimental duties. "Up to this period," wrote Captain Kincaid, "it had been a matter of no small difficulty to ascertain, at any time, the day of the week; that of the month was altogether out of the question, and could only be reckoned by counting back to the date of the last battle; but our division was here joined by a chaplain, whose duty it was to remind us of these things."

Unfortunately for Kincaid and his friends sickness spread among the troops and conditions became so unhealthy that Wellington decided to move away in the direction of Ciudad Rodrigo. By the second week in August that town was invested and a siege train from Britain, having been transported on barges to Lamego, was making the difficult journey overland to Ciudad Rodrigo. Until its arrival no serious attempt at breaching the walls could even be contemplated and the allies settled into cantonments, while maintaining a watch on the movements of the French around Salamanca.

Intelligence had reported French strength at 58,000, a figure which caused Wellington some unease, and, leaving the Light Division and Picton's 3rd Division to keep watch from El Boden, he withdrew his main force from the plain around Ciudad Rodrigo to the hills west of the city.

Meanwhile, pushing cautiously forward from Tamames, Marmont had sent his cavalry to investigate whether Ciudad Rodrigo was actually under siege or merely being invested. On 23 September the Imperial Cavalry, led by Montbrun, crossed the Agueda ahead of the infantry to find General Picton's 'Fighting Third' dispersed over a wide area around El Boden, a position too extensive to be adequately defended and where communications were vulnerable due to the crossing points over the river frequently being rendered impassable because of the sudden rains.

Two days later, without waiting for the infantry, cavalry scattered the English pickets, driving them across the Azara, while Montbrun attacked Picton's division, turning the heights on which they had been posted. A battery of six field guns, which had earlier opened fire from the crest of the hill, were limbered up too late to avoid capture and were taken with their crews. The guns did not remain in the possession of the French for long, however. The 5th formed line and, after delivering a shattering volley, the regiment swept forward with the bayonet against the dragoons who, breathless and in disarray after their charge up the rocky slope, were no match for determined infantry. The guns were recaptured and the dragoons driven down the slope.

Meanwhile, the men of Picton's division, outnumbered as they were, fell back from the high ground and, as Marmont's column closed on their rear, the order came to disengage and, united with the 5th and 7th regiments, Picton withdrew across the plain towards Guinaldo. At several points during their retreat it seemed that nothing could save them from annihilation in the face of repeated cavalry attacks, but, by adopting the proven tactic of forming square, the enemy were beaten off and the retreat continued in good order, supported by the British dragoons and Hussars of the King's German Legion.

One confrontation between individuals was remembered for an act of chivalry rendered by an unknown French cavalry officer. Rapidly closing on the one-armed Captain Felton Hervey of the 14th Dragoons, he was about to cut him down when he noticed the Captain's empty sleeve. In one rapid movement the Frenchman turned the downward sweep of his sabre into a salute and swerved away.

On the 27th, five miles south of El Boden, General Pakenham's brigade came under attack from a strong French force at Aldea de Ponte. The village was twice taken by the French and re-taken by the Fusiliers and Cacadores. These actions brought young Robert Knowles his baptism of fire, but any nervousness he might have felt was quickly forgotten with the order to "Form line and advance".

Lieutenant Knowles, being the senior officer in his Company, led it into battle against Marmont's corps whilst "balls flew about our ears as if in a hailstorm," reported the young man later. One grazed Knowles' cap and another cut the strap of his canteen in two, but, although men were falling all around him, the eagerness of his redcoats to close with the bayonet left the lieutenant quite unconscious of any feeling of fear.

The affair at El Boden brought Wellington's campaign of 1811 to a close and on 1 October the respective armies retired to their winter quarters, the British around the Coa, where, from its narrow front, the position could not be easily turned, and the French to the valley of the Tagus.

Now that active campaigning was suspended for the winter, Wellington's troops, for the first time in many weeks, found themselves with little to do outside of normal picket duties. Sport played a major part in the army's leisure activities and the Irish, notoriously restless when not engaged in fighting the French, relieved their aggression with bare-knuckle contests. The ban on the use of firearms did not deter the wildfowlers from adding to their rations with duck or rabbit, while, as ever, the pursuit of the fair sex occupied much of the troops' leisure hours:

"We invited the villagers, every evening, to a dance at our quarters. . . . We used to flourish away at the bolero, fandango and waltz, and wound up early in the evening with a supper of roast chestnuts," wrote John Kincaid. However, he added, "We found that the cherry cheek and sparkling eye of the rustic beauty furnished but a very poor apology . . . for an opportunity of once more feasting our eyes on a lady."

Among the officers fox hunting and hare coursing were favourite pastimes and a pack of hounds was even sent out from England, the cost being met by a few of the wealthier cavalrymen. Occasionally a meet provided the huntsmen with some unlooked-for excitement, as was experienced by Captain Gronow taking part in his first hunt. At first all went well, but then the quarry crossed to the French side of the river, followed by the rest of the pack, much to the consternation of a group of voltigeurs under instruction. Alarmed by the sudden appearance and hallooing of the hunt, the class took to its heels, but the sport terminated abruptly when the French, believing themselves to be under attack, opened fire on the huntsmen, fortunately without effect.

Thoughts of campaigning may not have been uppermost in the minds of most of Wellington's soldiers at that time, but a renewal of the siege of Ciudad Rodrigo was very much the concern of their Commander-in-Chief. The long-awaited siege train had been assembled at Almeida and on 8 January 1812 steps were taken to put the fortress town once again in a state of siege.

For the troops who had been brought up to positions just five miles from the fortress which guarded the northern approach to Spain the contrast with their previous quarters could not have been more severe. Their inadequate rations were transported with difficulty over the atrocious roads and at times the fatigue parties were obliged to scour the woods for fallen acorns as a substitute for bread.

The village in which the 7th Fusiliers were billeted had only twenty small cottages in which to accommodate 700 men and, in writing to his parents, Robert Knowles could state with conviction that, "Few people at home would envy me my present situation". Rain fell in torrents and those officers fortunate enough to have secured reasonably comfortable quarters suffered no less than the others who had to be content with a hastily constructed shelter of branches and bracken. A peasant's cottage was, in the opinion of Captain Ross-Lewin, "the worst possible of all winter abodes".

John Mills, writing home, could justifiably complain that "roofs which despise the vulgar accomplishment of keeping out rain do not inspire the same sensations of comfort that a comfortable fireside, and the certainty of no trickling water upon the head are accustomed to do in England." The Portuguese occupants of his billet seemed to Ross Lewin, "the very picture of misery". Wrapped in coarse brown blankets against the icy draughts, they huddled together in the one corner of the room which was free from the drips which spilled with monotonous regularity from various parts of the boarded ceiling.

Although given the facility of a large wooden chest on which to sleep, thus avoiding the rats, the Captain of the 32nd Regiment was unable to escape the torment induced by the flea-infested bedding provided by his host. He, however, was marginally better off than an officer of the 34th who discovered that the wet earth was to be his bed for the night. Ensign George Bell, who might have expected more comfortable quarters, wrapped himself in his cloak and prepared a bed of bracken. "How did you sleep?" he was asked after his first experience of bivouacking in inclement weather. "Slept like a fish," he replied. "I believe they sleep best in water."

Ciudad Rodrigo stands on high ground on the north bank of the Agueda, dominating an extensive plain. To the left and right were the convents of Santa Cruz and San Francisco, both of which had been fortified by the French after the town had fallen to Marshal Ney in 1810. The defence works, although not as formidable as those of Badajoz, were nevertheless immensely strong. The wall which enclosed the mediaeval town and its labyrinth of cobbled streets was thirty-two feet high with masonry counter-scarps rising to twelve feet, whilst the suburbs were protected by two fortified convents on its flanks. Since its re-occupation by the French, Ciudad Rodrigo's 2,000-strong garrison, led by General Berrie, who had succeeded Reynaud, possessed a plentiful supply of firearms, cannon and ammunition with every expectation of holding out until relieved by Soult or Marmont.

Four divisions had been allocated as working parties to the engineers concerned with the excavation of batteries for the thirty heavy siege cannon and the digging of trenches in the frost-hardened ground. This wearisome business was shared by each division and, as a result of much hard labour by day and night, parallels and seven battery positions were completed by 11 January, despite a harassing fire from the garrison.

The time was fast approaching for an assault on the citadel, but first the outlying convent of Santa Cruz needed to be overcome before an additional parallel, thought necessary by the engineers, could be excavated close to the curtain wall.

On the 13th work began and that night three companies from the 52nd successfully stormed the convent for the loss of six men killed and twenty wounded. It had not escaped the garrison's notice that, with a change of shifts, there happened to be a brief interval when the trenches were barely manned and on the evening of the 14th, as the working parties were being relieved, a sortie from the citadel rushed the trenches, overturned the gabions and would have succeeded in spiking the guns had not the engineers and a few workmen put up a spirited fight until reinforcements obliged the French to beat a hasty retreat.

The outlying redoubt of San Francisco, north of Santa Cruz, dominated the town and, after a bombardment from 27 siege guns the following evening, a breach was made and the convent fell to a storming party from the 40th Regiment in less than twenty minutes. The French, under pressure from several points, then abandoned both convents, deciding in favour of concentrating all their resources in the defence of the fortress.

The inclement weather which had heralded the New Year now worsened to such an extent that the troops engaged in digging the trenches were obliged to seek the shelter of the outlying villages, which meant that the parties working on the second parallel, because of its position, had to ford the icy waters of the Agueda in order to relieve each other every few hours, an operation which the garrison always celebrated with a cannonade from every gun and mortar which could be brought to bear. Although much of the shot flew harmlessly wide, so numerous were the cannon balls which buried themselves in a hill a mile north of the town that Wellington's troops commonly referred to it as "plum pudding hill". On one notable occasion, a 13-inch mortar shell dropped in a trench occupied by a working party from the 52nd Regiment. Almost everyone there threw themselves to the bottom of the trench, including George Napier, now a major in the 1st battalion, the one exception being the battalion's most notorious character who ran up to the still-smoking shell and, striking the fuse with a blow from his spade, knocked it out. The Irishman then picked up the iron sphere and presented it to the major with the comment, "There she is for you now your honour. Be Jasus, she'll do you no harm, since I knocked the life out of the crature!" A relieved George Napier felt that the least he could do was to give the man a dollar with "leave to get drunk – on the assumption that he would reach the cantonments safely".

The stress of continuous work under fire was not eased for the redcoats by the difficulty of digging trenches in the frozen ground. The casualties and the constant interruptions caused by the bombardments were becoming intolerable and finally a decision was made to work only at night. Lieutenant George Simmons was placed in charge of one such group employed in carrying up baskets of earth to build a protective wall around the siege cannon. It was exhausting work, rendered no less dangerous by the glare of fireballs thrown over the walls of the fortress three hundred yards distant. Several times Simmons faced the hazard of crossing open ground regularly swept by grape and on each occasion he lost several of his men. It was with profound relief that he finally received confirmation that the engineer was satisfied that the pile of gabions was high enough.

By the 18th the second parallel had been completed and an additional seven siege guns joined with the other twenty-seven in battering the curtain wall. The next day two breaches were judged to be sufficiently wide to permit of an assault and Lord Wellington, knowing that

Marmont would be straining every nerve to raise the siege, issued written orders for an attack timed for 7.00pm that evening. The plan provided for the Portuguese to create a diversion on the other side of the town half an hour before Picton was due to carry the main breach. Whilst Craufurd's Light Division attacked the smaller of the two breaches, Pack's brigade was directed to escalade the southern curtain wall.

As the hour for the storming drew near, Sir Thomas Picton addressed the 88th. "Rangers of Connaught, it is not my intention to expend much powder this evening. We'll trust entirely to cold iron."

In the fading light the men detailed to storm the breaches marched out of their cantonments and halted a mile short of the town to allow volunteers to be called to form a 'Forlorn Hope', comprising a section of twenty-five men and two sergeants, led by a subaltern.

A similar band of volunteers, known as '*Les Enfants Perdus*', was employed by the French, whose rankers, unlike their British counterparts, were usually promoted to officer rank should they survive. Among the volunteers waiting for the order to 'Stand to Arms', few experienced a greater degree of trepidation than did Edward Costello. The young rifleman was conscious of "a silence and solemnity among the men around him more intense than anything he had before experienced". As he speculated gloomily on his chances of survival, Costello's reverie was broken by the harsh voice of General Robert Craufurd addressing the stormers: "Soldiers! The eyes of your country are upon you. Be steady – be cool – be firm in the assault. The town must be yours this night. Once masters of the wall, let your first duty be to clear the ramparts and in doing this keep together."

Three hundred yards away the massive black silhouette of the fortress stood out against a sky threatening snow, and when at 7.00pm a signal rocket blazed a fiery arc above the trenches the stormers dashed across the ground to meet a hail of musketry and grapeshot. The Forlorn Hope, led by Lieutenants William Mackie of the 88th and John Kincaid of the 95th, both of whom miraculously escaped without a scratch, was forced to the left of the breach, but the main party scrambled up the steep slope of the glacis with Major Napier in the lead. Slipping and scrambling over the loose stones, Napier was close to the top when he staggered and almost brought down Edward Costello. A musket ball had shattered his elbow. Having ensured the Major was not mortally wounded, Costello clambered over the broken masonry of the lesser breach only to be seized by the throat in what was to become a life or death struggle. Bent almost double beneath the weight of the Frenchman, Costello was beginning to lose consciousness when the artilleryman was tripped and bayoneted by a rifleman in Costello's own company.

Several yards away, General Craufurd stood directing the stormers through the breach when a musket ball struck his chest, hurling him into the ditch. Away to the right, the men of Picton's command were attempting to scale an almost perpendicular mass of rubble in the face of bursting grenades and the fire from two field pieces which enfiladed the main breach. Private Donaldson, stumbling over the broken stones, overheard General Henry Mackinnon complimenting the youngest officer in the Company on his bright new pelisse. "Come Beresford," the General called. "You look a fine lad. You and I will go together." A commitment which was to prove deadly for them both.

Hard-pressed on both flanks as well as the rear, the defenders began to waver, and, when more redcoats began to pour into the fortress they retreated into the town. It was then that a frightful explosion shook the ground close to the main breach, sending up a column of flame and smoke. General Mackinnon, together with many of the stormers who had taken the left-hand circuit of the wall, was blown high into the air. His death was regretted by the brigade of the Coldstream Guards and, it was said, by Napoleon himself, with whom he had formed a friendship when, as a cadet, he had become a regular visitor during Mackinnon's period of residence in Paris.

Ensign Grattan, only a few yards from where the mine was detonated, was blown into the ditch. He lay there stunned amongst the rubble with his clothes smouldering and only the prompt action of his sergeant saved the young Ensign from being trampled underfoot in the rush from the scene of the explosion. Captain John Kincaid was equally fortunate, for he had taken the right-hand circuit of the wall and so escaped the fate of most of those who had turned in the direction of the mine.

The huge French mine, which fortunately had erupted before most of the attacking troops had reached the main breach, had brought down a large section of the curtain wall, thus giving access into the town which the Highlanders of the 94th were quick to exploit. Lieutenant Mackie, who had miraculously survived the explosion, found himself in solitary possession of an area immediately beyond the breach where he was quickly joined by others of his Company.

The garrison, faced with increasing numbers from the 3rd Division, now lost heart and in less than two hours from the start of the assault General Berrie, together with eighty officers and 1,700 other ranks, offered themselves up as prisoners to the victorious allies. One unexpected result was that of General Graham acquiring the services of the

Governor's French cook. The man, a non-combatant, had hidden in a chimney. When the redcoats entered the chilly room, a fire was lit, whereupon the cook came scrambling down, much to the amusement of the General, who offered him a place in the mess.

Now that the town had fallen, there followed the indiscriminate looting and acts of rape which usually the fate of a town taken by storm. Frenzied redcoats ran riot, firing at every window which indicated that the room was occupied and often at individuals, as in one incident when Captain John Cooke was engaged in conversation with the regimental barber in the town square and the unfortunate man was struck by a musket ball. "He fell dead at my feet," wrote Cooke, "and his brains lay on the pavement."

As ever, the liquor stores were the main targets and the drink naturally fuelled the mob's savage behaviour. The frightening appearance of drink-crazed devils with powder-blackened faces and blood-stained tunics bursting into a room paralysed the occupants, who, not daring to interfere, were forced to endure the screams of their womenfolk as they were dragged out of hiding.

"The scene of rapine I am told," wrote Ensign John Mills, "beggared all description. The town was on fire in many places, every house was ransacked; in short, for the whole of the night it was given up to pillage."

Only after some hours was a minimum of order restored, chiefly from the act of General Picton in lashing out at marauding soldiers with a broken musket barrel. Their fury spent, the victorious troops of Picton's 3rd Division matched out of the town, "dressed in all varieties imaginable," reported Edward Costello, "some with jackboots, others with white French trousers, others with frockcoats with epaulettes, some even with monkeys on their shoulders." As they marched past to the cheers of the Light Division, a bemused Wellington was heard to mutter to an equally astonished staff, "Who the devil are those fellows?" They were, of course, the infamous Connaught Rangers.

"The sound of the drums died away," commented Lieutenant Grattan, "the division was no longer visible, except by the glittering of their fire-locks; at length we lost sight of even this and we were left alone, like so many outcasts, to make the best of our way to the hospitals in Badajoz."

Private Donaldson, sickened by the acts of violence he had witnessed, made his way out of the town and towards the breach in the wall. Here the silence was broken only by the moans of the wounded and he found that the calm expression on the faces of many of the dead contrasted sharply with the contorted faces of the frenzied mob he had left behind in the town. John Mills, in a letter to his mother, described the chaos at the point of entry to the town: "The scene such as it was when I saw it, stripped of half its horrors, was beyond all imagination . . . one continued mass of friends and foes lying dead – caps, clothes, arms, cannon balls, ammunition, beds, chairs, wearing apparel, legs etc, filled the streets. Those who saw this scene on the morning after describe it as dreadful beyond expression."

Attention to the wounded close to the scene of conflict was often crude and hasty. Amputation was the only means of saving the patient from the consequence of gangrene. Performed without anaesthetic, much depended on the surgeon's skill and speed to lessen the onset of shock. George Napier was unfortunate, for, due to poor light and blunt instruments, it was at least twenty minutes before his operation was completed. "I must confess that I did not bear the amputation of my arm as well as I ought to have done," wrote the Major of the 50th. "I made noise enough when the knife cut through my skin and flesh. It is no joke I assure you. . . . I then thanked him [the surgeon] for his kindness, having sworn at him like a trooper while he was at it . . . and proceeded to find some place to lie down and rest."

The fall of Ciudad Rodrigo had been accomplished in just eleven days but at the cost of many dead, including one of Wellington's most able lieutenants. In a small room above the one in which George Napier lay recovering from the amputation of his arm General Robert Craufurd, after suffering greatly for most of a day and a night, died from his wounds and was buried where he had fallen at the foot of the breach. His coffin was borne by six sergeants from the Light Division and was followed by Lord Wellington and a retinue of high-ranking officers, many of whom found it difficult to contain their emotion. Wrote Lieutenant Colonel Bingham of the 53rd, "There are many circumstances which make a military funeral striking, but this was particularly so, and there were more tears shed on this occasion than at funerals in general."

A stern disciplinarian, 'Black Bob' had forged the Light Division from a band of selected personnel into an elite force whose efficiency became a byword in the Peninsula. Craufurd held a theory that a march which did not deviate from a straight line was not only the shortest route but also the least fatiguing. So well trained were his men that they would march unhesitatingly through the deepest stream rather than break the line of march by taking advantage of a ford or bridge. It was perhaps an unconscious tribute to his methods that, after the funeral, the burial party, faced with an ice-encrusted pool some fifty yards across, marched knee deep through the freezing water rather than taking a path around the edge.

One barrier to Spain had been overcome, but there remained Badajoz and in the middle of February the army was once again in motion.

Leaving a division on the Agueda, Wellington moved rapidly upon the Tagus and, crossing that river, established his headquarters at Elvas on 6 March. Five days later three divisions, the Light, third and fourth, crossed a pontoon bridge over the Guadiana with the objective of investing that formidable fortress town.

Chapter 13

THE BREACH AT BADAJOZ

The capture of Ciudad Rodrigo had secured the British army's line of communication from the north and, reinforced by fresh troops from England and the additional Cacadore regiments, Wellington was determined that the continued presence of French troops in Badajoz should no longer present a threat to southern Portugal. Late in January the army was again on the move and, as he marched with his battalion across the plain of Albuera, Private Wheeler was astonished to find the bleached skeletons of last year's battle still visible. Rusted iron cannon balls, broken equipment, muskets and clothing still littered the ground, but more disturbing to the soldier of the 51st was the sight of long earthen ridges from which the whitened bones of arms and legs projected, betraying the haste with which the dead had been buried.

On 14 March a pontoon bridge brought up from Abrantes was laid across the Guadiana and the allies began their slow build-up on the Spanish border. By the middle of the month 25,000 troops and a siege train comprising sixteen 24 pdrs, twenty 18 pdrs and sixteen heavy mortars floated up by barge were ready to play their part in reducing the walls of the fortress.

Against a garrison outnumbered by five to one, Wellington was confident of a successful outcome of the siege. Equally assured of defeating this, the third attempt to take the city, was the Governor, General Armand Phillipon. He had already experienced two sieges and was well prepared for this one. Breaches in the wall made from a previous attempt had been filled in and the approach to the exposed west wall had been provided with mines fused to explode at the first hint of trouble. Indeed, no defensive measure which might add to the security of the garrison had been neglected, even to the damming of the Rivallas Brook which, if demolished, would inundate an area in front of the Trinidad Bastion.

A close examination by Wellington's engineers on the 16th persuaded him that the bastion of La Trinidad was the weakest part of the curtain wall and for the next nine days, despite heavy rain, work forged ahead on a system of trenches and parallels essential to a successful prosecution of the siege. It was soon recognized as being dangerous and uncomfortable work and for that reason was chiefly undertaken at night, supervised by General Kempt, whose watchfulness was proverbial among those who made up the working party. Captain McCarthy of the 50th was amused to hear from his men that the General's frequent visits to the trenches almost always ended with the homily: "Well, work away boys; there's One above sees all."

Fortunately for the labouring troops, the timing fuses of the French shells were so erratic that the shells either burst too soon or so late that the working party had ample time to scramble clear of the trench, although in one instance a shell destroyed most of the previous night's work.

Possession of the Picurina in the south-east sector of the town was a necessary preliminary to the capture of the Trinidad Bastion and on the night of the 25th, after a fierce cannonade, the fort was stormed by 500 men from the 3rd Division under the command of General Kempt. Despite a stiff resistance, the redcoats led by the General forced their way up the steep glacis and through three rows of palisades to carry the fort at the expense of some 300 casualties. Its capture enabled a second parallel to be completed, together with a sufficient number of gabions for the protection of the working parties and by the end of March three batteries of heavy-calibre siege guns were knocking large chunks of masonry from the curtain wall. The Portuguese gunners had profited by their experience with the earlier siege artillery and the batteries now included 18 pdrs and 24 pdr howitzers sent up from the coast and supplied with powder and shot from the Portuguese garrison at Elvas. Because of a shortage of wheeled transport, to supply the cannon in sufficient quantities, mules and a team of sweating militiamen would stagger into the Picurina fort every day, having carried a score of 18 or 24 lb cannon balls over 12 miles of rough undulating countryside. In this fashion a daily supply of shot and shell ensured that the artillery maintained a relentless bombardment of the Santa Maria bastion and the curtain wall with just a short pause to allow the guns to cool.

Seven miles to the north, at Campo Mayor, the concussion from the heavy cannon shook the roof of the church and Walter Henry, an assistant surgeon in charge of a convoy of sick, could plainly hear a crackle of musketry in the intervals between the explosions. As the bombardment reached a crescendo, the assault troops grew impatient for an order which would end their suspense and send them against the fortress. The long uncomfortable hours spent crouching in wet and muddy trenches and the recollection of previous unsuccessful attempts to take the town had

136

increased the feelings of apprehension so graphically summed up by Lieutenant Gleig: "In the first place, time appears to move upon leaden wings, every minute seems an hour, and every hour a day. . . . On the whole, it is a situation of higher excitement, and darker and deeper feeling, than any other in human life."

Events were now moving towards their climax. At noon on 5 April, two breaches were inspected and declared practicable and a rumour circulated among the troops that the attack was to take place at sunset. Private Lawrence and his bosom companions 'Pig' Harding and George Bowden had been quartered in Badajoz after Talavera and were familiar with the jewellers and silversmiths of the city; together they discussed a plan for robbing them. All three agreed that a certain silversmith would prove the most rewarding and, in the event of becoming separated, it was arranged that they would meet there. Now, however, came the order for the storming parties to assemble and the three friends took their place with the ladder party to await the order to advance.

In fact the rumour proved false, for the attack was to be delayed 24 hours to allow time for a third breach to be knocked in the curtain wall. This was duly accomplished and, in the knowledge that both Soult and d'Erlon were marching to relieve the garrison, Wellington ordered that the assault was to be made at 10.00pm the following night – Easter Sunday. The plan called for Picton's 3rd Division to stage a diversionary escalade of the castle wall in the north-east, while the 4th and Light Divisions stormed the main breach between the Trinidad and Santa Maria bastions. In a further bid to distract the defenders from the main objective, the 5th Division was to assault the San Vincente Bastion to the north-west while a mixed force of British and Portuguese demonstrated against the San Roque Lunette in the east. In the unnatural silence following the end of the bombardment men fidgeted with their accoutrements, swallowed nervously or lifted canteens to parched lips. Preparations for the storming of the fortress began to take shape. Ladder parties were organized and bundles of fascines and bags of hay were distributed to ease the drop into the ditch in front of the main breach, estimated at some six feet.

At zero minus one the Forlorn Hope was paraded and a half pound of bread and a gill of rum was served to each man. Private John Green of the 68th had fought in a score of battles without sustaining so much as a scratch, but as he advanced in the darkness he was struck by an uneasy thought: "You will be in hell before daylight". "A feeling of horror swept over me," he wrote, "such as I had never before experienced."

Shortly before the appointed hour a fireball arced across from the bastion of Santa Maria, throwing into sharp relief the outline of the fortress and every object that lay within a hundred yards. It was quickly extinguished by a shovel of earth and a few minutes later the 3rd, 4th and Light Divisions took up their positions along the edge of the great ditch. Captain Kincaid, looking up from the beginning of the glacis, could plainly see the heads of the defenders lining the parapet, a slight ground mist hiding him and the others from observation by the sentries.

The Forlorn Hope crept forward to lower the ladders into the ditch when, perhaps alerted by a dislodged stone, a sentry challenged and, receiving no reply, discharged his musket into the darkness. The alarm had been raised and before the crouching redcoats could rise to their feet they were illuminated by a sudden blaze of light as flaming carcase, fire-balls and other combustibles burst around them.

The sudden transition from night to day came as a shock to Captain McCarthy: "Some idea may be formed of its refulgence," he explained, "by supposing it possible that all the stars, planets, and meteors of the firmament, with innumerable moons emitting smaller ones in their course, were congregating together, and descending upon the heads of the besiegers."

From the entire length of the ramparts, now bright with torches, a storm of grape and musketry tore into the assembled redcoats to wreak dreadful carnage among their closely packed ranks. Harding fell at once with a mortal wound and William Lawrence stumbled beneath the weight of his ladder as two fragments of iron struck his knee and a musket ball, passing through his canteen, grazed his thigh. Private Green was in the act of throwing a grass-filled bag into the ditch when a ball tore through the fleshy part of his thigh and smashed into his wrist. Four men were sharing the weight of a 30-foot ladder with Edward Costello. As they rushed forward, crouching low, three were struck and the ladder fell upon the young rifleman, pinning him to the ground. Unable to crawl free, Costello was drenched in the blood from the bodies of the ladder party who had fallen across him and, had it not been for the sack of grass against his chest, might well have suffocated.

After a lengthy struggle Costello freed himself from a heap of corpses and, without his Baker rifle, he rushed blindly towards the glacis with a crowd of stormers as the ditch behind him became ever more congested with the bodies of the slain and the struggling wounded. Above them, Phillipon's men taunted the attackers with derisive cries of "*Entrez! Entrez!* Why don't you come into Badajoz?" accompanying the invitation with an avalanche of stones, rocks, grenades and even cartwheels from dismantled gun limbers.

As an increasing number of redcoats from the 4th and Light Divisions vied with each other to climb the ladders or claw their way up to the breach, the great ditch became a death trap from which it was increasingly difficult to either advance or retire. Into this chaotic mass of struggling humanity the defenders lobbed live shells and grenades, whilst barrels of gunpowder with short spluttering fuses rolled down the glacis to engulf the redcoats in a pillar of fire.

"The roaring of cannon, the bursting of shells, the rattle of musketry, the awful explosion of mines and the flaring sickly blaze of fireballs seemed not of human invention," wrote Robert Blakeney, "but rather as if . . . heaven, earth and hell had united for the destruction alike of devoted Badajoz and its furious assailants." It seemed that Kincaid was correct in describing the conflict "as respectable a representation of hell itself as fire, and sword, and human sacrifice could make it."

In the blaze of musketry, McCarthy fell, his thigh fractured by a ball which struck him as he attempted to climb the glacis. "I instantly seized the trousers and turned over the limb to preserve existence," he reported, "and, being in a spot most exposed to the guns, I requested some men to carry me out of the stream of fire."

Although McCarthy was eventually rescued from the ditch, he was left in a perilous position until late in the afternoon of the following day. It was to be the middle of May before his fractured limb was set by a surgeon.

Despite the horrendous losses – more than 2,000 had fallen already – there was no shortage of men eager to press forward in response to the bugles continuously sounding the advance. Prominent in the assault was Lieutenant Harry Smith and an officer of the 43rd. Linking arms, they struggled to mount the rubble of the main breach in the teeth of a hail of flying iron and masonry. Within a few seconds most of the men around Smith, including his companion, had been knocked over and the Rifle officer, his tunic ripped open by the chips of stone splintered by musket balls, found himself to be the only unwounded member of his Company.

William Lawrence, weak from loss of blood and in a state of shock following the death of his two friends, was persuaded to go to the rear. "My wounds were still bleeding," remembered the Sergeant of the 40th, "and I began to feel very weak; my comrades persuaded me to return, but this proved a task of great difficulty, for arriving at the ladders I found them filled with the dead and wounded hanging, some by their feet, just as they had fallen and got fixed in the rungs." The climb left Lawrence utterly spent and he crawled away from the glacis on hands and knees, barely conscious of the lead whistling past his head. Once out of range, he rose to his feet, only to find himself just a few yards from Lord Wellington and a group of staff officers. A grey-faced and haggard-looking Wellington, having enquired after Lawrence's wounds, questioned the progress of the assault before directing him to a surgeon of the 40th who had improvised a dressing station in the lee of a hill.

Lord Wellington had every reason to fear the worst, suspecting that the breach made in the curtain wall was insufficiently large, for the scene at the main ditch was truly horrific, piled high with bodies. The French had profited from the delayed attack by creating a number of ingenious *chevaux-de-frise* in the breach. Among them heavy wooden beams, chained together and bristling with razor sharp sword blades, obstructed the approach and doors studded with spikes and loose planks embedded with jagged pieces of metal covered the slope leading up to the opening in the wall.

Time and again small groups of brave men would make a fruitless attempt at forcing a passage, even to the extent of lassoing the upturned blades, but the few who managed to reach the top of the glacis were clubbed, bayoneted or thrown headlong to the foot of the wall. Climbing over the rubble, Captain John Cooke was within yards of the *chevaux-de-frise* when he received a blow "which deprived me of sensation". On recovering from his fall, he looked about him and a scene reminiscent of Dante's *Inferno* met his gaze. "To exaggerate the picture of this sanguinary strife is impossible," he later wrote. "The small groups of soldiers seeking shelter from the cart wheels, pieces of timber, fireballs, and other missiles hurled down upon them; the wounded crawling past the fireballs, many of them scorched and perfectly black, and covered with mud . . . and all this time the French on the top of the parapet, jeering and cracking jokes, and deliberately picking off whom they chose."

Such was the intensity of the fire directed against them that many of the wounded were hit several times as they crawled to shelter behind the heaps of corpses.

Among the wounded lay Edward Costello. A musket ball had passed through the lower part of his leg and another had drawn a bloody furrow across his forehead. Screening himself as best he could behind the bodies, he lay there listening to the awful sounds of battle. "Screams, groans, bugle calls and the angry shouts of the combatants mingled with an endless roar of cannon fire and musketry, whilst the glare from exploding barrels of powder threw into sharp outline the struggle going on around me," he wrote.

As Lieutenant George Simmons, in a frenzy of frustration at the lack of progress, stamped on a potfire which threatened to draw attention to his men from sharpshooters, six hundred yards away Ensign Grattan was stacking barrels of powder against the dam the French had built at the San Roque Lunette. His attempt to demolish it failed, for, in seeking the advice of an engineer, Grattan was struck down and assisted to the rear. The area in front of the Lunette remained flooded and several Fusiliers from the 4th Division who had survived the murderous conflict at Albuera were drowned in twelve feet of water.

Two hours had elapsed and Wellington's troops were no closer to overcoming the obstacles in the breach than they had been at the beginning of the assault. The 4th and Light Divisions had suffered appalling losses and, in the knowledge of such carnage, Wellington considered calling a halt to the storming of the main breach.

Picton's 3rd Division, meanwhile, were engaged in a desperate attempt to escalade the castle wall, a feat considered impossible by Phillipon's engineers. Led by the General in person, wearing a faded blue coat and the celebrated wide-brimmed top hat, he and his men rushed forward to raise the heavy greenwood ladders against the wall. A few broke under the weight of the climbers, others were pushed away by the defenders using long poles shod with iron, but, as one thirty-foot ladder toppled with its climbers, another took its place. Scores of men were shot down or bayoneted as they struggled to reach the top of the wall and among the casualties was General Picton who, struck on the foot by a musket ball, was carried to the rear.

Contrary to the expectations of the French, success was within reach, however, for pressure from the men of Connaught and redcoats from the 45th began to take effect and at length cheers from the mass of redcoats struggling to mount the ladders betrayed the fact that a footing had been gained on the ramparts.

Jumping from the wall, Lieutenant Robert Knowles was greeted by a blast of grape which killed his corporal but merely shattered Knowles' light infantry sword. Miraculously, apart from cuts and bruises, the young lieutenant had suffered no serious injury and, picking up the dead man's musket, he dashed along the battlements with the rest of his Company killing or disarming all who barred their way. Eventually. outnumbered ten to one, the castle's defenders retreated to the keep where, in a desperate hand-to-hand struggle, they obstinately contested each flight of stairs.

At the San Vincente Bastion General Leith's 5th Division, after a short delay, had managed to force a passage through a secondary breach to join Picton's men in the streets of the town. A relieved Wellington heard the news as he was about to recall the Light Division and Robert Blakeney, who was nearby, found himself surrounded by a crowd of Spaniards who had gathered to watch the storming. Shouting in Spanish that Badajoz was taken, Blakeney was astonished to hear the noise of musket fire from behind the walls. In fact the redcoats were firing upon each other as troops from the 5th Division coming from the other side of town encountered resistance from the soldiers of Major General Walker's brigade. In the dark and the general confusion the two groups continued to exchange shots until the coming of daylight revealed their identities.

Now that the breaches were no longer defended, thousands of troops rushed to join those of the 3rd and 5th Divisions and General Phillipon, realizing the futility of further resistance, retired across the Guadiana where he was to surrender the following day. In the town, groups of redcoats, half-crazed from the horrific experience of storming the breaches, lost no time in seeking out the liquor stores. Bands of drunken soldiers reeled down the streets in a search for women and plunder. No civilian was safe while the frenzied mob roamed the cobbled streets and alleys, for, wrote Blakeney, "Men, women, and even children were shot in the streets for no other apparent reason than pastime."

By daybreak the sufferings of many of the wounded had been terminated by death, but the period of calm which succeeded the thunder of explosions, "was now more awful to us than the raging of the battle," commented Captain McCarthy.

At Campo Mayor surgeon Walter Henry of the 66th, knowing that the next day's march for the sick in his charge was to be a short one, delayed his departure and rode over to Badajoz. He crossed the bridge over the Guadiana after little more than a half-hour's journey expecting to find an orderly scene in which the dead would have been buried and attention given to the wounded. In sharp contrast to his expectations, the surgeon was aghast to learn that the wounded had been abandoned and forgotten in the drunken orgies that had followed the fall of the town.

It was an unwritten rule that a town which refused terms of surrender and was subsequently taken by storm was a legitimate target for plunder, but the events which followed the fall of Ciudad Rodrigo and Badajoz by any standards were truly inexcusable. In Badajoz, among those seeking refuge in the officers' camp early the next morning were two sisters from a high-born Spanish family. The eldest, her ears torn and bleeding, begged for protection from the depravity of the mob roaming the city streets. The youngest, just fourteen years of age, caught the eye of Johnny Kincaid, but for Lieutenant Harry Smith the encounter led to deeper feelings, for within a matter of weeks the young Juana Maria de los Dolores de Leon became his bride. The union, against all the judgment of his friends, proved enduring and in later years Juana was to accompany him on various campaigns. Eventually, when, as Sir Harry Smith, her husband became Governor of the Cape, she was to lend her name to a South African township, the site of another famous siege almost a century after Badajoz.

The sacking of Badajoz continued unchecked for two days and a night, during which time, wrote William Grattan, "every insult, every infamy that human invention could torture into practice was committed." On one occasion a sergeant struck Ensign Blakeney with his halberd for being prevented from joining in the plundering of a Spanish house. Blakeney

142

snapped his pistol in the sergeant's face. It misfired, but was enough to bring the man to his senses, after which Blakeney deemed it prudent to retire.

The nature of the plunder varied widely according to the whim of the plunderers. Ensign George Bell was astonished to see a powder-blackened redcoat staggering beneath the weight of a longcase clock, accompanied by another equally begrimed soldier bent double under a broad looking glass on his back. The Portuguese do not seem to have taken an active part in the looting, but individuals had their own methods for acquiring a share of the spoils. They were content to play a waiting game as many a redcoat discovered to his cost when, awakening from a drunken slumber, he found that his prize had disappeared.

In the days following the capture of the town, the most puzzling feature was the callous indifference shown to the suffering of the wounded, whose pleas for assistance often fell upon deaf ears. Captain Kincaid, riding towards the river on the third day after the fall of the city, was aghast to find two grievously wounded Highlanders. Each had lost a leg and had lain there unattended although hundreds of their comrades had passed within easy call. William Surtees did what he could to alleviate the suffering of the wounded and, with the assistance of the few redcoats still sober and willing to help, he later removed as many from the ditch as was humanly possible, but many more remained where they had fallen. neglected and forgotten. So depressed was Surtees by his experiences that he later confessed, "At this time I think I was fairly tired of life, so disgusting and so sickening were the scenes the last few days presented."

On the evening of the second day Lord Wellington rode into Badajoz with his staff, to be immediately surrounded by a group of drunken redcoats. "There he comes with his long nose," George Bell heard one shout. "Let's give him a salute!" and a volley of ball cartridge whistled over the heads of the officers on Wellington's staff.

Such licentious behaviour could not be allowed to continue and, after the miscreants had disappeared, a Portuguese brigade was brought into the town accompanied by the Provost Marshal and a gallows. "We generally hang or shoot half a dozen fellows, not withstanding every soldier is a gentleman and a man of honour and receives votes of thanks from both Houses of Parliament," was Samuel Rice's facetious reply to a query from a friend. In fact, no one was hanged, although a soldier in Costello's Company had the noose placed around his neck, the sight of the gallows being sufficient to bring the mob to its senses, and order was restored after 72 hours of unbridled violence.

Wellington had paid a high price for his success. As the sun rose on that April morning the full extent of the dreadful slaughter became apparent. The great ditch in front of the main breach was a scene of horror. Surgeon Henry, who had delayed the start of his convoy of sick to visit the site, was appalled by what he found: "There lay a frightful heap of fifteen hundred British soldiers, dead, but yet warm, and mingled with them some still living, but so desperately wounded as yet to be irremovable. . . . There they lay, stiffening in their gore – body piled on body – involved, intertwined, crushed, burned, and blackened – one hideous and enormous mass of carnage."

Returning to his charges at Campo Mayor, Walter Henry heard the church bells pealing and found crowds dancing in the street celebrating the victory. "Rejoicing!" he commented, "after what I had just witnessed! . . . after the piteous moans and dying ejaculations; after the blood-cemented pile of slain still fresh in my eye; rejoicing after all this!"

In the flooded area of the Trinidad Bastion, a score of bodies floated in the discoloured water and Ensign Robert Blakeney, examining the site the morning after the assault, with the stench of burnt flesh still hanging in the air, noticed that far from being able to force an entry through the main breach, the bodies of just two redcoats lay on the castle side of the wall. It was said that Lord Wellington, after visiting the glacis where lay the massed dead of his two elite divisions, could not keep the tears from his eyes and only succeeded in controlling his distress by castigating the Government for its meanness in restricting his funds.

Once order had been established in the town, the garrison was marched away as prisoners to Elvas. During a pause in his work of attending to the wounded, Surtees watched with interest as they passed him on the road. From their downcast and dejected manner it occurred to the Quartermaster of the 2/95th that, far from regarding their plight with resignation, many feared for their safety. Soon after their departure, the army marched away to the north. William Grattan watched them go from his hospital bed, whilst Kincaid rode with them, the remembered sounds of cannon and musket fire still ringing in his ears.

The heavy casualties suffered by his battalion had brought promotion to John Cooper. Now a sergeant of the 1/7th Fusiliers, he had charge of a party of sick and wounded who were unable to walk. After several muleteers had refused their services, Cooper was determined to requisition the next suitable transport. "I grew desperate," he wrote. "An empty car came up; I ordered my men to get into it, but the driver would not stop. I threw their knapsacks into the car; he threw them out again. Enraged, I drew my bayonet, took it by the small end and, swinging round, gave him such a blow on the mouth with the heavy end as stunned him. Then I got them into the car and he drove on, holding his mouth as if he had the got the tic."

Among those conveyed to the hospital at Elvas was Private Lawrence, where the sight of so many corpses being brought out of the building completely naked and thrown into carts "like so many pieces of dead wood" was sufficient to speed his recovery and in less than a month Lawrence was back with his regiment.

In the same hospital Rifleman Green lay in his first bed for almost three years. It was more comfortable than any billet he had ever known, but it seemed to the young Green Jacket as he lay in pain listening to the groans of his wounded comrades that it was a stiff price to pay for such unaccustomed luxury. Unlike Lawrence, John Green was to spend many months at Elvas whilst surgeons considered amputation. Finally, still troubled by his wounds, Green returned to England and his native Leicestershire, where a grateful Government awarded him a pension of nine pence a day in recognition of his gallant service.

The capture of Badajoz had cost some 4,760 casualties, with the Light and 4th Divisions losing 30 per cent of their effective strength, but Wellington now controlled both north and south passages into Spain and only Soult and Marmont stood in the way of Wellington's next objective, that of freeing Salamanca from the possession of the French.

Chapter 14

SALAMANCA SUMMER

The news that Badajoz had fallen to the British was conveyed to Marshal Soult by a handful of survivors from the garrison, who, faced with the alternative of spending the remainder of the war in a prison hulk, fought their way through the British lines. Soult, who was two days' march from Badajoz, showed little surprise. The Marshal was more concerned with the activities of the Spanish Generals Morillo and Ballesteros outside Seville.

Lord Wellington, now that his divisions had been brought up to strength, turned his attention towards mounting an offensive against Marmont and the Army of Portugal, which had retired from the country-side around Ciudad Rodrigo to Salamanca.

In his diary entry for 24 May Ensign John Mills had written: "It appears improbable that we shall remain long quiet. The mysterious silence kept about our future operations makes me think that something will soon be done. The enemy has of late shown so decided a weakness that we are justified in attempting anything in which our supplies will bear us out."

The odds on a successful undertaking were in Wellington's favour, for Napoleon's Russian campaign had deprived his armies in Spain of a great many experienced troops, but before he could cross the Tagus Wellington was faced with the problem of repairing a centuries-old bridge at Alcantara which the British had rendered impassable by destroying the central arch in 1809. This Roman bridge, 150 feet above the river, had been left with a gap of 90 feet between the broken arches, a problem great enough to tax the ingenuity of the most capable of Engineers. The solution provided by Major Robert Henry Sturgeon of the Royal Staff Corps was in its way quite revolutionary by the standards of the times. Using ship's cable tensioned by windlasses, his men arranged for chains of wooden sleepers to be lashed tight to the cables in such a way as to form a stable platform and, in so doing, create the first suspension bridge in Europe.

Wellington was now ready to cross into Spain with three columns of infantry totalling 43,000 men, half of which were British. Although he was free to move into either northern or southern Spain, having control of the two corridors, Marshal Soult's Army of the South and Marmont's Army of Portugal could still communicate by means of a pontoon bridge floated across the Tagus at Almarez, which was the only means of crossing upstream from Toledo. Lord Wellington was aware of the danger and Sir Rowland Hill was given the task of destroying it. He left at once from Almandraleja with 7,000 troops and six howitzers, and on 18 May his column reached the fortified Pass of Miravete less than two miles from the bridge of boats, guarded on the south side by Fort Napoleon and on the north bank by Fort Ragusa.

Following a close inspection of the fortified position, Hill came to the conclusion that any attempt to carry the bridge by direct assault would be decidedly risky. A much better plan would be to engage the attention of the defenders with a feint attack, while Brigadier Howard with the 50th advanced on Fort Napoleon from the broken ground of the sierra where ample cover existed to enable him to close without sustaining too many casualties.

The French, convinced that the bridge could not be attacked without first overcoming the garrison at Miravete, were astounded at daybreak on 19 May to see the 50th and part of the 71st descending the hill by way of a mountain track. As the redcoats rushed from cover a score of men fell, but the attack was pressed home with such vigour by the ladder parties that a foothold was soon established on the ramparts and, after a brief resistance, the Prussian defenders of the fort fled in such haste that those who gained the pontoon bridge ahead of their comrades cut the moorings, to leave some 200 of their number prisoners of the British.

A similar panic overtook those in Fort Ragusa under attack by the 71st, for, after suffering a short bombardment from guns captured at Fort Napoleon, the Garrison Commander abandoned the fort without firing a shot. He was later tried by the French on a charge of cowardice and executed. The bridge was later dragged to the south bank and burnt.

Among the great quantity of stores abandoned by the French in their haste was an "ample supply of provender sufficient to rejoice the heart of any half-starved warrior," wrote a delighted Captain Patterson. "Collected together in knots and parties, with the greensward for our tablecloth, we feasted most sumptuously, drinking to our foes in their own generous wine, and wishing that, in future campaigns, our adventures might be terminated in an equally agreeable and fortunate manner."

Sir Rowland Hill, in destroying the bridge of boats, could now retire to his former quarters at Merida satisfied in the knowledge that he had carried out Wellington's instructions to the letter. Now that the communications between Marshals Soult and Marmont had been cut, Wellington turned his attention towards the north of Spain and on 12 June, "a day of glorious sunshine," remembered one redcoat, his three columns passed through Ciudad Rodrigo for Castile. His soldiers were in excellent spirits, anxious "to tap some more French claret", but as the wooded landscape gave way to a vast sunbaked plain with scarcely the shade from a single tree their buoyant mood was soon deflated by the suffocating clouds of dust which enveloped every column. In the searing heat the redcoats suffered agonies of discomfort from their tight tunics and the leather stock worn around the neck. Above the marching columns dozens of vultures circled and Lieutenant Tomkinson, as he shaded his eyes against the glare, could not help thinking what a terrible fate it would be to lie wounded and not have the strength to fend them off.

At length the Guarena was reached, now reduced to a shallow stream of brackish water, and men and horses rushed to quench their thirst, regardless of the fact that the pool was thick with mud. Ahead lay Salamanca, a city famed as a seat of learning, and when, on the morning of the 17th, the advance party cautiously felt its way into the suburbs they discovered that Marmont had abandoned the city during the night, leaving just 700 men to man the three monasteries which commanded the only bridge over the Tormes.

For three years the citizens of Salamanca had been subjected to French occupation and the entry of the British was greeted with the wildest enthusiasm, even to the nuns fluttering handkerchiefs from grated windows.

"Many absolutely cried for joy," wrote Captain Warre, "and we were embraced or had to shake hands with everybody we met." Even Lord Wellington, much to his annoyance, was hugged and kissed.

Although the French had evacuated the city, three fortified monasteries, San Vincente, San Gaetano and La Merced, which overlooked the great Roman bridge with its twenty-seven arches, were to prove a thorn in the side of the troops charged with their reduction. Ensign Mills was puzzled by Marmont's tactics. "What his meaning can be in leaving men in the forts here is impossible to imagine," he wrote. "The Spaniards affect to be delighted to see us – I almost doubt whether they are in earnest."

The bombardment of the three small forts began badly, for the battery was poorly protected and, as a result, the unfortunate gunners suffered a number of casualties from French musket fire. An attempt to mine the counterscarp of San Vincente was thwarted by the vigilance of a guard dog and it was only after two days of sporadic bombardment that the lower wall was breached, bringing down the roof and burying a number of the defenders. Finally, on 28 June, after red-hot shot had set San Vincente on fire, the garrisons of all three redoubts surrendered and the men from Clinton's 6th Division were allowed to relax.

Thirty-six cannon, 700 prisoners and a quantity of provisions had fallen into British hands, but the twelve days it had taken to reduce the forts had enabled Marmont to gather reinforcements and take up a strong position along the line of the Douro at Tordesillas. Now that his army had grown to 42,000 with the arrival of General Bonnet's division, Marmont felt confident of retaking Salamanca and on 17 July the Marshal crossed the Duero and began a series of movements designed to outflank Wellington's right wing. The British Commander-in-Chief, however, was no stranger to such tactics and for the next four days the two armies marched and counter-marched on a parallel course to the Tormes, with Marmont's troops occasionally crossing the shallow river to threaten the allies on either flank. "It was a fine sight to see the two armies in motion at the same time," wrote John Mills. "They moved parallel to each other and at no time were more than two miles distant. They passed along a hill and we along the bottom."

It was during one such encounter that Lord Wellington and Sir William Carr Beresford came close to becoming prisoners of the French. The incident was witnessed by Captain John Kincaid and his Riflemen, who watched in astonishment as Wellington, his Staff, two guns of the Horse Artillery, and a mixed body of French and British cavalry thundered past their picket in a confused mass, with the men of the 95th unable to interfere for fear of hitting their own men.

The next day the hostile armies faced each other across the Guarena where they remained within gunshot of each other, marching on parallel lines along the river banks. "The weather dreadfully hot by day and cold by night," confided Major Rice to his diary. "We are lying in corn fields without the smallest covering. . . . How the men stand this severe work is to me astonishing . . . my brains are baking into a paste."

The following two days were spent in attempts by each Commander to outmanoeuvre the other. The French soldier was less encumbered, which gave Marmont a distinct advantage and his greater mobility forced Wellington to cross the Tormes during the night of the 21st away from Salamanca under a darkening sky with distant peals of thunder betraying the approach of a violent storm. The river crossing was made as the first large drops of rain began to fall and, as the electrical disturbance grew, St Elmo Fire played about the points of the soldiers' bayonets to such a degree that many were dazzled by its brilliance. Private Wheeler, sheltering from the torrential rain beneath the branches of a Spanish oak, had a fortunate escape when, having just vacated the spot to converse with a friend, a bolt of lightning split the tree in half.

The rising wind and the rolling peals of thunder so terrorized the horses of the 15th Dragoons that dozens broke free from the picket posts, trampling their riders in the confusion. Ross-Lewin caught the bridle of one loose horse and, as he fought to restrain it, the darkness was rent by a vivid blue flash and he caught a glimpse of "expanding nostrils, eyeballs almost starting from their sockets and a mouth white with foam. I never saw terror more forcibly pictured in the appearance of any animal," remembered the Captain of the 1/32nd. "His whole form was paralysed and trembling."

"The thunder in awful claps echoed through the wood," confirmed an anonymous private soldier. "The flashes of lightning were vivid, and in quick succession; the rain fell in torrents and, what added to our distress, was we were exposed to the open air, not having a tent or anything else to cover us."

"About midnight the storm ceased," wrote John Green of the 68th, "the morning was beautiful, the sun rose without a cloud, and everything had a most enchanting appearance."

The morning of the 22nd saw the respective armies north-east of two odd-shaped hills known as the Arapiles which were shortly to become the pivotal point of the battle. Of this pair, the southernmost hill or Greater Arapile, as it was known, was in the possession of a brigade of artillery from General Jean Pierre Bonnet's Division, following an earlier confrontation with the Portuguese.

Just before 1.00pm the battle opened with a heavy cannonade on the Portuguese who were forced to retire as two columns, led by Generals Thomières and Maucune, drove in the British light troops, before extending towards the plateau in front of the Greater Arapiles. The manoeuvre was badly carried out by Thomières who had rashly allowed his left flank to advance too far ahead of Maucune. The French columns were now spread out across 4 miles of open country with a rapidly growing gap between their centre and left flank.

While this movement was taking place Lord Wellington had seized the opportunity to snatch a cold lunch. An aide stood watching the movements of the French from a position on the Lesser Arapiles. Wellington paused in his consumption of a chicken leg. "Tell me, what are they doing?" he asked the aide. "Extending rapidly to their left, my Lord," came the reply. "The devil they are," exclaimed Wellington. "Give me the glass." A few moments passed whilst he studied the enemy columns and then, snapping shut the telescope, he exclaimed to his Spanish liaison officer, "By God! Marmont est perdu!" The British Commander had seen that the French divisions, perhaps tired after their long march, were no longer in support of each other.

It was close on 4.00pm and Wellington, mounting 'Copenhagen',

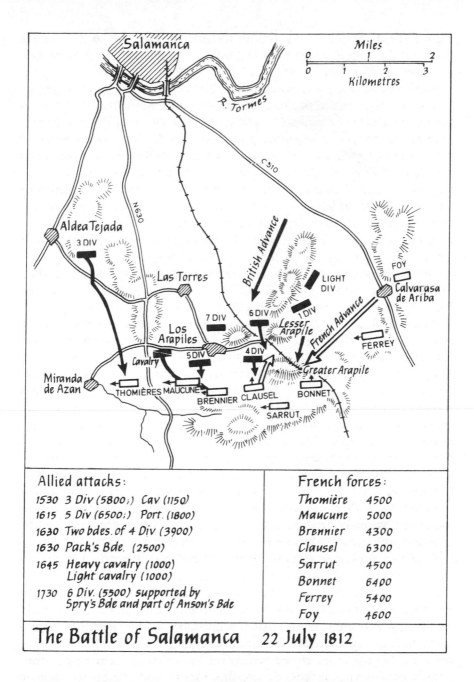

Allied attacks:

1530 3 Div (5800;) Cav (1150)
1615 5 Div (6500;) Port. (1800)
1630 Two bdes. of 4 Div (3900)
1630 Pack's Bde. (2500)
1645 Heavy cavalry (1000)
      Light cavalry (1000)
1730 6 Div. (5500) supported by
      Spry's Bde and part of Anson's Bde

French forces:

Thomière	4500
Maucune	5000
Brennier	4300
Clausel	6300
Sarrut	4500
Bonnet	6400
Ferrey	5400
Foy	4600

The Battle of Salamanca   22 July 1812

immediately despatched his staff officers with orders for an attack which would cut the French in two. Turning to his brother-in-law, Edward Pakenham, commanding the 3rd Division in the absence of Picton, Wellington tapped him on the shoulder. "Ned, d'ye see those fellows on the hill? Put your division into column and drive 'em to the devil!" "I will my Lord," replied Pakenham, "if you will give me a grasp of that conquering right hand."

The battle which opened on Sunday, 22 July was to go down in history as the one upon which Wellington was content to rest his reputation as the most successful British General and it opened with the Portuguese cavalry and the 14th Dragoons charging into the leading regiment of Thomières' brigade while the twelve battalions of the 3rd Division fixed bayonets and uncased their colours. A level plateau of sand and scrub almost half a mile in length stretched before them and, as Pakenham's troops marched steadily towards the heights, flame and smoke erupted from the muzzles of twenty cannon drawn up on the ridge. As the redcoats drew near, French shot ploughed the ground about them as return fire from English batteries whirred through the air above their heads. Disregarding the roundshot which was tearing great gaps in their ranks, the men of the 3rd Division climbed the slope to close with the French. Grape and canister reduced their numbers, but rolling volleys from the 45th, 74th and 88th Regiments also cut swathes through the massed ranks of General Thomières' brigades and, shaken by the devastating rifle power of the British regiments, the French began to waver. In an incident which enraged the men of the Connaught Rangers, a Colonel of the 22nd Leger, in an attempt to encourage his men, picked up a musket and ran towards the oncoming Irish troops. Taking careful aim, he shot Major Murphy of the 88th and the sight of this popular officer being dragged lifeless along the front of his regiment excited the Irishmen to a frenzy. Pakenham, sensing the mood of that regiment, ordered Lieutenant Colonel Wallace, the brigade commander, "to let them loose", and, with a roar of rage, down came the bayonets as the Connaughts rushed headlong to close with the French. In the mêlée General Thomières was killed and, supported by the rest of the 3rd Division, the men of the 88th sent the demoralized French regiments reeling back until their pursuers were obliged to halt in order to recover their breath.

Further to the east, Leith's 5th Division, after enduring a heavy cannonade, attacked the blue-coated columns of Brennier's division. In a double line Portuguese and British troops crossed the heavily ploughed fields to engage the enemy. Despite the thinning of their ranks, the allies moved up the slope in closed formation to decimate the tightly packed French columns in a fierce fire fight. Brennier's troops were hustled down the reverse side of the hill and barely had time to form square before the heavy brigade, "twelve hundred big men on big horses" led by General Edward Le Marchant, supported by Anson's Light cavalry, swept towards them with a thunder of hooves.

The fresh young conscripts of the 22nd Leger began to shuffle and show signs of unease. Their musketry became ragged and, although a few saddles were emptied, Le Marchant's dragoons crashed through the hastily formed square trampling the terrified youngsters underfoot and inflicting terrible wounds with their long cavalry swords. Many of the conscripts, half-blinded by blood gushing from head wounds, staggered towards the ranks of Leith's infantry which, moved by feelings of pity, closed about the Frenchmen and saved them from total destruction. The cavalry, now in a mixed body, went on to charge a third column some fifty yards from the fringe of a wood. Again the discipline of the French square was poor and it rapidly broke up in confusion. Small groups ran for the protection of a fringe of trees, but were quickly cut off by the horsemen, who, excited to a frenzy of blood lust, made sure that few escaped. Brennier's vanguard, hurrying to the support of their comrades, were attacked on the march and scattered, but not before a murderous discharge of musketry from no more than twenty yards emptied a score of saddles, including that of Le Marchant, who dropped with a mortal wound at the edge of the copse.

"The men reserved their fire with much coolness," wrote a French officer, "until the cavalry came within twenty yards. Then they poured it in on the concentrated mass of men and horses with deadly effect." He went on to state, "Nearly a third of the dragoons came to the ground, but the remainder had sufficient command of their horses to dash forward. They succeeded in breaking the French ranks and dispersing them in utter confusion over the field."

The Divisions of Pakenham and Cole had defeated the French left wing, but to the east of the Arapiles it was a different story. In that quarter Pack's Portuguese were at grips with Bonnet's battalions. Advancing through waist-high rye grass, the 4th Cacadores were met with a crippling volley. The Portuguese had scarcely recovered from this blow before Bonnet's men were among them with the bayonet. The officers tried to rally their men, but with little success, and the triumphant French troops, who had been reinforced by Clausel, turned their attention to the 4th Division, now reduced to just two brigades.

"The firing of both armies commenced in such a way as I have never heard before," observed John Green. "It was like the long roll of a hundred drums without an interval." Case and roundshot from the French batteries on the hill ploughed furrows through the ranks of Cole's Division and, when first Leith and then Cole fell badly wounded, a condition close to panic gripped many of the redcoats.

Wellington, recognizing that the crisis had been reached in this battle for possession of the Arapiles, immediately committed his considerable Reserve to meet the 12,000 troops launched by Marshal Clausel in support of Bonnet. The light, made worse by the smoke and dust rising in dense clouds from the slopes of the Arapiles, was rapidly fading, but, despite this handicap, the 5,500 soldiers of Clinton's 6th Division pushed rapidly across the uneven ground, their path lit by blazing patches of dry gorse and the muzzle flashes from the cannon on the heights.

The resolute advance of Clinton's three brigades was met with equal determination by Clausel's men and for a short time a furious exchange of musketry took place without either side giving ground. Captain Ross-Lewin soon found himself in the thick of the action, but his role in the battle was over sooner than he might have wished. While he was still yards from the French first line, his arm was shattered by a ball and he was taken to the rear. Weak from loss of blood, Ross-Lewin was led to an outhouse in the village of Los Arapiles filled with wounded men, whose pleas to have the dead removed rang in his ears for the rest of the night.

By committing his Reserve at just the right time Wellington had turned the fortunes of his hard-pressed divisions. By 10.30pm the battle was over save for the occasional skirmish among the trees to the east. The British, too exhausted to think of pursuit, flung themselves down among the detritus of battle, leaving the wounded to the tender mercies of the Spanish peasantry.

Lieutenant Robert Fernyhough had not been in the Peninsula long enough to become accustomed to the shameful treatment meted out to the defenceless wounded and he was dismayed to find that even the least shreds of dignity were denied them. Incensed that a brave man should be so humiliated as to be stripped of his clothes, he soon put the peasant to flight and earned the grateful thanks of the Frenchman who, in addition to three musket wounds, had also suffered a severe gash from a sabre.

In sharp contrast to the behaviour of their menfolk, the Captain from the 3/95th discovered that the Spanish women were sympathetic to the wounded of both sides. "Indeed," wrote Fernyhough, "it was not uncommon for them to be seen supporting the walking wounded or carrying their pack and musket."

As to the provision of material comforts, the British wounded were perhaps worse off than the French, for, being six months in arrears of pay, they were unable to purchase even the basic necessities. Robert Knowles, who had been wounded in the closing stages of the battle, wrote bitterly to his father complaining of the plight of his fellow officers who were forced to sell their horses and even their uniform epaulettes to avoid starvation.

Thanks to his magnificent troops, Salamanca was Wellington's greatest victory of the Peninsular War and, referring to it in Paris after Waterloo, he wrote: "I never saw an army receive such a beating". The opposing forces had been roughly equal in numbers, but, compared with the allied casualties of 4,732, the French left 6,000 dead and wounded on the field, together with an unknown number of prisoners, in a battle which lasted little more than six hours. Three French Generals had died, Thomières, Ferey and Desgraviers. Bonnet was gravely wounded, while Marshal Marmont, galloping to rally one of his broken squares, was struck by a shell fragment which "shattered his left arm and tore open his side". He was to carry his arm in a sling for the rest of his life.

Early the next morning 450 dragoons of the King's German Legion were again in the saddle in pursuit of the French retiring on Valladolid. So numerous were the small wooded areas in that part of Castile and so rapidly were the French retreating that it was late in the afternoon before the Hanoverians overtook the three battalions of General Foy's rearguard at the small village of Garcia Hernandez.

Riding as a screen to the infantry were several squadrons of light cavalry which were attacked so vigorously that they were forced to retire, leaving the infantry columns to rely upon hastily formed squares for protection. A volley from the kneeling front rank brought down many of the riders, but, undeterred, cavalry of the K.G.L and four squadrons of heavy dragoons led by Baron George von Bloch, a man so short-sighted that he had to be pointed in the right direction, swept on, separating at the last moment in order to attack the square from two sides. A bristling hedge of bayonets faced them at ground level, while four standing rows of muskets exploded in a rippling line of flame and smoke. Men and horses crashed to the ground, but, in falling, one horse collapsed across a group of defenders, kicking and flailing to create a gap in the blue-coated wall. The oncoming horsemen were quick to take advantage and, hacking away with their sabres, they opened up a lane which was quickly exploited by other dragoons.

Once a square had been broken apart, there was little the infantry could do to save themselves and this case was no exception. In a matter of moments two battalions of the 76th Line were scattered and dispersed. A second square formed by the 6th Leger shared a similar fate and Foy's battalions were soon in full flight, leaving 1,200 of their less fortunate comrades dead or wounded on the plain.

"The contest ended in a dreadful massacre of the French infantry," wrote an English officer. "The ponderous weight of the heavy cavalry broke down all resistance; and arms lopped off, heads cloven to the spine, or gashes across the breast and shoulders showed the fearful encounter that had taken place."

At the end of July, when Clausel's shattered divisions were nearing Burgos, having abandoned the hospitalized wounded in Vallodolid, Lord

Wellington, certain that the French Marshal was in no position to undertake a fresh campaign, turned his attention to Madrid.

The march south to the Spanish capital was unopposed. Everywhere the victorious redcoats were received with acclaim and gifts of wine and fruit were pressed upon the not ungrateful soldiery.

Segovia, famous for being the site of the Alcazar, was reached on 7 August, San Ildefonso, a favourite summer residence of the Spanish royal family, two days later. Here, 50 miles north of Madrid, Wellington rested his troops to allow the right wing to close up before resuming his advance on the 11th. As the vanguard of the allied army neared the seat of King Joseph's government, the approach roads became crowded with Spaniards of both sexes, many of whom joined hands with the marching redcoats.

"Our division marched right in front," wrote William Wheeler proudly. "We were the first regiment that entered Madrid. . . . At the distance of five miles from the gate we were met by the inhabitants, each had brought out something. . . . The load represented a moving forest, from the multitude of people carrying boughs." Private John Green of the 68th agreed. "The bells of the different churches rang, the ladies waved their handkerchiefs from the windows, and every countenance beamed with joy."

Wellington's troops were favourably impressed by the flowers strewn in their path by the pretty Spanish girls, but less so by the insistence of Spanish males on kissing their liberators. The combination of breath reeking of garlic and moustaches stiffened with sweat and dust was altogether too much for Private Wheeler. He considered the experience as "like having a hair broom pushed into one's face that had been daubed in a dirty gutter".

On the 12th Lord Wellington, accompanied by the guerrilla leaders Don Carlos and Julian Sanchez, entered the gates of the city to the pealing of bells and the "Vivas" of the crowds thronging the spacious squares. "The manner in which the inhabitants received him was beyond belief," reported Lieutenant Henry Hough, who thought Madrid was infinitely superior to London. "He was surrounded and nearly dragged from his horse and Viva! Viva los Inglises! was only to be heard."

The travel-stained and perspiring redcoats marvelled at the ornate fountains, the streets hung with gold and silver draperies and the magnificent white stone buildings, but, as always, it was anticipation of the wine and fruitful liaisons with the young women that did most to lift their morale. The ladies of Madrid certainly made an impression upon the 22-year-old John Mills. Writing to his mother, he confessed: "The Spanish women wear large veils which they put on most gracefully. They waltz extremely well. They dance figure dances and country dances

– the former they excel in I think. They move their arms most gracefully. . . . You will begin to think I am likely to fall in love with them. I could do such a thing to be sure as I think there are a great number of pretty women here."

Captain John Kincaid, on approaching the city, had speculated on the probable nature of his reception. For the past four years the people of Madrid had enjoyed a generally peaceful occupation under King Joseph Bonaparte and profited from his benevolent rule. The most popular opinion among Kincaid's fellow officers was that they were likely to be regarded as something of a nuisance and it was therefore all the more gratifying to find themselves so heartily welcomed by the majority of the citizens who had remained.

Joseph had retired with 17,000 of his troops and a large retinue to Ocana, and those left behind in Madrid lost no time in celebrating their liberation with a series of fêtes, balls, drinking bouts and parties. The festivities proved to be an expensive undertaking for Wellington who generally gave a ball or a dinner almost every night. On 23 August he wrote to Lord Bathurst: "It will be necessary that the Government should either give me additional pay . . . or that they should allow me to charge some of the expenses . . . or I shall be ruined."

Among the less costly of the entertainments offered by the Spaniards was the national sport of bull fighting. Bull fights were seen for the first time by many Britons and were regarded by most of the redcoats with mixed feelings. Lieutenant George Simmons thought the bull fighters displayed "the greatest intrepidity and courage", while Private Donaldson could not understand how "such a cruel and disgusting exhibition could be so much encouraged in Spain."

Whatever their pleasure, Wellington's troops, for once, did not drink to excess and discipline remained at a fairly high level, encouraging their Commander-in-Chief to believe that, once his army was rested and its deficiencies made good, the time had come to resume the pursuit of Marshal Clausel who was retiring upon Burgos with the Army of Portugal.

Chapter 15

'THIS CURSED CASTLE'

As a result of the defeat at Salamanca, French dispositions in Spain began to fragment. The Army of Portugal was in the process of abandoning Valladolid. King Joseph, who had fled Madrid with an enormous entourage, took refuge with Marshal Suchet at Valencia, while in the north the scattered troops of General Caffarelli's Army of the North were there only to assure communications, but had recently fought a number of minor actions against the guerrillas supported by Admiral Popham. Rear Admiral Sir Home Popham, sailing from Corunna with two men o'war and several frigates, had landed marines at a number of places along the coast, eventually culminating in the seizure of Santander, a port which in the coming months was to replace Lisbon as the allies' major supply base.

It was General Bertrand Count Clausel whom Wellington considered to be the greatest threat and, leaving Hill to occupy the Spanish capital, he left Madrid on 1 September with 21,000 troops for Burgos by way of Arevalo. Six days later he crossed the Douro, but, since the allied army completed no more than six miles a day, Clausel easily outdistanced them to reach Burgos in good time to re-equip his divisions. Then, in pain from the wound he had sustained at Salamanca, he handed over command to General Joseph Southam who promptly withdrew to Briviesca, leaving General Dubreton and 1,800 men to garrison the castle.

Lord Wellington entered the town on the 18th with the 1st and 6th Divisions and two Portuguese brigades, a total of 12,000 allied troops, while the remainder of his army covered the siege and prevented the Army of Portugal from interfering.

The old castle of Burgos, the birthplace of the legendary El Cid, was in a poor state of repair, though the French had added several new palisaded earthworks, but its real strength lay in a powerful battery of guns sited in the old Keep overlooking the town. As in most of his sieges, Wellington seems to have initially declined the use of heavy artillery, for he had brought just three iron 18 pdrs with a limited supply of powder and shot. At a later stage they would be supplemented by five brass 24 pdrs, but, until these were brought up from Salamanca, the three iron guns comprised the sum total of the allied siege artillery. Burgos castle was invested on 19 September and that same afternoon skirmishers from the Light Division drove the French pickets into their earthworks and, when darkness fell, the outlying hornwork which commanded the approach to the castle was attacked in the light of a full moon. In this short bloody encounter the stormers of the 42nd, supported by companies of the Highland brigade and Pack's Portuguese, advanced gallantly to the walls, but their ladders proved not to be long enough and they were driven back in disorder, having suffered some 400 casualties. Only a determined sortie by the light companies of the 1st Division led by Major Edward Somers-Cocks retrieved the situation. This courageous band of no more than 140 scaled a nine-foot palisade without the help of ladders, scrambled into the rear of the earthworks, causing the French to withdraw and the outer hornwork to fall into the hands of the British. The capture of this bastion prepared the way for an attack on the castle walls and at midnight on the 22nd 400 stormers from the 1st Division assaulted the castle, supported by a company of Portuguese and a party from the Brigade of Guards.

Unfortunately this attempt at escalade without the benefit of a preliminary bombardment was a dismal failure, for in the darkness the Portuguese lost their way and the defenders, alerted to the danger, drove the men of the 1st Division back to their trenches before they even came close to scaling the 25-ft high masonry wall.

Following this débâcle, it was decided that only a full-scale siege operation would deliver the castle into the hands of the besiegers and the next day work was begun on a parallel and a sap to zig-zag towards the western face of the outer wall. In his diary entry for the 26th John Mills wrote: "The siege of this place promises fair to rival that of Troy in duration. Every day shows the deficiency of our means, the strength of the place and the ingenuity of the garrison – in the refinements of war they far exceed us."

With the approach of autumn the weather began to change and for the next few weeks Wellington's troops spent a frustrating and tedious period of inactivity sheltering from the inclement weather in crude huts built from brushwood, or shivering in the rain-soaked trenches.

"From the moment we first invested this cursed castle," wrote William Bragge, "the weather has proved particularly unfavourable to our operations, having scarcely ceased raining the whole time, accompanied by occasional high winds and very severe nights. . . . You can easily conceive the state of such a camp on low ground," continued the disgruntled Lieutenant in this letter to his father, "after three weeks' rain which has almost filled our trenches with mud and water as well as the camp."

A mood of discontent and resentment of authority was rapidly growing among the besiegers, nurtured by the fact that the clothing of a good many of them was in a threadbare condition, whilst some even lacked the basic necessity of a greatcoat or blanket.

When, on 29 September, Captain Harry Ross-Lewin set out to rejoin his regiment, his wound now completely healed, he met on every stage of his journey wounded men returning from Burgos to the hospital in Salamanca. Almost all held pessimistic views on the chances of the siege ending in success and it seemed to the Captain of the 1/32nd that repeated failures were having an adverse effect upon morale. It was a view shared by Ensign John Mills, who wrote on 1 October: "Lord Wellington seems to have got into a scrape – his means are most perfectly inadequate and he has already lost a 1,000 men."

A further cause for concern was the poor performance of the artillery and a shortage of roundshot. It was reported that a reward of sixpence was offered for each enemy shot brought in to the British artillery park, but, whatever the truth of this, the heavy siege guns which had been brought up to supplement the three iron cannon were found to be so inaccurate that two were withdrawn, their effectiveness hardly justifying the expenditure of powder. Worse was to come, for 'Thunder', 'Lightning' and 'Nelson', as the three iron guns were called, were not long in action before the French had disabled two of them – a timely warning for the gunners to pull back to a less exposed position.

In the early hours of 8 October, during a heavy rainstorm, the garrison made a sortie which drove Wellington's men from their position close to the castle wall and allowed the French to destroy a new parallel and carry away the entrenching tools. After a fierce encounter during which Major Cocks of the 79th, an intellectual and a favourite of Wellington's, was shot dead as he attempted to rally the working party and repel Dubreton's sally from the castle, there grew a spirit of discontent which even affected Wellington himself, who declared that he would like to abandon "this damn place".

The Spanish autumn was drawing to a close before the allies enjoyed a modicum of success on 1 October when a 1000 lb mine was fired beneath the outlying church of San Roman to bring down a part of the north wall. The springing of the mine was the signal for an assault against three separate points. A mixed body of Portuguese and Spanish troops led by Colonel Browne seized the ruins of the church, while the Coldstream Guards and a Company from the King's German Legion stormed the western and northern walls of the castle, gaining the top of the ramparts and staying there for a short period. However, in the darkness the supporting companies missed their way and all three groups were beaten back in the face of regular volleys of musketry and grape and the demoralized survivors retired to their rain-soaked trenches having lost half of their number.

A month had been spent in front of Burgos to no good purpose and, although part of the perimeter defences had fallen into the hands of the British after four assaults and the loss of 2,000 men, it seemed increasingly unlikely that the castle would ever fall to the besiegers. On the 21st a decision was taken to abandon the water-logged trenches and in the evening preparations were made for an immediate retreat.

It was with feelings of profound relief that the 1st Division and Pack's Portuguese Brigade passed through the cobbled streets to head a retreat which was eventually to take the army from the bleak and featureless terrain around Burgos, across the Douro and by way of Salamanca, back to Ciudad Rodrigo and Portugal. Concealed by an overcast night sky, the troops marched across a stone bridge spanning the River Arlanzon in pouring rain, followed by the artillery whose gunners had muffled the wheels with straw, leaving no sound but the tread of boots.

"There was something peculiarly awful in the night march of so great a body of men," recalled Ross-Lewin. "The cautious silence, the dead hour, and the consideration that in an instant the guns of the castle might be sending death among us."

But in the poor light the garrison did not see them and, had it not been for a body of Spanish lancers whose clatter across the bridge drew the garrison's attention to the movement of troops, the withdrawal would have been completed without incident. Fortunately, in the darkness and the conditions prevailing, range and direction were uncertain and in little more than an hour the army, together with its baggage and artillery, was across the river and on the road to Torquemada, an important town in this wine-producing region.

In Madrid, some 150 miles to the south, General Hill faced a potentially dangerous situation in that the Tagus was exceptionally shallow and presented no great obstacle to the passage of troops. It was known that the combined armies of Joseph Bonaparte and Marshal Soult were nearing the capital and, to the relief of Sir Rowland Hill, orders reached him on the 29th instructing him to leave Madrid and retire with all possible haste to the west of the country.

The directive came as a surprise to many of Hill's officers, who tended to blame the reluctance of the Spanish General Ballasteros to co-operate with the British for the decision to vacate Madrid. Yet when a Spaniard accosted Moyle-Sherer in the street with the accusation, "Why, why did you come hither if you did not calculate on maintaining possession?", the young lieutenant was forced to admit that he could give no satisfactory answer.

On the last day of the month Hill's troops marched out of Madrid and, as Captain Leach walked the silent streets to bid farewell to a Spanish friend, he could not help but contrast the sombre mood of the citizens with the joy they had expressed just three months earlier. Particularly galling to the troops were the jeers and taunts thrown at them by the young women. Even Edward Costello, with all his charm, failed to win a kiss from his "dark eyed Clementeria" at their moment of parting.

As Costello and his comrades in the 1/95th left the Spanish capital behind, the vanguard of Wellington's divisions had already completed a march of 26 miles which brought them to one of the finest wine-producing areas in northern Spain. "The whole of this is grape country," wrote Ensign Mills. "The wine had just been made and deposited in large vaults in the vineyards – they were soon found out." Presented on every side with unique opportunities for slaking their thirst, it was inevitable that fully two-thirds of the army should become totally incapacitated. Long strings of mules carrying insensible burdens draped across their backs became an all too familiar sight. "The conduct of some men would have disgraced savages," wrote an indignant Sergeant Wheeler. "It was no infrequent thing to see a long string of mules carrying drunken soldiers to prevent them falling into the hands of the enemy." These inebriates, however, were more fortunate than many of their fellow redcoats who, lying helpless in the wine cellars, were soon murdered by the furious Spanish villagers.

The last days of the retreat were misery to both Sir Rowland Hill's column retiring on Alba de Tormes and to Lord Wellington's on a path to Vallodolid. Many roads were all but impassable after the heavy rains and the movement of supply wagons and artillery became a logistical nightmare. The plight of the infantry can be imagined as they sloshed through the glutinous mud. Every step demanded an effort by the exhausted soldier who, on more than one occasion, would extricate himself from an ankle-deep morass only to find that his shoes had remained in it when he lifted his feet.

For both columns the retreat was becoming a severe test of stamina and hundreds fell by the roadside overcome by the sheer physical effort of struggling along, weighed down by rain-soaked clothing, a musket and a heavy knapsack. Even Wellington appeared haggard and drawn. "He wore an oilskin and looked extremely ill," commented an officer of the 32nd, "which was not to be wondered at considering the anxiety of mind and the fatigue of body which he was enduring."

For Hill's troops hardship was made no easier to bear from the knowledge that their large iron cooking pots were with Wellington's baggage train moving on a parallel path some twenty miles to the north. Particularly aggrieved were those troops who had retained a portion of their meat ration. With no means of cooking it, the blood oozing from the undressed beef had turned their issue of bread into a sticky inedible paste, which could only be thrown away, and they were obliged to satisfy the gnawing pangs of hunger with handfuls of maize. A captain in the 1/32nd, having endured two days of acute hunger, in desperation purchased what he understood to be pork from a Spanish muleteer. Ross-Lewin ate it with relish, but became so ill after the meal that he barely found the strength to resume the march. A rumour to the effect that it was sometimes the practice of Spaniards to slice the flesh from a corpse when they were unable to procure anything else did nothing to relieve his nausea. For years afterwards the mere mention of pork was sufficient to cause Captain Ross-Lewin to recoil in revulsion.

On 9 November Wellington and Hill joined forces in front of Salamanca, while, Soult having arrived at Alba de Tormes the previous day to take command of Joseph's forces, the respective armies faced each other on the site of the 22 July battle. The next day passed in manoeuvring and deployment as Wellington formed by the Arapiles and waited to see whether the French would give battle.

The rain, which had been falling steadily since daybreak, now increased to a torrent, threatening to turn the area into a bog in which men and horses floundered, and Joseph, with only a few hours of daylight remaining, allowed the allies who were on the higher ground, to retire towards Ciudad Rodrigo. It was a decision which did not please a high-ranking French General, who bitterly criticized Joseph's refusal to give battle. Wrote Baton Maximilian Sebastien Foy: "We had an army stronger by a third than Wellington's and infinitely superior in cavalry and artillery. . . . The chance had come of beating the English – perhaps of driving them from the Peninsula. This grand opportunity . . . was allowed to slip."

Had Wellington been forced to stand and fight, it might well have ended in a catastrophic defeat for him. Large numbers of troops had already fallen out by reason of sickness or exhaustion and as many again through straggling. In one instance, the 1/82nd Regiment suffered so many stragglers that their Colonel was placed under arrest. As it was, Soult's cavalry, in just two days, took 1,800 prisoners, including General Paget, and by the evening of the 18th, when the army crossed the Huebra, a tributary of the Douro, to arrive back in Ciudad Rodrigo, Wellington s losses in the retreat from Burgos were in excess of five thousand.'

In a letter to his mother, Major George Ridout Bingham castigated the troops under his command. "Our men are so greedy of drink, and so utterly careless of the consequences, that a night march, a retreat, or a forced march of any kind costs us as many men as a smart skirmish."

To an equally furious Wellington, the blame lay not so much with the men as with the officers' failure to discipline them. An order of the day, restricted in circulation to senior rank, expressed his irritation: "I must draw your attention, in a very particular manner, to the state of discipline of the troops. . . . I am concerned to have to observe, that the army under my command has fallen off, in this respect, in the late campaign, to a greater degree than any army with which I have ever served, or of which I have ever read. Yet this army has met with no disaster; it has suffered no privations, which but trifling attention on the part of the officers could not have prevented . . . nor has it suffered any hardships, excepting those resulting from the necessity of being exposed to the inclemencies of the weather, at a moment when they were most severe."

Despite its confidentiality, the contents of the letter became widely known and was viewed with dismay by many junior officers both in the Peninsula and in Britain: "I was very sorry to see Lord Wellington's Letter to his Generals commanding Brigades and Divisions at full length in the rascally London Newspapers with suitable remarks by the Editors, one of whom coolly observes the Army was in a state of mutiny," confided Lieutenant Bragge to his father. "My own opinion is that Lord Wellington never wished or intended the aforesaid letter to be published, nor was it, I believe, in many instances read to the Troops but to the officers only."

"The Army is not a little out of humour with his Lordship at present," wrote Ridout Bingham. "He affirms the Army suffered no privations except such as they were exposed to from the severity of the weather; but the wearied famished wretches who perished by numbers on the roads, and were left unburied, and half devoured by dogs and wolves, as an encouragement I suppose to others, is a refutation of this accusation," and, in a reference to Lord Wellington, he added, "It is always the practice of the great to kick from under them the stool by which they have been exalted."

Lieutenant Robert Fernyhough, himself so ill from physical exhaustion that he only narrowly escaped falling into the hands of the French, wrote of the losses suffered by his Company, to his brother in England. After describing the hardship and deprivation he had undergone during the retreat, he pointed out that less than one third of the men who had left England with him were now alive.

What might have been termed a year of fluctuating fortune, however, could be offset by a considerable number of achievements. Southern

Spain was free from French occupation, important fortresses had been captured, and the activities of Wellington's troops in the 1812 campaign had everywhere encouraged guerrilla activities. These bands, led by such men as El Capuchino, El Pastor, Mina and Longa, gave the French no rest and Captain Marcel of the 69th Leger was obliged to confess: "Time and again the division ran its races, sometimes on the heels of El Pastor at other time on those of Mina or Longa, but they were useless fatigues . . . we often managed to get lost in this pathless, mountainous country . . . the enemy was always better informed than we were, and had inevitably just left when we arrived."

Now, as details of Napoleon's dreadful losses in the snows of Russia became common knowledge, speculation grew among Wellington's officers as to whether the Emperor would withdraw from Spain in order to rebuild the Grande Armée for further campaigns in Russia. Lord Wellington, who had recently been created Duke of Ciudad Rodrigo by the Spaniards, was unconcerned, for he was even then planning a campaign for the beginning of 1813 with the objective of driving the French out of northern Spain once and for all.

A rigorous programme of training was laid down and undertaken with enthusiasm by troops determined to prove that Wellington had been misguided in his condemnation of them. Tons of powder and thousands of flints were expended in musket practice and each new battalion undertook a course of field training until the required standards had been raised to match those of the veteran battalions. By early May most could form a square from line or column in less than a minute regardless of the nature of the terrain, and ease of movement was greatly increased by adopting the practice of discarding heavy greatcoats on the march and with the provision of lightweight cooking pots to replace the ubiquitous heavy iron kettle.

Kincaid could write enthusiastically: "It did one's very heart good to look at our battalion that day . . . each daring, bronzed countenance, which looked you boldly in the face, in the fullness of vigour and confidence, as if it cared neither for man nor devil." "An excellent spirit pervaded the army," confirmed Blakiston. "It possessed the most unbounded confidence in its commander, and confidence is the soul of battle."

One problem which troubled Wellington was the increased activity of bandits, roaming the countryside in the guise of guerrillas, who, far from being of assistance in the fight against the French, availed themselves of every opportunity to prey upon the Spanish peasants. Journeying from Lisbon to join his regiment, Ensign William Thornton Keep was dismayed that a once beautiful country could be left in so destitute a state. "The roads are infested with bandits," he wrote, "who find no difficulty to escape justice and thus utterly prevent all travelling on them by the peacefully disposed."

With the arrival of fresh regiments from England, Lord Wellington's Anglo-Portuguese army had grown to 81,000 with an additional 14,000 troops marching to join him from Cadiz. In addition, Wellington had 21,000 Spaniards under his command with a further 12,000 active on the northern seaboard against Clausel.

On 21 May the allies broke up their winter cantonments to begin the campaign of 1813 with a movement directed at turning the enemy's position on the Douro and ultimately of driving them over the Pyrenees and into France. To Sir Rowland Hill was given the responsibility of taking 30,000 men on a route through the Tagus Valley in an advance on Madrid, whilst General Sir Thomas Graham, with twice that number, began a 200-mile trek with the objective of outflanking King Joseph's forces at Medina. After a brief skirmish with the enemy, Hill overran Salamanca on the 26th and, leaving a token force in the town, continued his advance, leaving Wellington to ride across 50 miles of rough country to visit Graham where the Elsa met the Douro near Zamora. Graham's 60,000-strong army had for the past seven days laboured manfully to cross the mountain wilderness of the notorious Tras-os-Montes towards Zamora. This particular route had been considered all but impassable by the French and certainly at various stages of the precipitous climb the infantry were obliged to crawl up on hands and knees, whilst the artillery had to be manhandled and lowered on ropes. The advance, difficult as it was, met no serious obstacle until the Elsa was reached. An usually heavy rainfall had swollen the river to such an extent that it had become a fast-flowing flood seen by one observer to be "as wide as the Thames at Windsor". Lord Wellington, while recognizing that a crossing could be a hazardous undertaking, was nevertheless anxious to complete it before Joseph learned that the greater part of the allied army had left Portugal and did not plan to return.

On the last day in May the crossing began, with the foremost companies cautiously feeling their way against a strong current and swirling waters which even at the ford were knee-high. The 51st crossed successfully, although drenched to the skin, and then came the turn of the rest of the infantry, with many grasping the stirrup leather of a Hussar for added security. Eventually the ford became so congested with men and horses that several lost their footing and were left floundering in the surging brown torrent, with desperate redcoats clinging to the tail of a horse. With the arrival of pontoons secured with guide ropes from the opposite bank, the remaining divisions and horse artillery completed the crossing before nightfall. It was a feat which the French thought impossible, and when news reached Joseph that Wellington threatened his line of communication with Vitoria he again abandoned Madrid, taking the main route to Burgos.

For the first two weeks of June Wellington's army advanced steadily across the plain of Old Castile, passing through a countryside studded with acres of vineyards and waving corn. The passage of such a large body of troops with a baggage train caused an immense amount of damage to the crops. In the wake of such destruction, Captain William Tomkinson had every sympathy for the plight of the peasant farmers. But, as he tactfully remarked to a group of angry villagers, "You must not mind your corn if we can but get the enemy out of the country."

Villarcayo and Medina de Pomer were passed on the 16th before Wellington wheeled eastward in an attempt to outflank the French, moving from one range of hills to the next so rapidly that it caused a corporal to remark, "We had scarcely time to count the valleys".

Meanwhile, Joseph Bonaparte had arrived at Burgos on the 13th only to find that the old fortifications were in a state of disrepair and, not having time to strengthen them, he stayed just long enough to destroy the castle and surplus stocks of powder before moving on. Twelve miles away, George Bell was awakened from his slumber on a makeshift bed of bracken as the ground shook. The young subaltern, still half asleep, drew himself up into a sitting position and, with painful memories of the siege, exclaimed, "Thank God! There goes Burgos!"

The fact that the destruction of the castle had been bungled soon became common knowledge among the troops. "In a few hours we heard that the enemy had blown up the inner walls of the castle with so little skill," reported Private Green, "that thirty men of the garrison perished by the explosion."

Several hours later Lord Wellington rode with his Staff to inspect the defences which, ten months before, had defied his every attempt to overthrow. A few French troops were still in the vicinity of the town and Wellington was seen by Sir Richard Henegan to be in some danger from a group of the enemy's cavalry not 300 yards from where his Chief was conversing with the staff. A rise in the ground concealed Wellington from immediate observation by the enemy vedette and Henegan was relieved to see them ride away.

The allied advance continued at a fast pace and the next few days saw the dust-covered columns progressing toward Vitoria through a rugged wilderness of rock-strewn hills and mountain ridges with only the occasional glimpse of a fertile valley to relieve the monotony. After twenty miles of boulders and slippery shale Johnny Kincaid, depressed at the thought of traversing as much rough ground ahead as he had left behind, suddenly found himself looking down on the Valley of the Ebro and at one of the loveliest panoramic views he had ever seen. Spread out before him were sparkling rivers, green meadows, and extensive vineyards. The effect upon his men was electric.

"The influence of such a scene on the mind can scarcely be believed," wrote Kincaid. "Five minutes before we were all as lively as stones. In a moment we were all fruits and flowers, and many a pair of legs that one would have thought had not a kick in them were in five minutes after, seen dancing across the bridge, to the tune of 'The Downfall of Paris'."

That night Johnny Kincaid rested in a cottage garden "with his head on a ripe melon and his gaze on a cherry tree", without a disturbing thought to trouble his slumber. Not nearly so sanguine was Captain Blakeney. "For my part," he confessed, "I had seen and heard enough to convince me that we were on the eve of a great battle; and in the thoughts naturally engendered by that opinion, I lay awake a greater part of the night."

The next day, after crossing the Ebro by way of the mountain bridges at San Martin and Puente de Arenas, the advance was resumed, but now in pouring rain along the bank of the river. Vitoria was now little more than 20 miles distant and the infantry, despite their arduous march to the Ebro, were full of confidence and spoiling for a fight. So close were they on the heels of Joseph's tired and dispirited soldiers that, as one Peninsula veteran remarked, "They could smell the frog-eaters' baccy and onions".

Vitoria, the capital of the Basque province of Alava, with its splendid background of the Pyrenees, is set in a valley bounded by the winding River Zadorra. It was, then as now, an important road junction with routes to Bilbao, Bayonne, Trevinho and the Ebro Valley, whilst another road, little better than a country lane at that time, runs eastward to Salvatierra and Pamplona.

Lord Wellington, conscious that a victory over Joseph was a necessary preliminary to an early invasion of the south of France, deployed his 80,000 troops with care. The very nature of the Zadorra Valley afforded an attacking force the opportunity of mounting several simultaneous assaults from widely different points and the allied Commander was prepared to launch four massive columns at Joseph's overstretched divisions which occupied a front of almost eight miles.

The first column, led by 'Daddy Hill', was instructed to enter the valley from the south-west through the Puebla Pass and advance along the ridge in a feint attack. Further north, two columns under Sir Thomas Graham were to strike at Vitoria from the rear, cutting the vital Bayonne road. In the centre, the Earl of Dalhousie, with the 3rd and 7th Divisions, was required to bring his men up to the hills from the west and attack the bridges over the Zadorra, while the Light Division and a Hussar brigade under Wellington's personal command attacked the right flank of Joseph's Army of the South.

At daybreak on 21 June Lord Wellington's dispositions were complete and the allied army prepared for a battle which, if successful, would be the first step in the expulsion of the French forces from the whole of Spain.

Chapter 16

RICH REWARDS AT VITORIA

Whatever reluctance King Joseph might have shown, it was now impossible for him to avoid giving battle and, as the sun rose giving every indication of another bright, hot, summer day, Marshal Jourdan rode out with Joseph to review the troops drawn up as if on parade. The various colourful dispositions of infantry and cavalry were clearly visible to Surgeon Walter Henry two miles away on the heights west of the river. In the clear air Walter Henry could plainly see groups of French officers moving from one assembly to the next in their tour of inspection. "This was the first time I had seen a powerful army preparing for battle and the sensation was exciting, exhilarating and intoxicating," he wrote. "I was young and ardent. . . . I longed to join in the struggle and throw physic to the dogs."

Surgeon Henry was just one of many admiring the colourful martial display, for, in order to follow the progress of the battle, every possible vantage point was crowded with viewers, not all of whom were hoping for an allied victory. They were not kept waiting, for soon after 8.00am the battle opened with Morello's Spanish corps climbing the rock-strewn slopes of the Puebla Heights to reach the summit unopposed. Once there, among the rocks and trees, they became hotly engaged with the French defenders.

"It was a heavenly morning, bright and sunny," remembered Auguste Schaumann, "when, at about eight o'clock, we heard the rattle of musket fire behind the lofty heights on our right. It ultimately spread to the very ridge of the hills, and was slowly extended towards the left."

Twelve miles to the north Sir Thomas Graham was beginning his drive against General Reille along the Bilbao–Vitoria road. Reille's division put up a strong resistance, but, unable to stem the advance of so many troops on their front, they were forced back on the Zadorra where Graham's men in close pursuit battled to dislodge them from this vital river crossing. The German Commissary waxed eloquent in his description of

170

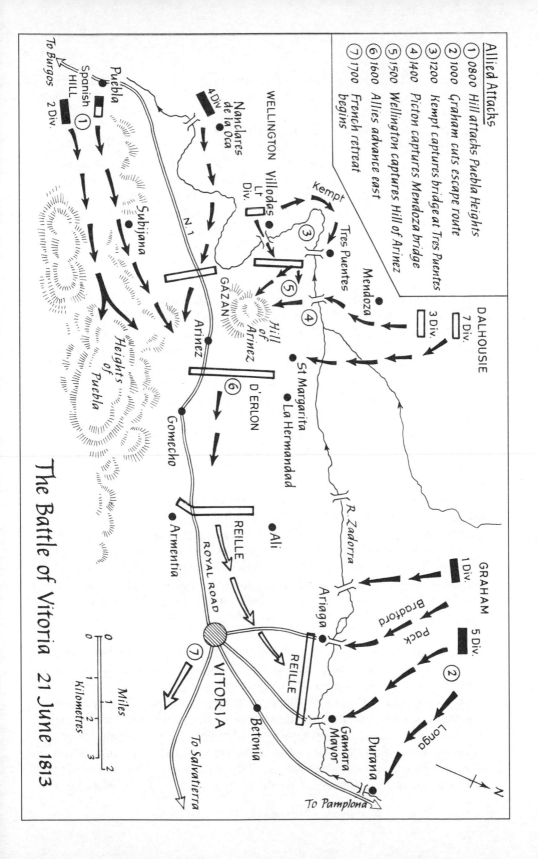

The Battle of Vitoria 21 June 1813

Allied Attacks
1. 0800 Hill attacks Puebla Heights
2. 1000 Graham cuts escape route
3. 1200 Kempt captures bridge at Tres Puentes
4. 1400 Picton captures Mendoza bridge
5. 1500 Wellington captures Hill of Arinez
6. 1600 Allies advance east
7. 1700 French retreat begins

To Burgos
Spanish HILL
2 Div. (1)
Puebla
Nanclares de la Oca
4 Div.
Subijana
Heights of Puebla
WELLINGTON
Villodas
Lt Div.
Kempt (3)
Tres Puentes
Mendoza
DALHOUSIE
7 Div.
3 Div.
GAZAN (5)
(4)
Hill of Arinez
St Margarita
La Hermandad
N.1
Arinez
(6)
D'ERLON
Gomecho
Armentia
Ali
REILLE
ROYAL ROAD
R. Zadorra
Ariaga
GRAHAM
1 Div.
Bradford
Pack
5 Div.
(2)
Longa
REILLE
Gamara Mayor
Durana
VITORIA
Betonia
(7)
To Salvatierra
To Pamplona
N

Miles
Kilometres
0 1 2 3
0 1 2

the scene: "The bright morning sunshine, the gloomy wooded hills, the flash of muskets, the rolling thunder of the fire, and the wonderful shapes formed by the smoke in and out of the groups of trees covering the hills, lent a picturesque grandeur to the scene."

Joseph had expected an attack from the west across the Zadorra, but he was uncertain as to which was to be Wellington's main assault and which was merely a diversion. Marshal Jourdan, who had left a sick bed to advise Joseph, was sure that the troops massing at the Villodas bridge were simply demonstrating and that the real threat would come from Sir Rowland Hill's corps. Jourdan's view prevailed and General Eugene Villatte was ordered to take the 3rd Division to the Puebla Heights where the Spaniards were battling desperately to maintain their position among the pine trees.

Most of Wellington's troops had been sitting on their knapsacks in anticipation of an order which would send them into battle. Among them was Thomas Pococke. "We had not a bit of tobacco and were smoking leaves and herb," he confessed. "Colonel Cadogan rode away and got us half a pound of tobacco a man, which was most welcome." Shortly afterwards the Highlanders of the 1/71st found themselves climbing to the assistance of the Spaniards, where they quickly became embroiled in a bitter clash with the blue-coated columns of Villatte's elite troops. "Scarcely were we upon the height when a heavy column, dressed in greatcoats, with white covers on their hats, exactly resembling the Spanish, gave us a volley," wrote Pococke, "which put us to the right about at double quick time."

Led by a piper playing 'Hey Johnny Cope', the Scots then charged over the broken ground and, as the sun's rays slanted through the trees to drive away the early morning mist, they may have caught a glimpse of a dense mass of French infantry before a tremendous rolling volley thinned their ranks to deprive them of most of their officers, including Colonel Cadogan, who fell at the head of his men. The dazed survivors soon recovered their composure and, together with the 50th Foot, joined the Spaniards in a fierce encounter which spilled across the summit as the allies attempted to drive in the French left flank.

Marshal Jourdan, aware of the danger, detached troops from his centre to reinforce Villatte's hard-pressed Reserve, but the weight of the combined British and Spanish force proved too great and the French were forced to give ground. Wellington, seeing the forward surge of his red-coated infantry, turned in triumph to his Staff and announced that the Heights of Puebla had been carried. In taking the heights the 1/71st, in addition to losing almost all of their officers, had also lost more than 700 men and, as Pococke remarked of the survivors, "There were not 300 of us on the height able to do duty, out of above 1,000 who drew rations in the morning. None spoke, each hung his head in mourning for the loss of a friend and comrade."

Shortly before noon a Spaniard was conducted to Lord Wellington's headquarters with a vital piece of intelligence. A bridge over the Zadorra at Tres Puentes two miles to the north had been left undefended. The Commander-in-Chief acted immediately by sending Colonel Barnard with a battalion of the 95th, led by the Spanish guide, to investigate. Moving off at their customary fast pace, the Rifles reached the bridge without incident and it was not until Kempt's brigade had crossed to the opposite bank that the enemy became aware of the danger. A French battery stayed just long enough to fire off two rounds, one of which decapitated the unfortunate Spanish peasant, before limbering up and retiring at speed.

Two columns, those of Hill and Graham, were now heavily engaged. A third, the 7th Division, commanded by Lord Dalhousie, had found the broken ground to the west difficult to negotiate and had yet to join with Sir Thomas Picton's 3rd Division as instructed by Wellington. Picton now awaited its arrival with mounting impatience. Earlier he had bitterly disputed the obligation of his 'Fighting Third' to be encumbered with scaling ladders and other unnecessary impedimenta during the march, and waiting for the 7th Division had not improved his Welsh temper.

The planned attack on the Mendoza Bridge was thus held up and, as yet another aide galloped up to seek a reason for the delay, the Commander of the 3rd Division could no longer contain his irritation. Rising in his stirrups, Picton shouted at the Staff officer, "Have you any orders for me, Sir?"

"None," replied the aide.

"Then pray Sir, what orders *do* you bring?"

"Why, that as soon as Lord Dalhousie with the seventh division shall commence an attack on that bridge, the fourth and sixth are to support him."

Raising the blackthorn stick he habitually carried, Sir Thomas leaned across his horse's mane and bellowed, "You may tell Lord Wellington from me, Sir, that the third Division under my command shall in less than ten minutes attack the bridge and carry it and the fourth and sixth may support it if they choose."

Turning to face the grinning redcoats behind him, the General addressed them with a familiar oath: "Come on ye rascals! Come on ye fighting villains," and, in his old faded coat of blue and top hat, Picton spurred the cob across the bridge to the opposite bank. As he watched him, an amused Kincaid observed, "Old Picton rode at the head of the third division dressed in a blue coat and round hat, and swore as roundly all the way, as if he had been wearing two cocked ones."

Half a mile to the west of Mendoza, Kempt's brigade was in an isolated and dangerous position, having crossed the bridge at Tres Puentes only to find themselves closely engaged with a strong force from General Gazan's Army of the South, which considerably outnumbered them. A growing number of casualties thinned Kempt's three battalions and his fire power was further diminished by a number of misfires from the flint-lock muskets they used. It was an experience not unfamiliar to the redcoat and was easily remedied by scraping the flint clean before clearing the touch hole by means of the long brass picker which hung from the soldier's belt. In doing so, however, the soldier had only his bayonet with which to defend himself and it was with some relief that Kempt's men greeted the arrival of Picton's 3rd Division.

The riflemen of the 95th, skirmishing ahead of the main body, were soon hotly engaged with the voltigeurs of d'Erlon's Army of the Centre around the village of Arinez. The French defended stubbornly and, in running forward to take up a new position, Rifleman Edward Costello was bowled over from the impact of a musket ball striking his leather pouch. Dazed by the fall, Costello, who imagined himself to be gravely wounded, was relieved to discover that the ball had merely torn away the pouch, leaving him with nothing more serious than an ugly spreading bruise.

Equally fortunate was Rifleman John Green. In the act of loading his Baker rifle, a ball tore the ramrod from his grasp and, seconds later, "a grapeshot struck the top of my cap and carried away the rosette with part of the crown. Had it been three inches lower, I should have been no more."

General d'Erlon's troops were fighting desperately to hold their position in the village, each street being contested as fiercely as any experienced by the 95th at Fuentes de Onoro some two years before. "At one period," recalled Johnny Kincaid, "we held one side of a wall . . . while the French were on the other side, so that any person who chose to put his head over from either side, was sure of getting a sword or bayonet up his nostril."

The general din of battle had by now reached a crescendo with the massed cannon of both sides engaged in a tremendous duel which raged unabated for an hour. Sergeant William Surtees, who, as Quartermaster of the 2/95th, had no role to play in the fighting, found himself drawn by an insatiable curiosity to the crest of a conical hill which promised to afford a panoramic view of the battlefield. He found the extensive plain covered with cavalry, infantry and artillery of the respective antagonists and, as Surtees gazed in awe at this display of military might, the crashing reverberations from musketry and cannon almost stunned his senses.

The fire from the enemy artillery was intensifying and, as Captain Harry Smith stood by his horse with a loose rein, observing the exchange of fire between a battery of Ross's brigade and its French counterpart, his horse suddenly collapsed. He could find no visible wound and it remained a mystery to him until an artillery officer explained to the startled Rifle officer that his horse had probably been knocked over by the wind from a passing cannon ball.

Sir Thomas Graham's troops had been greeted with a storm of musketry and, as Sergeant Cooper turned with an encouraging word to a Fusilier on his right, a ball tore the knapsack from the man's back without harming him, while, a few yards from Kincaid, a shell exploded, kicking up such a cloud of dust and smoke that his horse reared and bucked so violently that Kincaid found it difficult to retain his seat. As he strove to control his mount, a voice Kincaid recognized as Lord Wellington's, called out "in a tone of sharp reproof" to "stop showing off your horsemanship, Sir, and look more to keeping your men together."

Severe though the artillery fire and musketry was, it could not halt the men of the 4th Division who were advancing in a double line through fields of ripe wheat. By late afternoon, as the threat to their flanks increased, Gazan's Army of the South was near to the point of collapse. The whole of the enemy's first line, outnumbered by the allies, began to fall back from the centre of the valley, at first in an orderly fashion, but then, as it became increasingly clear that the day was lost, small groups breaking away from the conflict were at first followed by hundreds, and then thousands as the non-combatants joined the soldiers in a rush from the battlefield.

By 4.00pm the battle was virtually over. The French fell back on Vitoria and, lacking horses for the artillery, the cannon were spiked and abandoned.

"In all directions there was nothing but fire, smoke, moving columns, troops forming squares or occupying heights, dead and wounded men and horses, and shelled houses and trees," reported Auguste Schaumann, "whilst weapons of all kinds, forage caps, strips of uniform, cartridge boxes, paper cases, buttons and shoes covered the ground."

It had been Wellington's instructions that the Spanish infantry, whose uniforms closely resembled those of the French, wear a patch of white cloth on their left arm. Now, in the closing stages of the battle, a number of Frenchmen employed the ruse of wrapping a piece of white linen around their arm in order, perhaps, to approach near enough to loose a volley against an unsuspecting foe. Corporal Lawrence, with several of the 40th, surprised one such band close to a wood and were about to engage them when they were stopped by an officer who had noticed that the soldiers wore white armbands. The French, after discharging a ragged volley, fortunately without effect, made their escape through the trees. "I never in all my days of campaigning saw men in such a rage as ours were with that officer," commented William Lawrence.

Ahead of the victorious allies lay the city of Vitoria, almost hidden in the drifting clouds of smoke and dust. The valley and the road to the mountains soon became notable for a proliferation of carriages and wagons bumping furiously over the uneven ground, as the fleeing occupants were goaded to even greater exertions by the knowledge that British Hussars were close on their heels. A cart which the driver, in his haste, had overturned on the road to Pamplona blocked one line of vehicles and Joseph Bonaparte, caught up in the mêlée, only escaped capture by leaving his coach in favour of a horse and riding off at speed escorted by his personal guard of Cuirassiers. Marshal Jourdan, ill with a fever, also fled on horseback, leaving behind his sword and Marshal's baton.

Lieutenant Bell passed Joseph's carriage upset in a ditch and noticed with interest that the fine silk linings and draperies had already been ripped apart by a crowd of perspiring redcoats. Faces black with grime and powder, they were busily searching for anything of value. Ensign William Thornton Keep could sympathize with their action. "It is a fine chance for some of our poor fellows," he wrote, "many of them obtaining 50 or 60 guineas each as wagons loaded with money fell into their hands. The spoils of the day pretty well compensate for its toils, to some of these heroes, and they are certainly deserving of it, for there is no describing what they endure in these campaigns."

Many, it was true, would leave much wealthier than they had been at the beginning of the battle, but others, equally deserving, were less fortunate. George Bell hastily snatched up a sack which, when opened, disclosed a cold chicken, a few maps and a flask of wine, the sum total of his share of the plunder that day, and Bell rode on, understandably disappointed with his find. Private John Green fared little better: "A crown piece, some children's frocks, two flutes, an English Bible, and a few other small articles, were all that fell to my share," he confessed regretfully.

Nevertheless, many of Green's comrades made their fortune and in one case all promotion in the ranks of the 14th Light Dragoons was stopped for three years following the theft of King Joseph's silver chamber pot, eventually to be used as a punch bowl in the officers' mess. Such was the loss to the Military Chest from undeclared plunder that an accurate figure would be difficult to assess. That of John Cooper probably reflects an estimate prevailing at the time: "In the course of the night the money wagons taken from the enemy were plundered of perhaps nearly seventeen million francs," he wrote. "One of my company got his pockets filled with doubloons and dollars."

Perhaps the most prized trophy taken that day was Marshal Jourdan's baton, by Corporal Fox of the 18th Hussars. It was sent to the Prince Regent, who, in turn, presented Wellington with a specially commissioned British-made baton with his compliments: "Your glorious conduct is beyond all human praise, and far above my reward. . . . You have sent me among the trophies of your unrivalled fame the staff of a French Marshal; and I send you in return that of England."

Close upon the heels of Joseph's broken battalions rode the British Hussars and Light Dragoons. Their route to the city gates was festooned with abandoned cannon and overturned limbers, but by ruthlessly forcing a passage through the panic-stricken crowds of camp followers, the leading squadrons galloped into the city in pursuit of the enemy. The narrow cobbled streets were soon echoing to the clash of steel as the troopers strove to prevent the French infantry who were guarding the retreat of Joseph and his entourage from dragging them from the saddle. Indeed, every street was so crowded with soldiers and civilians that it seemed to Auguste Schaumann most improbable that anyone would ever reach the exit on the other side of the city.

Standing near the German Commissary, a captured French officer summed up the situation as he saw it. "It's no wonder you gained a victory," he complained bitterly to Schaumann. "For you have an army while we are nothing but a travelling brothel."

Schaumann did not disagree, for, as he later wrote, "The unmarried ladies belonging to the French army, most of whom were young and good-looking Spanish women, dressed in fancy hussar uniforms and mounted on pretty ponies . . . were first robbed of their mounts and their jewels, and then allowed to go. But as all they wanted was protection and a new lover, both of which they soon obtained, they were to be had for the asking."

At dusk any further pursuit of Joseph's army was abandoned, but, with the road to Bayonne blocked by Sir Thomas Graham, the only escape route now open to the refugees was a narrow track to Pamplona. Wellington's soldiers were obviously feeling the strain of almost five weeks of continual marching, but an equally plausible explanation for the delay in following the French lay in the accumulation of the loot of five years' occupation. The plain was littered with the wrecks of carriages, chests, spilt jewels, silverware and gold plate. Even late arrivals were able to profit from the riches to be found in the many boxes and abandoned wagons.

"At dusk the head of our column came upon some wagons," wrote Captain Blakeney. "Someone called out, 'They are money tumbrils'. No sooner were the words uttered than the division broke, as if by word of command, and in an instant, the covers disappeared from the wagons, and in their place was seen nothing but a mass of inverted legs. . . . The scene was disgraceful, but at the same time ludicrous."

Edward Costello, now a sergeant in the 1/95th, with a single blow from his musket persuaded a Spanish muleteer in the service of the French to release his hold on a small but heavy portmanteau. Its contents amounted to £1,000 in gold and silver Spanish dollars which Costello, in his turn, only narrowly preserved from the attention of three troopers of the 10th Hussars.

When darkness descended and the bivouac fires flared into life, the allied camp took on the appearance of an illuminated fairground, with soldiers capering about dressed in all manner of silken clothing or drunkenly staggering beneath the weight of a trunk of silver dollars. Little of value was ever recovered for the Treasury, for even the local peasantry made sure that a portion fell into their hands. "Much fell to the share of the peasants of the country," observed George Ridout-Bingham. "Perhaps they are the people to whom in justice it ought to belong."

The few who had failed to obtain a share of the loot were soon making up for it from the profits made from the sale of hams, tobacco and Cognac, and, with brandy fetching a high price – Wheeler paid 40 dollars for a bottle of Cognac – they had little cause for complaint.

The defeat of the French at Vitoria signalled the end of King Joseph's reign over the Spanish people and effectively ended French resistance in Spain, paving the way for Wellington's assault on the gateway to the south of France. News of the British victory reached every national capital with astonishing speed and gave renewed hope to the rest of occupied Europe.

French strength at the time of Vitoria had been in the region of 100,000 men and, taken in proportion to the relative size of the respective armies, their casualties had not been excessive – 756 killed and 7,000 wounded or taken prisoner. Their loss in artillery, however, had been enormous. From a total of 153 cannon at the start of the battle the French had managed to save just two field guns and not a single caisson. Allied casualties amounted to 5,148 and it is interesting to note that Richard Henegan, in his capacity of Military Commissary, calculated that, from ball cartridge expended and the casualties inflicted, only one musket shot in four hundred and fifty-nine took effect – confirmation either of the inaccuracy of 'Brown Bess' or of the low standard of marksmanship prevailing in the heat of battle.

Of more concern to Lord Wellington was the army's failure to follow up its victory with a vigorous pursuit of the French. In a despatch to Earl Bathurst, the Secretary of State for War, notable for its scathing criticism of both officers and men, he wrote: "We started with the army in the highest order, and up to the day of battle nothing could get on better; but that event has, as usual, totally annihilated all order and discipline. The soldiers of the army have got among them about a million sterling in money . . . the night of the battle, instead of being passed in getting rest and food to prepare them for the pursuit of the following day, was passed by the soldiers in looking for plunder. The consequence was that they were totally knocked up. . . . We may gain the greatest victories, but we shall do no good until we shall so far alter our system as to force all ranks to perform their duty."

Nevertheless, Bonaparte's ambition of adding Spain to his empire had received a mortal blow, for by the end of June only three strongholds remained in the possession of the French: Pamplona at the foot of the Pyrenees, San Sebastian in the north-west and the fortified town of Vera.

Chapter 17

BATTLE FOR THE PYRENEES

When Lord Wellington resumed his advance on 23 June, with Joseph's forces little more than a day's march from the border, he had left a city in which movement of every kind had been brought to a halt by as many as 3,000 abandoned carts, wagons and carriages. Lieutenant Moyle-Sherer, sent back to take command of a Company of the 34th, found the streets blocked by gun carriages, dead horses and rubble of every description. Carts filled with a mixture of English, Spanish, Portuguese and French wounded competed for space with long trains of commissariat mules, which threatened to close all but the broadest avenue to the city's gates. The townspeople had been so long under the yoke of French occupation that, it seemed to Sherer, "every face wore a look of astonishment, as if their recent liberation was as yet impossible to understand."

The battalions in pursuit of Joseph's forces retreating on Pamplona were being subjected to irritating delays as brigades, bivouacked in unfamiliar territory, took the wrong road or were late in assembling. Captain Norman Ramsey, celebrated for his exploit at Fuentes de Onoro, after disregarding orders to remain with his battery in his present location, proceeded under his own initiative and became hopelessly lost. A furious Wellington, concerned at losing part of his artillery train, placed Ramsey under close arrest where he remained for three weeks until his Colonel successfully interceded on his behalf.

Insubordination such as Ramsey's and the absence of men continuing to search for plunder so delayed pursuit of the French that Joseph and Jourdan with the main body were allowed to reach Tolosa during the evening of the 23rd where the corps reformed, Reille taking the road to San Esteban and Joseph, with the Army of the Centre, maintaining the rearguard. Maximilien Foy, having learned of the disastrous defeat, withdrew across the Bidassoa and, after leaving a garrison in San Sebastian, occupied Tolosa and prevented the allies from cutting off the retreat of the rest of the French army.

An irritated Lord Wellington expressed his annoyance in another letter to Earl Bathurst on 9 July: "I do not know what measures to take about our vagabond soldiers. By the state of yesterday, we had 12,500 men less under arms than we had on the day before the battle. . . . There may be some whose youth, indiscretion, or bad habits may lead into irregularities. These must be restrained; discipline, subordination, and good order must be established among all."

In spite of the delays which had occurred, Joseph Bonaparte was chased along the single road to Pamplona, where, after a brief skirmish, the French were forced to abandon one of only two cannon they had salvaged from their defeat at Vitoria. "They robbed and plundered everywhere," complained Ensign George Bell. "Women and young girls were found on their own hearthstones outraged and dead; houses were fired and furniture used for hasty cooking. Such is war!"

Unable to inflict further damage on Joseph's army, Wellington left Sir Rowland Hill to invest Pamplona on 23 June and, after sending Graham with 10,000 men to besiege San Sebastian four days later, he despatched his advanced brigade to oust French pickets from the mountain passes along the Bidassoa, after which he called a halt to secure his rear before advancing towards the Pyrenees.

Joseph Bonaparte, having reached the Pyrenees with an army of 50,000, also re-organized his forces, General Reille taking the road to San Esteban, while the Army of the South, led by General Gazan, crossed via the Roncesvalles Pass to St. Jean-Pied-de-Port, arriving on the 27th. General Drouet d'Erlon, with the Army of the Centre, after taking an alternative route via the Maya Pass, halted there to await instructions.

Napoleon Bonaparte was in Dresden when he learned of his brother's calamitous defeat and he reacted with fury. Then, far from yielding to a mood of despondency, he immediately relieved Joseph of his command and prematurely retired Marshal Jourdan, both of whom were ordered back to France in disgrace. Marshal Soult, who happened to be with the Emperor, was given specific instructions: "You will arrive in Paris on the 4th where you will go and see the Minister of War. . . . You will be in Paris for no longer than twelve hours. From there you are to continue your journey to go and take command of my armies of Spain."

In compliance with his orders, the new Commander-in-Chief of French forces arrived in Bayonne on 12 July to institute a strict programme of training designed to win back the territory lost by Joseph in Spain.

Marshal Nicolas Jean Soult, Duke of Dalmatia, known to the British troops as the Duke of Damnation, had the reputation, even among his contemporaries, of being a surly, unscrupulous character. Although cautious in his approach to tactical problems, he was nevertheless an efficient administrator. Certainly, within a few days of taking command, he displayed an astonishing degree of activity. His first task was to instil into the disillusioned soldiers a measure of the spirit which had once earned them a reputation of being the Emperor's 'Invincibles'. In addition to raising morale, he ensured that the old and vulnerable defence works of Bayonne were made good and, in addition, designed a series of forts to be erected on the approaches to the town. Having achieved his initial objectives, his priority now was to secure the line of the Ebro and relieve Pamplona and San Sebastian. In order to achieve this, the Army of Spain was created. Formed from ten infantry and two cavalry divisions grouped into three equal bodies, the right wing was given to General Reille, the centre to d'Erlon and the left wing to Clausel. The three divisions were supported with a total of eighty-six cannon, giving Soult a total strength of 90,000 infantry and 7,000 cavalry.

The Pyrenees, stretching from the Atlantic coast to the Mediterranean, provide a formidable barrier between France and Spain. On the French side it takes the form of great buttresses rising from the plain at right angles to the principal range, whilst on the southern side a series of steep mountain peaks extend in an irregular pattern deep into Spain. In 1813 the roads on the Spanish side of the mountain range were little better than cart tracks, with the movement of large bodies of troops restricted to just three routes into France: through the Roncesvalles Gap to the town of St. Jean-Pied-de-Port, a coastal road crossing the Bidassoa near Irun, or from Pamplona through the Maya Pass to Bayonne.

Lord Wellington had confidently assumed that Soult would attempt to relieve the garrison in San Sebastian under siege by Graham since 27 June; therefore it was with some astonishment that he learned on 25 July of French movements through the passes at Maya and Roncesvalles rather than along the coastal road to San Sebastian. Soult, however, had decided that the road to San Sebastian was too well guarded and he would achieve a greater measure of surprise by attacking Pamplona, with the possibility of falling back on San Sebastian, once the garrison in Pamplona had been relieved.

On that Sunday morning, the 25th, it had been Lieutenant Joseph Moyle-Sherer's duty to mount an outpost with the 2/34th at the eastern end of the Col de Maya. In spite of the distractions occasioned by the spoils from Vitoria, Sherer's picket was alert, for the captain of a neighbouring picket had reported movements which he believed to be nothing more serious than a change in position of the French skirmishers. In fact, it was the beginning of a move by Drouet d'Erlon to take the high ground above the Maya Pass and, as Stewart's troops busied themselves with the sundry chores of camp life, their activities were abruptly interrupted by the sound of musketry.

Sherer's outpost was quickly overrun by d'Erlon's voltigeurs, who, unencumbered by bulky knapsacks, had infiltrated every ravine and watercourse. The 2/34th fought desperately to contain the French, but, after a short but violent resistance in which two-thirds of Sherer's men became casualties, the survivors were forced back to where the Highlanders, led by Brigadier Pringle, held the heather-topped ridge. Moyle-Sherer readily acknowledged that he owed his life to the action of a French officer who beat up the levelled muskets of his men as they closed upon him and he was taken prisoner to the rear.

Several hundred tirailleurs, supported by a strong column from the 6th Leger, went on to attack the Highlanders of the 1/92nd and in little more than a half hour succeeded in driving the Scots from the high ground to a position among the rocks barely fifty yards wide where the Highlanders fought stubbornly for twenty minutes to stem the advancing tide of General Darmagnac's division.

"They stood there like a stone wall," wrote George Bell of the 34th, "overmatched by 20 to 1, until half their blue bonnets lay beside those brave northern warriors. When they retired, their dead bodies lay as a barrier to the advancing foe. Oh, but they did fight well that day; I can see the line now of the killed and wounded stretched upon the heather, as the living retired, closing to the centre."

Firing regular volleys, the men of the 1/92nd inflicted such heavy losses upon Darmagnac's troops that at one point in the battle the French officers had difficulty in persuading their men to advance beyond a line of heaped corpses. In the end superior numbers prevailed. Despite the gallant behaviour of the 34th and 92nd Regiments, which had allowed the rest of General Hill's command to withdraw in good order to the Bazten Valley, at the end of the day d'Erlon's men were firmly in possession of the Maya Pass, having inflicted more than 500 casualties on Pringle's brigade and taken four mountain guns. It was in this engagement that Ensign William Thornton Keep distinguished himself by saving the regimental colours of the 28th Foot. The standard bearer of the 28th, while carrying the colours, fell shot through the heart. Ensign Keep immediately took them up, exclaiming that "the colours of the 'slashers' should never want a person to display them to the enemy." In a letter to his father, Thornton Keep explained, "A violent zeal seized me to preserve the Colours not caring for my life, and I pitched myself head-long down the ravine, grasping most tightly to the staff. Through bushes and briars I rolled. . . . Rough stones rattled down with me, and it was some time before I put my feet to the ground. . . . Colonel Belson and the officers were highly rejoiced to see the Colours again, which they feared were lost."

Lord Wellington, when informed of d'Erlon's successful forcing of the Maya Pass, immediately rode to the position taken up by Sir Rowland Hill at Irurita behind the upper Bidassoa, where he found that General quietly awaiting d'Erlon's next move. The French Marshal, however, with his forces enveloped in fog, could do little more to exploit his success and had come to a temporary halt.

Although Wellington was relieved to find Hill in no immediate danger, he was disturbed by the absence of reliable information concerning events on his right flank. There, 20 miles to the south-east, Sir Lowry Cole with the 4th Division, Byng's brigade and Morillo's Spaniards, held the Pass at Roncesvalles barring the way to Pamplona. Thick mist had also slowed Clausel and Reille's advance from St. Jean-Pied-du-Port, giving the defenders time to deploy among the high passes north-east of Pamplona. Leaving Morillo's Spanish troops on the plateau, Byng led his brigade down to a position among the rocks where a narrow defile of 300 yards prevented the French from extending sufficiently in width to avoid crippling losses.

In the desperate fighting which took place at Roncesvalles, there occurred one of the rare incidents of a bayonet fight. John Kincaid later gave a description of the action: "The moment was fraught with disaster, when a gallant Centurion [Captain George Tovey] a choice spirit of the old 20th, at once came forth in character . . . in sight of the whole division, he with his single company, with desperate and reckless charge, dashed into the head of a whole column of French infantry which had already gained the heights, overthrew them, and sent the whole mass rolling headlong and panic-stricken into the valley below."

In Tovey's Company of eighty men, "a powerful man by name of Budworth, returned with only the *blood-soiled* socket of the bayonet on his piece stating that he had *killed away* until his bayonet broke," an indication of the bitter close-quarter fighting that marked 25 July. For almost four hours the French battled to dislodge the 20th, 31st and 66th Foot, but it was not until mid-afternoon, with the summit wrapped in fog and the ammunition of the defenders running low, that Sir Lowry decided that the risk of his slim force being enveloped by the enemy was too great. Despite Wellington's instructions not to withdraw, he ordered the regiments to retire along the road to Pamplona as far as Sorauren. His decision to evacuate the area might be open to question, but with the entire Roncesvalles area wrapped in low cloud, reducing visibility down to less than fifteen yards, it was perhaps a wise decision.

At 5.00pm the troops moved off, leaving the seriously wounded to the ministrations of the French surgeons, or, as one or two of their more pessimistic comrades observed, to the greater chance of mutilation by mountain wolves.

Cole's was an orderly retirement, despite the necessity for the exhausted redcoats to tread cautiously over fog-shrouded tracks strewn with loose rocks and masses of nettles. Fortunately there were few stragglers and, when the 1/71st halted for the night, Sergeant Cooper, in calling the roll, was agreeably surprised to find that not a single man missing.

Much to the chagrin of the French Marshal, Cole's withdrawal had gone unnoticed and it was not until the following morning that Soult resumed his advance. He was still 30 miles from Pamplona and every hour that passed was of the greatest importance if he were to reach the garrison of 3,000 before Wellington.

Lord Wellington, who had been with General Graham at San Sebastian, immediately rode south to where Sir Lowry Cole had consolidated his position in an area free from fog four miles north of Pamplona. The high ground occupied by the 5th Division comprised a ridge one and a half miles long, bordered by a fast-flowing stream with the mountain village of Sorauren lying at the foot of its western edge.

In addition to Anson's and Ross's brigades, Cole had been joined by Byng's and Cambell's, while further west Picton's Division and two Spanish battalions had taken up a position overlooking the Arga Valley beyond the range of the garrison's guns in Pamplona.

On the morning of the 27th a lone figure wearing a grey frock coat and a low-crowned cocked hat spurred onto the field to a storm of cheers from the troops assembled there. The calls echoed down the line of redcoats. "Nosey has come! See – old Nosey! Nosey!" The Portuguese, not to be outdone, set up their own chant of "Douro! Douro!" as Wellington, on his horse Copenhagen, doffed his hat in acknowledgment of a greeting which had clearly carried to Clausel's troops on the hills in the background.

The British Commander-in-Chief had dismounted beside a rocky outcrop where he accepted a telescope proffered by an officer on his Staff. Directing the glass towards the position occupied by Soult and a group of his Generals, Wellington is said to have remarked, "Yonder is a great Commander, but he is a cautious one and will delay his attack to ascertain the cause of those cheers, that will give time for the sixth division to come up and we shall beat him."

Indeed, Soult seems to have been in no great hurry to begin hostilities, spending much of the afternoon asleep beneath the shade of a mountain oak. Eventually, at noon on the 28th, a limited action began, by which time Pack's 6th Division had reinforced the 4th Division and the Portuguese, while Sir Rowland Hill was marching rapidly towards the battle area along the road from Maya.

The battle began with three columns from Clausel and Reille's command advancing towards the hill occupied by the 4th Division and the Portuguese. The British infantry, deployed in their usual fashion of two standing ranks, waited impassively against the skyline and watched the blue-coated figures cross the valley to begin the long laborious climb towards them.

"The English there occupied an elevated hill, of which the slope was rather steep," remembered the Marquis de Chambray. "The first line could neither see the troops which were to climb the hill to attack it, nor be seen by them. . . . As soon as they appeared the English battalions fired, charged with the bayonet, and overthrew them, but did not pursue; on the contrary, after having remained some moments near the crest, they retired in double quick time, at the command of their General, resumed their position and gave three successive cheers."

Although outnumbered by more than two to one, the nature of the terrain prevented a flanking movement and, when attacked for the second time, the 40th were able to use the advantage in fire power that their double line gave them to devastating effect. The French, bunched together and tired from their ascent of the thousand-foot-high hill, had little stomach for this second encounter and, in the storm of musketry from Anson's battalions, the attack once again collapsed.

Later that day a French officer, requesting permission to remove the wounded, admitted that their assault had cost them several hundred casualties. Elsewhere, the French achieved a partial success against Wellington's left flank, when Taupin's brigades drove in the 7th Cacadores. The Portuguese, in giving way, had allowed the French to outflank Ross's brigade, which, after losing 130 men in a matter of minutes, was forced to retire to the next range of hills.

A constant discharge of musketry had been directed against the French and, through constant use, Private Green's musket misfired and he was obliged to fit a new flint. While doing so he was struck in the side by a ball and initially felt nothing. "In about ten seconds, however, I fell to the ground, turned sick and faint, and expected every moment to expire," he wrote. "I thought it was all over with me, being confident that I had received a mortal wound." He was assisted to the rear where the surgeon probed the wound, but was unable to extract the ball. It was to be late September, after a torturous descent of the mountain to the General Hospital at Passages, before his wound was dressed by a surgeon who clapped him on the back, "telling me I should soon be able to have another shot at the French," added Green.

A position lost by Major-General Ross was soon recovered by the 27th and 48th Regiments of Anson's brigade at the point of the bayonet and, aided by other sections of the 4th Division, they routed the French with such vigour that Lord Wellington, in his despatches, mentioned the "enthusiastic conduct of the 4th Division"; a compliment which earned it the sobriquet of 'The Enthusiastics' from the rest of Wellington's army.

By late afternoon the action at Sorauren had reached its climax, with the French everywhere being driven from the ridge, and with their defeat vanished Soult's last hope of relieving the starving garrison in Pamplona. Provisions for Marshal Soult's own army were at a dangerous level and, with little prospect of foraging in this mountainous area, the Marshal decided to leave Pamplona to its fate and ordered a general retreat.

The next morning saw a change of plan, however, for, now that Wellington had been joined by Dalhousie's 7th Division, it appeared to Soult that, with the majority of the allied forces at Sorauren, he would encounter little opposition in a march on San Sebastian.

That night the pickets were alerted by the sounds of movement coming from the French camp and, when the sun rose on the morning of the 30 August, masses of blue and white clad infantry could be seen picking their way over the rough boulder-strewn slopes to the village of Sorauren. The drawn-out columns presented a tempting target for Cole's artillery which only the day before had been hauled to the summit of a hill overlooking Sorauren. The batteries opened at once with roundshot which succeeded in spreading consternation among the ranks of Maucune's and Conroux's regiments as they entered the village. Stewart's 2nd Division from the west and Pakenham's battalions from the south were also engaged, but it was Cole's artillery which did most to force the issue and, as the village houses collapsed under a barrage of roundshot, the French retired towards the valley of the Bidassoa, hotly pursued by Sir Rowland Hill. The young George Bell was ecstatic: "Nothing could stand against the ragged redcoats of old England," he enthused.

The battle for the Pyrenees had been brilliantly successful, but at a cost, allied losses amounting to 7,000 killed and wounded, causing Wellington to admit that, "at one time it was alarming, certainly, and it was a close run thing. I never saw such fighting . . . it began on the 25th and excepting the 29th when not a shot was fired, we had it every day till the 2nd. The battle of the 28th was fair bludgeon work."

Soult was now in full retreat and in their flight along the Ostiz road French losses in men and material were almost the equal of the British. A convoy overtaken and captured by the 57th Regiment at Elizondo was found to contain thirty wagons of bread and brandy, which, together with the loss of his baggage train, was a serious embarrassment to the French Marshal. That his divisions should escape a mauling was due in some respect to Wellington's mistaken belief that Soult would retire by way of the Maya Pass, but by the judicious use of mountain tracks which made any outflanking movement virtually impossible his army reached the bridge over the Bidassoa at Echaler, pursued by only a single brigade of the 7th Division.

The footsore soldiers of Alton's brigade achieved a measure of success, coming upon Darmagnac's rearguard just as the mist was lifting, to pour volleys into the massed ranks of the French from across the river. Elsewhere, Soult's army continued its retreat down the French side of the Pyrenees with the Green Jackets of the Light Division in close attendance, every shot being answered by a hundred echoes.

The pursuit by the Rifles was quickly terminated by the descent of a belt of fog, but not before Lieutenant Simmons and his Company of the 1/95th had the satisfaction of driving the French rearguard across the border in full view of their civilian compatriots. The dense mist, which persisted for most of the day, prevented any further action, but the Green Jackets relieved their feelings by loosening huge rocks and rolling them down the French side of the mountain.

Lord Wellington, who was suffering from a severe attack of lumbago, called a halt to all further pursuit and on 2 August he ordered his weary troops to fall back on the positions they had occupied a week ago while he turned his attention to the next task, the reduction of San Sebastian.

Chapter 18

ADVANCE INTO FRANCE

Sited on a rocky promontory in the Bay of Biscay near the French frontier, the city of San Sebastian had been under siege since the end of June, but each of three attempts to seize it had been repelled with heavy losses to the stormers. Dominating the city is the Castella de la Mota, built on the summit of a sandstone hill 135 metres high, which at that time could only be approached by a narrow isthmus guarded on one side by the crescent-shaped harbour and protected on the other by a tidal river. On the landward side of the city's defences was a hornwork and a rampart known as the Santa Catalina, beyond which stretched a range of sandhills. To the west of La Mota at a distance of 800 metres rose the island of Santa Clara, steep enough to overlook the city walls and consequently of great tactical importance to a besieging force.

With the allies fully occupied in the Pyrenees, Sir Thomas Graham, without siege artillery, could do little more than invest the town, assisted by the Royal Navy who had blocked the port. The Governor, General Louis Emanuel Rey, in command of the 3,000-strong garrison, had profited from the absence of heavy cannon to repair the breaches made earlier in the siege and erect a loopholed boundary wall behind the river defences, both tasks being completed by prisoners of war, a fact remarked upon by Lieutenant Gleig, who, from his post near a battery, could see the men "labouring in full regimentals", a shrewd move by the Frenchman, who knew that the work would be carried out without a single gun being directed against the labourers.

It was not until 18 August that a large consignment of heavy artillery, including howitzers, were received from England, but, without the necessary roundshot, eight days elapsed before the reduction of the city's defences could properly begin. On the 26th a deluge of missiles ranging from 64 pdrs to mortar shells was directed against the walls of the city. One by one the enemy batteries were silenced and two huge breaches were made on the river side of the boundary wall. Other guns were directed against the earthworks of Santa Clara and an amphibious assault by a mixed force of marines and soldiers stormed the island under the cover of darkness. The small garrison of Santa Clara was overwhelmed and, five days later, a new battery was its contribution to the bombardment of Rey's defence works.

The siege artillery had by now increased to eighty pieces and on 30 August, as a violent thunderstorm raged overhead, three enormous explosions, the result of mines sprung by Graham's engineers, created massive breaches in the sea wall and orders were issued for an attack to be made at 11.00am the next morning.

A mist of rain blanketed the boundary wall, but, promptly on time, the guns ceased their relentless bombardment and, as the rain lifted, soldiers of the 5th Division, led by General Sir James Leith, scrambled out of the trenches to advance across the sand dunes which at low tide connected the city with the mainland.

The assault was met by a storm of musketry and hand grenades, and the attackers, caught in the open, suffered horrendous casualties. One courageous group did manage to reach the foot of the wall where they suffered further casualties when a prepared mine exploded, bringing slabs of masonry down upon their heads. A few resolute souls scrambled over the debris only to find that they faced a precipitous drop of thirty feet to the street below. Constant and accurate musket fire soon made the area in front of the wall untenable, although, despite the odds ranged against them, volunteers still struggled to surmount the obstacles, urged on by General Leith, until he too was struck down by fragments of a shell which burst at his feet.

At the main breach the glacis was littered with debris and choked with corpses. The morale of the survivors crouched close to the base of the wall was at a low ebb. Huddled together, they refused to leave the protection of the wall and, adding to the difficulties of the assaulting party, an incoming tide swirling across the sand bar threatened to bring the attack against the hornwork to a premature end.

At this critical stage of the assault, when the dismal spectre of failure stared General Graham in the face, an order was given which dramatically changed the fortunes of the storming party. Concerned at the manner in which the attack had ground to a halt, an artillery colonel suggested that the batteries should shift their target to the crest of the boundary wall from where the defenders were inflicting so many casualties on the attacking troops. Graham agreed and, from a distance of 200 metres, forty-seven pieces of heavy ordnance erupted in a ripple of flame and smoke to lash the parapet of the wall with a rain of iron to the left of the main breach. Captain John Cooke, waiting in reserve with the 43rd, wrote of the devastating effect achieved by this novel and risky undertaking: "The fire from the batteries was terrific, and the troops retired four or five yards down the slope of the breach, whilst the heavy shot passed over their heads, skimming the round tower, the ramparts, and the crest of the breach with a precision truly astonishing, so that the enemy could not show their heads, or discharge a single firelock."

At first, as splinters of stone flew all around them, the soldiers sheltering at the base of the wall shrank back in confusion, shouting to each other "to come away as our batteries have opened on us". But the naval gunners were masters of their trade and the guns they served were new from England. Few injuries were inflicted on the storming party. Against the enemy, however, the effect was dramatic. Solid shot ploughed along the top of the wall, while grapeshot swept away the marksmen lining the rampart, encouraging the assailants to make a fresh attempt against the breastwork.

In the early afternoon a bursting shell may have ignited a store of combustible material which in turn set fire to a powder store. The resulting explosion was so violent that many of the garrison perished in a sheet of flame and for a few moments friend and foe alike gazed in awe as a thick column of sulphurous smoke climbed high above the city. "In every direction these hapless beings fell by the force of the explosion," wrote Richard Henegan. "Legs and arms, heads, and headless bodies, showered over the ramparts among our men."

"The explosion was supposed to be caused by accidental sparks or loose cartridge papers falling on the train," commented Cooke. "Probably no one living knows the real cause . . . however, all the French soldiers near the spot were blown into the air and fell singed and blackened in all directions."

As the smoke cleared to leave a blanket of dust and ashes, Leith's troops became aware that the way ahead was clear of defenders and, with a roar of cheers, they rushed towards "every crevice that offered admittance". The few Frenchmen in the area were quickly overcome, but resistance was far from being at an end and a savage bout of hand-to-hand fighting spilled into the streets and across the square. Many of the houses were barricaded and each one was fiercely defended, but by 5.00pm resistance by all but the most determined groups had come to an end.

By noon the next day the city was firmly in the hands of Graham's redcoats and the Portuguese from the 5th Division, followed by the usual scenes of rampage and looting. Richard Henegan could write with feeling: "In a few short hours the stillness of peace had replaced the din of war, but not so were the ravages of man to be obliterated; the town was in flames, the wretched inhabitants homeless and beggared."

Equally disturbed by the scenes he had witnessed, Captain John Harley of the 47th wrote: "I went in the evening through the breach . . . The scene that presented itself to me was horrifying – the dead lying in heaps in the streets – the French and British lying side by side; and not unfrequently a drunken soldier of ours was seen amongst them fast asleep."

English, Portuguese, Spanish and French corpses were everywhere and before long an overpowering stench of putrefaction forced the men of the 5th Division to collect the bodies and build huge heaps of faggots in order to cremate them. The pitiable cries of the wounded were largely ignored, but, even when conveyed to the hospital, the attention they received was rudimentary in the extreme: "The hospital presented a most dreadful scene," observed John Harley, "for it was a scene of human suffering; friend and enemy had been indiscriminately carried thither, and were there alike neglected."

In the closing stages of the assault the Governor had withdrawn into the citadel of La Mota with 1,300 of the garrison. They were to remain there until 9 September, when the survivors were allowed to march out with the honours of war, largely ignored by the allied troops who were more concerned with a search for plunder, the profits from which their womenfolk were happy to share. "I have gone into a church," complained Captain Harley, "and found three or four of them seated together, dividing watches and jewelry, and, on my speaking to them, they asked me did I want to interfere with them, and desired me to go off about my business."

Outside in the street no attempt had been made to contain the numerous fires which had continued through the night and by morning more than half the city was a blackened ruin. Drunken soldiers reeled past Harley oblivious of the charred timbers which occasionally fell in a shower of sparks. Even the citizens seemed to the Captain of the 47th to be stupefied with horror, rooted to the spot even when the rumble of falling masonry sent the looters running to a safer location.

Daylight revealed that, of the six hundred buildings, no more than a few dozen were anything but smouldering shells and when Lieutenant Gleig explored the gutted streets he was appalled by what he found. Everywhere were burnt and scorched corpses and the only living people to be seen were the groups of redcoats diligently searching the cellars, not for survivors, but for wine or liquor which might have escaped the attention of earlier marauders. The scenes of depravity rivalled even those in Badajos and Ciudad Rodrigo. An officer barely escaped with his life when he was chased by men who had mistaken him for the Provost of the 5th Division, whilst a Portuguese who attempted to stop the rape of a Spanish girl was bayoneted in the market square.

George Gleig, in describing what was almost a daily event, wrote: "Here you would see a drunken fellow whirling a string of watches round his head, and then dashing them against the wall . . . the occasional laugh and wild shout of intoxication, the pitiable cries or deep moans of the wounded, and the uninterrupted roar of the flames, produced altogether such a concert as no man who listened to it can ever forget."

A little more than a week later he returned to San Sebastian with a party of officers anxious to examine the citadel which had held out so long. The trenches and battery sites outside the city had fallen into disrepair and the outlying cottages were roofless and perforated with cannon shot. It was not until the group had entered the walled city, however, that the true picture of desolation became apparent. Passing through the ruined gateway, Gleig and his companions found themselves in what had once been the main thoroughfare. It was now choked with rubble and lined on each side by smoke-blackened ruins. Broken bits of furniture draped with discarded clothing, rusted cannon balls, broken muskets, with here and there the decomposing remains of a French soldier, met their gaze. The stench of death and corruption was everywhere. Of the inhabitants, Gleig reported that he saw only six, and their "wild and haggard appearance as they searched the ruins of their homes" moved the group of British officers "to a chilly sense of the more horrible points of their profession".

The whole affair had been traumatic. The attacks against the city's defence works had cost the allies some 3,000 casualties and the destruction of a useful sea port which many Spaniards believed to be a deliberate act designed to reduce competition with Britain's own seafaring trade. Deliberate or not, Britain's interest in the rebuilding of San Sebastian's port evaporated with the news that both Prussia and Russia had resumed hostilities against Napoleon, shortly to be followed by Austria. This welcome move gave an immense psychological boost to Wellington as he laid plans for the invasion of southern France, an operation which was sure to be welcomed by his officers and men, who were anxious to meet the enemy on his own soil. Until then Kincaid and his brother officers found that their present passive role was not at all to their liking, for, as the Lieutenant pointed out in his memoirs: "Our souls . . . were strung for war, and peace afforded me no enjoyment unless the place did," and a quiet village in the Pyrenees had little to offer a restless character such as Johnny Kincaid.

Lord Wellington was now fully occupied with a plan of campaign, beginning with an assault against French positions on the high ground across the Bidassoa. With his usual eye for detail, fords across the river were sounded and marked by fishermen from Irun, who, by the very nature of their occupation, would arouse no suspicion in the minds of the French vedettes. The tidal mouth of the river was only weakly held by the enemy, who, because the water here was deep and almost a thousand metres wide, were convinced that a crossing was next to impossible. It was an assumption for which Soult was to pay a heavy price, for, as Wellington knew from the reports of two Basque fishermen, tidal levels would fall sufficiently in early October to permit the estuary to be crossed in one or two places.

On 6 October, following a few days of patrol activity calculated to divert the attention of French pickets further afield, troops of General Hay's 5th Division left the village of Fuenterrabia at midnight to march down to the river as an electrical storm lit up the dark clouds above them. The crossing began at first light with the redcoats immersed to the waist and holding musket and powder pouch above their heads as they waded across towards the mud flats on the farther bank. A mile upstream the Light Division had already begun an assault against the Grande Rhune which dominated the area. In a remarkably short space of time the surprised defenders were driven from their stations on the high ground along the Nivelle and that night the redcoats bivouacked on French soil for the first time.

Only in the west did Wellington's troops meet with stiff opposition. There the French had constructed two strong points at Puerto de Vera, but, following some fierce fighting, the redoubt fell to the 52nd and the 95th, after which what little resistance remained was quickly overcome.

Among the prisoners taken in this engagement were two bandsmen and, at Lieutenant Simmons's request and much to the amusement of the Riflemen, the French musicians did their best to give a rendering of popular tunes. The best efforts of the two seem to have been less than satisfying, however, for, as George Simmons observed, "What with alarm and fright, they made sad music of it."

On the last day of October came the news of the fall of Pamplona, taken without bloodshed. The garrison had endured a siege of almost four months, by which time every domestic animal had been eaten and, towards the end, rats and weeds were the only source of nourishment.

Meanwhile, as he waited for the arrival of General Hill's contingent, even then struggling through the snow-covered passes of the Roncesvalles, Wellington studied the terrain and debated with his staff a plan to attack directly at Soult's centre or attempt to turn his position by advancing Hill's corps through St. Jean-Pied-de-Port.

The cold weather season had set in with a vengeance and the troops, bivouacked in flimsy tents, suffered accordingly. Forage was not to be obtained and many of the cavalry horses were fed on grass, for supplies from naval vessels could not be relied upon, since even at Passages the Atlantic swell was such that ships rode to their moorings with the greatest difficulty. The few cattle driven in over snow-covered roads arrived in such a wretched condition that they were scarcely fit to eat.

Eventually conditions improved sufficiently to permit a reconnaissance to be made of Marshal Soult's defence lines and on the evening of 8 November baggage and tents were sent to the rear and an order was given for the troops to be prepared to move off under the cover of darkness. Lieutenant Edmund Wheatley looked back at the camp he had just vacated and was struck by a sobering thought: "Fires stood deserted, excepting a solitary drummer boy shivering with apprehension and cold, or a soldier kneeling to the fire, lighting perhaps his last pipe."

The next morning saw the army of 82,000 British, Portuguese and Spanish troops facing once again a stiff climb into the chilly mist-shrouded regions of the Pyrenees. As the men climbed higher they began to experience sudden squalls of snow and hail so violent that Thomas Pococke was obliged to shield his face with his knapsack, and once, in attempting to rise from a bed of bracken, Surtees discovered that his cloak had frozen to the ground. In the clear periods between the squalls Wellington's soldiers looked out on a magnificent panorama of snow-capped mountain peaks and deep green valleys. Lieutenant John Malcom climbed the rocks adjacent to his bivouac and was rewarded with a view which lived long in his memory. Surrounded by hills thickly covered with trees, he could see the Bay of Biscay spread out beneath him "like a sheet of glass to the horizon", with the Bidassoa appearing as "a silver ribbon unfolding to the sea". To his front the plains of France lay "like a picture book of chateaux and villages", while to his rear was "the wild and rugged scenery of the Spanish Pyrenees".

As the soldiers began the long descent of the Grande Rhune, the knowledge that this tiring march over loose scree and sharp rock was coming to an end lifted their spirits and gave fresh impetus to aching limbs. The regimental band struck up with a rendition of 'The Downfall of Paris' and even the tardiest of redcoats was quick to respond with a cheer and an accelerated pace. Before the day had ended Wellington and his staff were gazing down upon the French fieldworks which extended from St. Jean-de-Luz to the Nivelle.

The huts were not the usual basic construction of brushwood and turf but of sun-baked clay with thatched roofs, giving every appearance of a permanent occupation.

"Those fellows think themselves invulnerable," remarked Lord Wellington to Sir John Colborne, "but I will beat them out and with great ease."

"That we shall beat them out when your Lordship attacks," replied Colborne , "I have no doubt, but for the ease . . ."

"Ah Colborne, with your local knowledge only, you are perfectly right; it appears difficult, but the enemy have not the men to man the works and lines they occupy. They dare not concentrate a sufficient body to

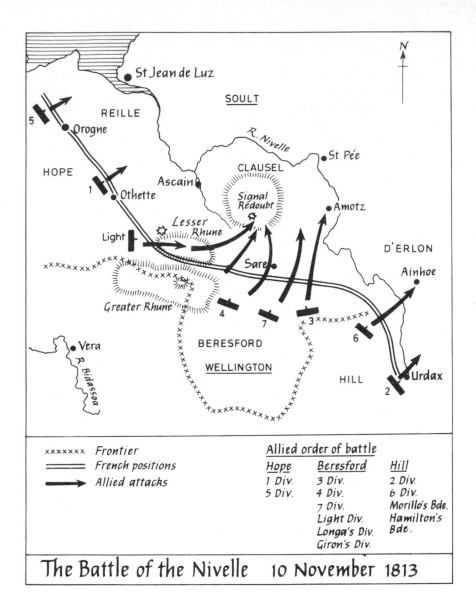

xxxxxx Frontier
====== French positions
➤ Allied attacks

Allied order of battle

Hope	Beresford	Hill
1 Div.	3 Div.	2 Div.
5 Div.	4 Div.	6 Div.
	7 Div.	Morillo's Bde.
	Light Div.	Hamilton's Bde.
	Longa's Div.	
	Giron's Div.	

The Battle of the Nivelle   10 November 1813

resist the attacks I shall make upon them. I can pour a greater force on certain points than they can concentrate to resist me."

Wellington then began an earnest conversation with Sir George Murray, his Quartermaster General, whilst Colborne and his aide, Lieutenant Harry Smith, stood in respectful silence. A plan of action was drawn up and approved by Wellington with the remark, "Ah Murray, this will put us in the possession of the fellows' lines."

The plan, converted into field orders by the Quartermaster, called for a thrust by columns of divisions between the village of Sare and the Nivelle on a front of three miles. A total of 20,000 troops were to be committed – the 3rd, 4th, and 7th Divisions commanded by General Sir William Carr Beresford, supported by cavalry and three brigades of horse artillery commanded by Colonel Dickson. The important task of storming La Petite Rhune was given to the Light Division and to General Francisco Longa's Spaniards, who, after consolidating the position, were to engage the enemy's flank.

To exert further pressure against the French, two Divisions, the 2nd and the 6th, were given the task of assaulting a ridge held by d'Erlon's Corps and, in a measure designed to obstruct any transfer of troops from Soult's right wing, four frigates would be sailing close inshore to cannonade the coastal towns of St. Jean-de-Luz and Socoa.

This ambitious scheme, which embraced a front of eight miles from La Petite Rhune to the sea, could not have been undertaken but for the manpower then available to Lord Wellington. Now, with an army which greatly out numbered his foe, he had every reason for holding the confident view he had earlier expressed to Sir John Colborne.

The first assault had been due to take place during the early hours of 10 November and long before daybreak Wellington and his staff assembled near a copse above the River Sare to witness the beginning of a new campaign.

Guided by a full moon, the men of the Light Division left the Grande Rhune to take up their position in a ravine less than half a mile from the enemy's earthworks. Promptly at 6.00am they left the deep shadow cast by the granite walls and, in seven columns, advanced across the spongy ground towards their objective. The 43rd, led by Colonel William Napier, headed for an incline between the marsh and a vertical wall of rock where lay the first of a series of stone redoubts. Since his Regiment faced an arduous climb before it could close with the enemy, Napier thought it prudent not to exhaust his men by quickening the pace. But the fire from the French batteries was now becoming trouble-some and he experienced some difficulty in restraining the redcoats from breaking into a run. In the event the problem was taken out of his hands by the action of an aide of General Kempt, who, galloping up behind Napier's men, urged them into a charge. The 43rd needed little encouragement and, with a wild cheer, they swept towards the strong-points, carrying their Colonel with them. Just as Napier had feared, long before the first line of earthworks could be reached, his men were quite blown. The attack petered out in the face of furious musketry. After a brief pause in the shelter of a rocky outcrop, while the men recovered their breath, Napier led his battalion against a dry stone wall only to see the defenders withdraw in haste, leaving the redcoats to capture the remaining redoubts in quick succession.

Further to the north, Beresford's Cacadores advanced in skirmishing order over difficult terrain. Opposition, which had been relatively light at the beginning, strengthened as the morning wore on and encounters with resolute groups of defenders became a frequent occurrence as the allied troops spread even further into the hills. The 95th, having secured their objective, joined with the 51st and 52nd in a joint attack on Signal Redoubt, an immensely strong position at the summit of yet another hill. The Green Jackets twice attempted to carry the fort by storm, only to be forced back on each occasion by a murderous concentration of musket fire.

In the fight around St. Jean-de-Luz Corporal Wheeler sustained a painful wound when a ball sliced through the fleshy part of both ankles, fortunately missing the bone. Lying helpless on the ground, he could do nothing to prevent a French Grenadier from robbing him of a few Spanish dollars. Wheeler, however, was soon to have his revenge, for, with the approach of the 51st, the Frenchman was obliged to beat a hasty retreat, leaving his musket at the Corporal's feet. William Wheeler was quick to put the opportunity to good effect and brought the Grenadier tumbling to the ground before he was many yards distant.

Away to Wheeler's left gunfire echoed through the wooded ravines where the 6th Division was drawn up on the heights of Ainhoe. Sergeant James Anton, waiting anxiously with the 42nd, could see little because of the mist, but from the increasing volume of noise it seemed likely that his battalion would not be kept waiting for much longer. As expected, when the mist lifted the light infantry was brought up to the edge of the wood just 100 yards short of the enemy's position. It was not long before shells were dropping through the trees to fall with disturbing accuracy among the closely packed ranks of the Highlanders. It took only a few such shells to convince the Colonel of the 42nd that, although "the trunks of trees might offer some resistance to cannon balls propelled horizontally, their leaves and branches afforded small protection against shells falling vertically," and he prudently moved his men to a safer site near the river.

After an uncomfortable period of enduring artillery fire without the opportunity of striking back, the Scots were at last ordered to advance in support of the Light Division. "It was an imposing spectacle," wrote Charles Cadell. "As far as the eye could reach, the masses of red jackets were seen moving to the points of the French lines in their immediate front. The cold and privation of the previous night were entirely forgotten."

Taking care to keep their muskets and powder pouches clear of the water, the men of the 42nd breasted the Nivelle and were soon actively engaged in driving the enemy pickets from their positions on the opposite bank. Ahead of them the sides of the mountain sparkled with muzzle flashes and the air reverberated with the dull boom of cannon.

Captain Blakeney, endeavouring to force a way through a tangle of brambles, was forced to call a halt in order to give his men a much-needed rest. After a short pause his men, now clear of the undergrowth, rushed forward with the regimental colour at their head. A discharge of grape met them and Blakeney stumbled and fell. A ball had shattered the bones in his leg. Propped up against a tree with shells and musket balls kicking up fragments of granite all around him, Blakeney urged his men forward until the noise of battle receded and he was able to crawl painfully down the slope in search of a surgeon.

Nowhere along the entire length of the five-mile front did Wellington's troops meet with a serious setback. Hill's division stormed and carried the heights of Ainhoe, while a force of British and Portuguese led by General Hamilton drove Darmagnac's forces from Espelette and forced Soult to order a retreat to a new position overlooking the Nive.

By mid-afternoon the outcome of the battle was beyond dispute. Three British Divisions, the 3rd, 6th and 7th, despite a heavy fire, had overcome every obstacle and the French were forced to withdraw, Clausel across the bridge at St. Pée and Soult to the neighbourhood of Bayonne. "It was one of the best contested fights I ever saw," enthused Cooke of the 43rd. "I considered myself no longer a recruit," stated James Anton. "I had now smelled the enemy's powder. . . . I had heard his bullets whistling past my ears, seen them dropping harmlessly at my feet and burrowing in the ground."

The next morning Commissary Henegan rode into the hills charged with recording the amount and nature of artillery captured from the French. Urging his horse along a steep path leading to a recently captured strongpoint, he found himself surrounded by Grenadiers who regarded him with some hostility. Gradually, as he conversed in fluent French, the atmosphere thawed and Henegan was invited to sample a flask of cognac. That this group had been actively engaged was evident from the number of unburied corpses. As the Commissary gazed about him, he noticed that several were bandaging their wounds, "whilst others sought relief from their injuries in bottles of alcohol". Close by one mortally wounded Grenadier a large poodle sat regarding its master with an expression of such devotion that Henegan was forced to turn away on the pretence of examining an unseated cannon.

In his tour of inspection, which embraced an area of some 30 square miles, Richard Henegan discovered 52 pieces of ordnance and a great quantity of ammunition. He also met a group of redcoats, who, had he questioned them, might have found it difficult to account for their movements so far from a military cantonment. Later that day he stumbled upon an isolated cottage where the body of a peasant farmer lay sprawled in the grass. The man had been clubbed to death and inside his home wrecked furniture and a young woman in a state of deshabillé, weeping bitterly, was enough for Henegan to attribute the atrocity to the group of redcoats he had passed a few hours earlier.

Chapter 19

CROSSING THE ADOUR

Early in November news of Napoleon's overwhelming defeat at Leipzig, culminating in his flight to Paris, had reached Wellington's headquarters at St. Jean-de-Luz, news which was indeed welcome, but, ironically, Napoleon's setback in northern Germany posed a problem for the allied advance in southern France. Marshal Soult, hoping to encourage the same degree of resistance to the allies as his divisions had encountered in Spain, took pains to spread propaganda among the civilian population to the effect that Wellington's soldiers were savages and would not hesitate to commit the most barbarous atrocities. But his attempt at promoting civil unrest proved less than successful, for, as one French villager was to explain to a British officer, "If the British soldier was terrible in the field, he was harmless enough when mixed with the people," a view endorsed by Colonel Bingham, who wrote: "On our entering France many of the inhabitants fled. They have now nearly all returned and, being for the moment relieved both from conscription and contribution, seem pleased with the change." "The French people returning are amazed at the bad opinion they entertained of us before our arrival," wrote Lieutenant Keep to his brother. "They have found their property safe, and now offer us all the comfort their homes can afford."

The most serious threat to Wellington's hope of winning over the civilian population came not from his own soldiers, but from the Portuguese and Spaniards. The men from these regiments, often on the pretence of obtaining supplies, scoured the outlying villages for plunder and a chance to revenge themselves for atrocities inflicted upon their own families by the French. Lieutenant Gleig of the 85th relates in his journal *The Subaltern* how, during a temporary halt in a village, a

Portuguese Company broke ranks and surged towards a group of cottages at the side of the road. Order was eventually established, but not before a musket shot and a piercing scream drew attention to the sudden appearance of a Cacadore from a cottage set apart from the rest. The man was quickly seized and, when questioned, readily confessed to the murder of one of the occupants. "He was quite unrepentant," reported Gleig, "explaining that he had taken an oath to kill the first French family he should encounter in revenge for the murder of his own parents."

Such acts were not so frequent among the Portuguese as they were among the Spanish troops and, in one particularly violent incident, Spanish malcontents sacked the village of Ascain, slaughtering most of the villagers. Lawless behaviour such as this could only serve to sabotage Wellington's good intentions and the Provost was instructed to bring to justice and hang any violator found guilty of such crimes. This tightening of discipline was immediately put into effect and the grim words of Major-General Edward Pakenham, "Let that scoundrel be hanged instantly," were enough to seal the fate of the accused even without a trial.

As a further safeguard in support of his policy to win over the civil population, Lord Wellington decided that, with the exception of Morillo's Division, all the other Spanish regiments were to be sent back across the Pyrenees, a move which enraged many of those whose only motive in accompanying Wellington was to avenge the barbaric treatment their countrymen had suffered at the hands of the French.

Commissary Auguste Schaumann remembered the mood in which the Spaniards took their leave: "They made a dreadful tumult as they marched away," he wrote. "The hatred of the English and particularly of Lord Wellington, who had them hanged whenever they robbed, manifested itself."

Unlike the Portuguese Cacadore regiments, who were respected by Wellington's soldiers, the Spanish troops had seldom found favour among the redcoats. "In their best days they were more like an armed mob than regularly organized soldiers," wrote Surtees, and George Simmons' opinion was scarcely more flattering: "We always know when the French are near – the Spaniards run away in every direction." Ensign Wheatley's diary entry for 29 November illustrates the strong feeling then prevailing: "A Spanish officer begged just now for a night's lodging in my room, which I refused for I hate a Spaniard more than a Frenchman."

On 9 December Hill's 2nd Division forded the Nive in two places close to the village of Cambo. "The French were under arms in a moment," wrote George Bell. "We took the stream, some killed and wounded went away with the current, for the French kept up a fire on us now, which was quite awful. We made good our footing on the right side, fought all day and, calling the roll at night, we found there were many widows."

With the loss of Wellington's Spanish divisions, the strength of the opposing armies was roughly equal and the next day, as Anglo-Portuguese columns continued to cross the Nive to advance along the coastal road from St. Jean-de-Luz, Marshal Soult ordered General Reille to counter-attack. The resultant savage encounter near Bidart against Sir John Hope's brigade helped Clausel to carry the plateau and march on Arcangues where he came up against General Hill's 2nd Division at St. Pierre d'Irrube. The French were in considerable strength and Lieutenant George Gleig, on a foray into the woods in the hope of bagging a hare for the pot, heard the noise of gunfire and hastened back to his bivouac as the crackle of musketry grew louder. The bugles had already called his battalion to arms and within a few minutes Gleig was marching with his Company towards the village of Arcangues. When the 1/85th breasted the hill Gleig was astonished to see that the red-coats were giving way to a mass of blue-coated infantry so dense that, in Gleig's eyes, they seemed to "cover the whole road as far as the eye could see".

Three divisions under Marshal Clausel, which had been skilfully concealed behind the trees and high hedgerows, had risen from cover to engage the Light Division north of the village. Some brisk skirmishing took place between the pickets and, as the light troops ran forward to lend support to the Green Jackets holding a line of trees bordering the road, Gleig's Company became embroiled with swarms of French tirailleurs intent upon wresting the wood from its British and Portuguese occupants. Initially caught by surprise, the allied troops quickly re-covered and, when darkness descended to bring an end to the fighting, small groups of skirmishers from each side became unavoidably inter-mixed in the blackness created by a dense mass of trees. Instead of the crackle of musketry, Gleig's ears were now assailed on every side by shouts and exclamations in a variety of tongues as British, Portuguese, Dutch, Germans and Frenchmen frantically sought to locate the where-abouts of their respective units.

As the first light of dawn began to filter through the trees Clausel resumed his attack, supported by a dozen cannon, in an attempt to force the position and reach St. Jean-de-Luz. Taking advantage of every scrap of cover, the tirailleurs met their British counterparts ahead of a column of infantry advancing to the beat of a drum. As the column approached the edge of the wood where the allied troops were drawn up in a double line the drummers increased their tempo until within a hundred yards, when the French raised a great shout of "*Vive l'Empereur*" and rushed towards them. Confident that his Cacadores would stand fast, Captain Bunbury was dismayed when, after an exchange of musket fire yards to his front, a mixed band of redcoats burst out of the mist to spread panic among his young soldiers. Unnerved by the sudden appearance of the French, many of the Portuguese threw down their arms and surrendered, but Bunbury had no wish to spend the rest of the war as a prisoner in Verdun and he ran for a gap in the trees as the advancing skirmishers peppered them with musket shots. Well in the rear and consequently an easy target, Bunbury was among the first to be struck down. A stab of pain lancing through the young officer's thigh brought him to a stumbling halt. Limping along and falling ever further behind, he was saved by the timely appearance of a squadron of 14th Light Dragoons who checked the flight of the panic-stricken redcoats by beating them about the head and shoulders with the flat of their swords, before riding on to engage the French. Fresh British troops were soon on the scene and, with the arrival of the Guards, Clausel's battalions were driven from Arcangues after a desperate struggle outside the village church.

Elsewhere, closer to the sea, General Sir John Hope was battling with three divisions against Reille's two infantry divisions and a brigade of Dragoons. At first the redcoats fared badly, with Campbell's brigade, and particularly the Portuguese, suffering severe losses from an enemy cavalry charge led by General Sparre. The battle raged for much of the day until Wellington arrived with reinforcements to blunt the impetus of Reille's attack.

For two days fortunes fluctuated as Soult endeavoured to prevent Wellington from encircling Bayonne. Then, on 13 December, as the morning mist lifted, massive French forces, outnumbering Hill's troops by as much as three to one, debouched from Bayonne to launch an assault on the three hills occupied by the Anglo-Portuguese battalions. Although the odds were very much in his favour, Soult was unable to outflank the British position and, after four hours of expensive frontal attacks, his battalions were forced to withdraw to their fortified lines between the Nive and the Adour.

In what was to be his last battle in the Peninsula, William Thornton Keep was wounded in the action around St. Pierre, a ball piercing the corner of his mouth, miraculously passing under his tongue to become lodged in his neck, fracturing his jawbone. "The consequence," wrote the young Ensign to his father, "has been an immense swelling, black as my hat, and frightfully disfiguring . . . the injury is not dangerous from the direction the ball took." Once the ball had been cut from Keep's neck, he went on to make a slow but full recovery from the injury.

For the next few weeks deteriorating weather conditions and the atrocious roads, which halted all but the lightest of baggage carts, severely restricted the movement of both armies. Marshal Soult seized the opportunity to strengthen his defences covering the approach to Bayonne, while Wellington's army withdrew to its winter quarters two miles from that city. Supplies were plentiful and Wellington's soldiers could look forward to a degree of comfort previously unknown in their mountain bivouacs.

Experience had taught the authorities that bivouacking in the open during inclement weather always resulted in increased sick returns, so for the winter of 1813 Wellington's men had been provided with tented accommodation. It was a move received with mixed feelings by many, for although canvas afforded greater protection than a roof of bracken, the soldiers were obliged to sleep fifteen to a tent and, in such crowded conditions, as James Anton discovered to his annoyance, late comers retiring for the night found it impossible not to stumble over their sleeping companions in the darkness.

During this period of inactivity, military life became almost tolerable. The French were surprisingly neighbourly and during daylight hours George Gleig, on a fishing trip, discovered that, providing he wore his red coat to establish his nationality, the French picket allowed him to cross to their side of the river and even pointed out where trout were to be found, an attitude of mind best summed up in a parting remark by a French officer to William Grattan: "We have met, and have been for some time friends," he said. "We are about to separate, and may meet as enemies. As 'friends' we received each other warmly – as 'enemies' we shall do the same."

Fraternization to this degree was perhaps an exception to the rule, but it was the festive season and for the first time in the war Wellington's soldiers were able to celebrate in some style. At Arcangues every man in Sergeant Cooper's battalion of the 7th Fusiliers contributed something towards a meal, whether it was a bottle of wine, a chicken or, in the case of the few who arrived empty-handed, some Spanish dollars. Several sheep were slaughtered and, to follow the main course of mutton, Cooper informs us that mince pies and puddings were baked. Apples made the rounds as a dessert and, to end the evening, the regimental band provided the music by which "many warmed their toes by dancing jigs and reels."

Apart from one or two minor skirmishes, the new year of 1814 found the armies passively facing each other, but then on 14 February Wellington began his new campaign by sending Hill to dislodge the

French from their positions on the Bidouze at St. Palaise, whilst General Hope with 30,000 troops was ordered to bridge the Adour and invest the city of Bayonne.

In mid-February the weather changed and for the next thirteen days the allies advanced steadily inland, forcing Soult to fall back on the high ground around Orthez to avoid being outflanked. This eastward thrust across the south of France, undertaken in conditions of drenching rain and sleet, was as arduous as any the Peninsula veterans could remember. After months of campaigning their tunics were threadbare and ragged from continual patching, but, although clothing could be repaired, the same could not be said for footwear and James Anton soon found himself marching barefoot over sharp stones. Fortunately for the footsore sergeant, the commissariat train was drawn by a team of bullocks and a timely issue of rawhide strips from cattle slaughtered on the road ensured that his discomfort was shortlived.

Towards the end of the month the weather, which had prevented large-scale military movements by either side, improved to the extent that Lord Wellington was able to see his plan for crossing the bar of the Adour come to fruition with the help of the Royal Navy. Bridging the Adour was notable for a remarkable feat of seamanship and engineering. Twenty-six hired coastal vessels were spaced uniformly across the 800 yards of tidal estuary and bound together with cables using ship's capstans. A platform of oak planks was then lashed to the two outer cables and the whole construction tensioned in such a way as to allow for the rise and fall of the Atlantic swells.

The first to cross were a detachment of Guards and the 60th Regiment, supported by forty artillerymen armed with 160 Congreve rockets. Some 1,200 Frenchmen moved quickly to repulse them, but, at a range of 300 yards, forty rockets, in a battery of ten abreast, were discharged, one salvo after another. Their effect upon the French was terrifying as can be appreciated from this description of their erratic path by the author of *The Bivouac*: "A twelve-pounder rocket laid on the ground and discharged without a tube by simply applying a match to the vent will run along the ground four or five hundred yards, seldom rising higher than a man's head; and, alternately rising and falling, will continue its course . . . and explode . . . scattering the seventy-two carbine balls, with which it was loaded, in all directions. . . . Should it strike against a stone it will bound off, and continue its terrible course."

The result of these repeated discharges was an immediate withdrawal of the French to the citadel in Bayonne, where they remained closely invested by Sir John Hope.

By the 23rd 15,000 troops of General Sir John Hope's command had crossed the Adour by means of the floating bridge to surround Bayonne, which obliged Marshal Soult to abandon the trapped garrison there and, in an attempt to stem Lord Wellington's relentless advance, take up a position a mile north-west of Orthez with 36,000 men and forty-eight cannon. Wellington had a numerical advantage in both men and artillery and he planned to attack Soult from three different directions. Cole's 4th division and Walker's 7th were to be sent against General Reille near the small village of St. Boes; the 3rd and 6th Divisions, together with the Light Division, were to combine in a frontal attack on General Droet d'Erlon at Orthez, while Beresford and Hill, assuming the other two assaults to be successful, would wheel in from Soult's left to cut Clausel's line of retreat.

Early in the morning of the 27th a turning operation by the 4th Division began with a brigade led by Colonel Ross, forcing the enemy to vacate a position they had held in a churchyard. As the fighting flared among the tombstones, the Scots of the 42nd formed a line, determined to drive Reille's battalions from St. Boes. The word to advance at the double was received with loud cheers by James Anton's Company. As they surged forward a ball plucked the bonnet from Sergeant Anton's head, but, showing a contemptuous disregard for the marksmen who had taken up positions behind loopholed walls and the windows of cottages, James Anton led a charge which scattered the French and put the Highlanders in possession of the village.

"No movement in the field is made with greater confidence of success than that of the charge," observed Anton later. "It affords little time for thinking, whilst it creates fearless excitement . . . strengthens every nerve, and drowns every fear of danger or of death."

Their hard-won success was short-lived, however, for Soult's artillery, coming to the aid of his tormented infantry, paved the way for a counter-attack which overran and captured the village's single street. General Sir Thomas Picton halted his column just out of artillery range, unable to advance and fulfil his role until Cole's Highlanders could regroup and drive the French from St. Boes.

The assault against Marshal Soult's right wing having stalled, Wellington revised his tactics by reinforcing Cole and sending the 3rd, 6th and 7th Divisions against the enemy's centre at Orthez, which allowed General Hill to cross the Gave de Pau and attack Soult's left flank. As Cole's and Walker's troops closed with the enemy they came under heavy fire from the guns of Soult's massed artillery and were forced to seek the cover of garden walls and the outlying buildings.

The 1/7th Fusiliers ran for the shelter promised by a nearby farmhouse, but the cannon balls and lead shot from bursting shells flying about the cobbled yard failed to dampen the spirits of the more incorrigible of Sergeant John Cooper's Company, for, while some Fusiliers kept up a retaliatory fire from the building, their comrades were actively engaged in seizing poultry for the pot. Others, breaking into the cellar, discovered a store of wine and spent the time in handing out copious draughts to the sweating and powder-blackened fighting troops.

At midday, after Hill had succeeded in turning Taupin's flank, the French began to give ground. Eventually, unable to contain the 6th and 7th Divisions pressing against his centre and fearing that his line of retreat to Toulouse would be cut, Marshal Soult ordered a general withdrawal eastward. His men had fought bravely, convincingly demonstrated by the many corpses on the plain above Orthez.

The French "had fought very obstinately," wrote George Simmons, adding as an afterthought, "Every cock ought to fight better upon its own dunghill."

A soldier of the 88th, noticing that a dead Frenchman bore the same colour facings and regimental number as his own, turned to Captain Ross-Lewin and remarked in astonishment, "Sun burnt me Sorr! But the frog-eaters have Connaught Rangers too."

The battle for Orthez had been a hard-won victory, with British killed and injured amounting to very nearly 2,000 men, including Lord Wellington who had sustained a bruised thigh from the impact of a spent musket ball. The French total of 4,000 killed, wounded or taken prisoner might well have been greater but for the fact that the ground was unsuitable for Wellington's cavalry. "Walked over the fields," read an entry in Wheatley's diary. "Full of dead. Saw horrible sights. Horrid trade."

Unlike Vittoria, there was little booty to be had and it was sheer fatigue that prevented the redcoats from following the French in close pursuit.

March began with heavy rain which turned fields into quagmires, causing carts to sink to their axle hubs in the atrocious rutted roads, which greatly impeded Wellington in his advance south-eastwards. The spent musket ball, which had struck the scabbard of his sword leaving a painful bruise, troubled Wellington for several days. He could only ride with discomfort and, as none of his lieutenants had the temerity to act without orders, Soult's demoralized battalions were allowed to continue their retreat along the right bank of the Adour without further molestation, reaching Toulouse three days before Wellington. However the weather, which had affected the allied advance, also slowed the progress of Soult's inexperienced conscripts bringing up the rear and

Tarbes fell to Sir Rowland Hill's forces on the 20th after a short but fierce encounter.

That night George Bell slept in a bedroom in Tarbes adorned with damask draperies, gilded mirrors and polished furniture. It was the first time the Ensign had slept in a bed since the occupation of Madrid.

The civilian population in that part of France, in common with a good proportion of Soult's conscripted soldiers, had long since lost their enthusiasm for the Bonaparte cause and the appearance of a British regiment marching through the streets was greeted everywhere with cries of "*Vive les Anglais!*" and demonstrations of loyalty to the Bourbons.

In Bordeaux, which Beresford's troops had entered on 12 March, the city's officials ripped the tricolour from their hats to replace it with the white cockade, exclaiming, "Long live the King. Long live the English".

Earlier, one hundred miles to the south at Bayonne, an uneasy truce which had existed between the French garrison and the besieging British forces since the middle of February was about to come to an end in a bloody confrontation. On 23 February, covered by a demonstration to engage the attention of the garrison, General Sir John Hope was ordered to establish a bridgehead across the Adour just west of the city and seize the outlying suburb of St. Etienne.

The 85th did not have an active role to play in the operation and Lieutenant Gleig, gazing across the broad waters of the Adour from a position on the sandhills, had a grandstand view of General Sir John Hope's attack. Clearly visible to him were the Portuguese Cacadores and riflemen of the King's German Legion spreading across a meadow and advancing upon a lengthy hedgerow behind which grey-coated infantry men, readily identified as French from their hairy brown goatskin knapsacks, waited to receive them.

George Gleig watched as the riflemen, running from tree to tree, paused to fire as and when the opportunity arose, while muzzle flashes and a drifting patch of white smoke rising above the hedge indicated that the voltigeurs were unwilling to retire without making a fight of it. Further afield, a crackle of musketry, punctuated by heavier explosions, betrayed the fact that Hope's troops were being hotly engaged in a bid to capture the suburb of St. Etienne. After little more than an hour Gleig became aware of a thinning in the ranks of the French troops holding the high ground above the town. A tangle of hedges and a screen of trees hid the attackers from his immediate view, but a lull in the fighting and the sight of a regimental colour streaming in the breeze was enough to convince the young lieutenant that St. Etienne had fallen to General Hill's division.

It had been a short but bloody encounter in which British losses had been twice those of the French, but Hill had reason enough to feel satisfaction. Bayonne was now completely encircled and at the mercy of Wellington's army.

Chapter 20

'NO MORE FIGHTING, LADS. NOW FOR OUR HOMES, WIVES AND SWEETHEARTS'

Having occupied Tarbes and Bordeaux, and encircled Bayonne in a ring of iron, Wellington began preparations for a final drive against Soult at Toulouse. Toulouse, a walled city with a population of some 50,000, had long been an important supply base for the Napoleonic armies and an assembly point for the conscripted regiments. It was effectively protected on its western side by the Garonne River which curved between the city and its suburb of St. Cyprien, and to the north and east by the Languedoc Canal, leaving only the southern wall of the city vulnerable to attack. The key to its capture lay to the east from an area known as the Heights of Calvinet, for if Wellington's troops could gain possession of this 600-foot-high ridge overlooking the city's eastern quarter siege artillery would rapidly render Toulouse untenable.

Lord Wellington began his operation on 5 April with a pontoon bridge being floated across the Garonne allowing 19,000 men from Beresford's contingent to cross to the opposite bank unopposed. Unfortunately, before the operation could be completed, the bridge was threatened by rising flood waters, leaving the engineers with little alternative but to dismantle it before the pontoons were swept away. Beresford's troops were thus marooned within sight of the 42,000-man garrison with a fast-flowing river at their rear. Incredibly, Soult neglected to take the opportunity of attacking while the odds were in his favour and, when challenged by one of his Generals, is reported to have replied, "You do not know what stuff two British divisions are made of. They would not be conquered so long as there was a man left to stand."

Beresford's men remained in their isolated and dangerous position for more than 24 hours until the flood waters had abated sufficiently to allow the pontoons to be floated at Croix d'Aurade, enabling General Manuel Freire's Spanish Corps to join them on the east bank.

The pontoon bridge was now taken up-river to facilitate Hill's posting with the 2nd Division to the west in front of St Cyprien. Sir Thomas Picton, with the 3rd and Light Divisions, was to cross the Languedoc Canal for a series of feint attacks against the city's northern side, while Beresford, with his strengthened divisions, was ordered to take them behind the Heights of Calvinet in preparation for an assault on the city from the east.

The battle for Toulouse began on Easter Sunday, 10 April, at 5.00am with a diversionary attack against General Reille at St Cyprien, while cavalry of the K.G.L swept along the east bank of the canal forcing a company of tirailleurs to seek the shelter of the city's wall. In the north Picton's 3rd Division and the Light Division became embroiled in heavy fighting around the Jumeaux Bridge over the canal and, in a reckless assault against an almost impregnable position, his troops were driven back repeatedly with heavy losses.

Further east, the main thrust against the Calvinet Heights began with a difficult march by the 4th and 6th Divisions across two miles of heavy, wet clay which reduced progress to a crawl and the passage of artillery almost to a halt. While the redcoats struggled through the heavy mud to their allotted position, two Spanish divisions waited impatiently for the signal to begin their attack. The mission given to General Manuel Freire's Galicians was the capture of a redoubt at the northern end of the Calvinet known as the Monte Rave, and the signal that would launch them against this strong position was to be the opening shot of a cannonade by Beresford's artillery, once his troops had reached a position where they could support the Spaniards.

In columns of three Beresford's men advanced towards their turning point a mile south of the Spaniards, as roundshot whirred through the air to fall with a splash into the river behind them. In his desperation that his own guns would never be able to get within range of the Monte Rave, the British General ordered the gun teams to manhandle their cannon to the top of a hill where they could at least silence the nearest French battery. Beresford's decision was to have tragic consequences for the Spaniards, who, hearing the discharge from his artillery, believed that the British General was in position to begin the main assault and so charged towards the redoubt unsupported by the 4th and 6th Divisions. Driving back a screen of voltigeurs to within sixty yards of the objective, they then encountered such withering artillery fire from the Calvinet that before long the air became fouled with dense black smoke and fountains of liquid mud tossed up by the bursting shells. The confused and deafened survivors fled to the shelter of a sunken road whence they refused to advance any further. Unhappily for them, the sunken road was vulnerable to enfilade fire and, faced by a discharge of grape from two mountain

212

guns and musketry from marksmen who had left the stronghold to target the helpless Spaniards, Freire's men threw away their muskets and poured back down the slope in a panic-stricken rout.

"They turned about and fled like chaff before the wind, amid the volume and dense clouds of rolling smoke . . . as if to veil from the enemy the great extent of their triumph," observed Captain John Cooke of the 43rd Regiment.

Lord Wellington, who had observed the débâcle through his telescope, turned in astonishment to an aide. "There they go, by God! Damn me if I ever saw ten thousand men run a race before!"

A regiment of Cantabrian Tiradores were the one exception, for, despite the devastating accuracy with which the French gunners plied the area with shot and shell, they remained at their post until ordered to withdraw.

The Spanish attack had failed dismally and at the northern end of the heights Beresford was coming under increasing pressure from the Imperial Guard of General Taupin's division. For a short time it seemed that Anson's and Lambert's brigades would be thrown back in disorder, but it was then that General Eloi Taupin committed a tactical blunder which had punished many a French battalion in earlier confrontations with the British and which was to cost him his life. Instead of deploying in line, he advanced with his entire force in close order column, presenting the redcoats with a target they could not miss. Roundshot and grape decimated the tightly packed brigades and, to add to the confusion, a battery of Congreve rockets was discharged to weave a fiery path through the French ranks.

"The rockets on the sandhills were discharged with terrific effect," wrote Captain Batty, "killing several men and blazing through it [the column] with the greatest violence."

"I had never before seen this rocket charge and I have never either since," confessed Sergeant William Lawrence. "By all appearance it was most successful."

The employment of this weapon in the field was entirely novel to the French and the noisy missiles tracing a twisting fiery trail before exploding to release dozens of musket balls caused Taupin's terrified troops to scatter in dismay. A sergeant of Grenadiers afterwards confessed to Gleig that, although he had been engaged in more than twenty battles, he had never experienced fear to the same degree as that day when a rocket passed harmlessly through his knapsack. "Such was the violence with which it flew that I fell upon my face, not stunned, but stupefied," confessed the Frenchman, "so frightful was the hissing sound which the missile sends forth in its progress."

Commented Lieutenant Gleig: "It [the rocket] skips and starts about from place to place in so strange a manner that the chances are, when you are running to the right or left to get out of the way, that you run directly against it; hence the absolute rout which a fire of ten or twelve rockets can create."

The brigades of Anson and Lambert were quick to take advantage of the confusion and as the French fell back the redcoats pressed forward with added vigour. General Taupin, struck by three musket balls as he endeavoured to rally his men, fell mortally wounded and with his demise the demoralized French withdrew down the reverse slope of the hill. Beresford's divisions were now in possession of one half of the Calvinet Heights and, following a halt to allow the artillery to come up, the light companies advanced towards the second line of earthworks.

Further south, the 61st Foot was reeling beneath a hail of grape, but the 42nd, impatient of delay, pressed forward, their path littered with heaps of tartan-clad dead and wounded. Such was the storm of lead that met them that a musket ball tore the halberd from Sergeant Anton's grasp and he felt the wind of another fan his face, while a third struck the hilt of his claymore and a fourth plucked the bonnet from his head.

Immediately in front of Lieutenant Malcom a soldier struck by a roundshot was splattered into an unrecognizable mess of flesh and bone. As the officer stared at the grisly remains in a state of shock, he felt a blow "as if from a huge club". John Malcom was barely conscious of the two Frenchmen rifling his pockets as he lay on the ground.

Plunging through the swirling clouds of smoke, the surviving Highlanders leapt into the earthworks and, after a few frantic minutes of hand-to-hand fighting, they drove the enemy out of the redoubt at the point of the bayonet.

"In a minute every obstacle was surmounted," wrote James Anton; "the enemy fled as we leaped over the trenches and mounds like a pack of noisy hounds in pursuit, frightening them more by our wild hurrahs than actually hurting them by ball or bayonet."

When Lieutenant Malcom recovered his senses sufficiently enough to look about him, two officers and sixty other ranks were all that were left from the right wing of his regiment. The battle flag of the 42nd, streaked with the blood of three successive standard bearers, lay against a wall, while on every side red- and blue-bonneted corpses bore grim testimony to the savagery of the fighting. As he sat contemplating this human wreckage of the conflict, Sergeant Anton found himself wondering whether "the spirits of these late enemies soared in friendship, sank in hatred, or whether every remembrance was annihilated in death".

By mid-afternoon the Calvinet was entirely in British hands, the French having retired with their artillery across the canal to seek refuge behind the walls of Toulouse.

While the Highlanders of the 42nd and the Camerons of the 79th were consolidating their gains, fresh reserves from Hill's Corps had reached the city and were battling their way through the suburbs of Toulouse. In a bloody bout of street fighting Soult's troops strenuously defended each barricade and many an unsuspecting redcoat fell victim to a concealed marksman. Lieutenant George Bell had a near brush with death. When walking down a long narrow street without an enemy in sight a musket ball whistled past his head so close that he felt the wind of it fan his cheek.

By late evening the fighting had slackened to little more than local skirmishes as Marshal Soult retired from Toulouse to Carcassonne, while Wellington, awaiting further supplies of ammunition and reluctant to add further to the 4,600 casualties he had already sustained, refused to cross the canal in pursuit of the beaten enemy.

The next morning, in the grey light of dawn, a detachment led by Lieutenant Bell cautiously felt its way through the now deserted streets and across a handsome stone bridge towards the great iron gates giving access to the walled city. The few citizens who were about at that early hour on 12 April quickly forced the heavy locks and young George Bell had the honour of being the first British officer to enter Toulouse, with the one exception of a Briton who had earlier been taken prisoner.

Later visitors were to witness the destruction of edifices and emblems of the Napoleonic years by a mob clamouring for the restoration of the Bourbon monarchy. Surgeon Walter Henry was not impressed and was outraged to see a particularly fine statue of Napoleon Bonaparte shatter when it toppled to the ground. "What a spectacle," he complained bitterly. "A crowd of wretches, who would have sunk into the very earth at the frown of the living man but two short weeks before, were now perpetrating this brutal indignity on the beautiful sculpture of Canova."

News travelled slowly and Wellington's soldiers marching through the city streets with drums beating and colours flying were largely unaware that two weeks earlier Paris had fallen, forcing Napoleon to abdicate at Fontainebleau.

"A strong rumour about peace prevailed," commented Ensign Close, "which gained ground everywhere." Welcome though such rumours were, Edmund Wheatley's thoughts were more concerned with personal comfort, and, after days of trudging over rutted roads and through quagmires, he was at last able to record: "I undressed for the first time in seven weeks." Whatever credence was given to the rumours of peace,

Ensigns Wheatley and Close were almost certainly ignorant of the fact that the battle in which they had recently been engaged had been fought three days after the ratification of a peace treaty and that thousands had perished needlessly.

Lord Wellington was informed of the news within an hour of entering the city. He was said to have exclaimed, "You don't say so! Pon my honour!", and allowed himself to spin on his heel while clicking his fingers.

After six difficult and bloody years, the war in the Peninsula was over, but unhappily the killing was not. At Bayonne the siege was in its tenth week when a report of Napoleon's abdication on 4 April was communicated to the French officers in the picket line by General Sir John Hope. The Governor, General Pierre Thouvenot, was a loyal Bonapartist and the news of the fall of his hero coming from an enemy source was, he thought, based merely on rumour. In fact Thouvenot had reasons of his own for rejecting Hope's tidings, for he was even then planning to strike a damaging blow against the besieging force. That the garrison was under arms and likely to make a sortie had been confirmed only the previous day by two deserters, but Major-General Andrew Hay, whose family had recently joined him from England, was unconvinced and his visit to the picket lines that evening was afterwards remembered for his optimistic prediction: "No more fighting my lads," he had said, "now for our homes, wives and sweethearts."

The siege had been conducted in a leisurely fashion from the very beginning and, with the news of Napoleon's downfall, vigilance was relaxed even further. Although experience had taught the redcoats that a careless exposure was likely to bring a musket ball about their ears, few believed that any blood would be spilled pending official confirmation of the peace treaty. It was with the greatest astonishment, then, that Lieutenant George Gleig and his fellow officers in the 85th were awakened in the early hours of 14 April by the sound of heavy firing.

In the picket lines those alerted by the single discharge of a musket by a surprised sentry barely had time to rub the sleep from their eyes before being run through by a French bayonet. The outlying pickets were quickly overcome by Thouvenot's men and within a few minutes of the break-out the 6,000-strong garrison had cleared the streets of St Etienne of British soldiers, save for a Company of the 38th who had taken refuge in the church. Fortunately for them and Captain Forster, there was only one entrance, which was quickly barricaded so that only one person at a time could gain admittance. Although cut off and surrounded, the men of the 38th resisted every attempt by the French to take the church, which was soon to become the focal point of an allied counter-attack.

Immediately upon the alarm being raised, Sir John Hope and General Hay had hurried to the scene, unaware that St Etienne was in the possession of the French. They were not to know that they were riding into a dangerous situation, for Thouvenot's men had flooded into the suburbs and were busily rolling up the pickets which had been cut off in the initial breakout. Walking wounded were passing on their way to the hospital as the two Generals and their escort of Lancers spurred their mounts along a sunken road towards the sound of musketry. Before the group had even reached the outskirts of St Etienne French soldiers were to be seen approaching on both sides of the road and, caught off guard in the dim light, the escort barely had time to pull their horses round before a volley of shots brought down Sir John and his horse. The Lancers, alarmed by the sudden appearance of the French, wheeled about in dismay, leaving the General pinned by his leg beneath the dead body of his horse. It fell to the Adjutant, Captain William Herries of the 9th Dragoons, to dismount in an attempt to free him, but it was too late. Sir John Hope, who was further wounded in the foot from a shot by an English picket, was taken into Bayonne, together with Herries and an aide, as prisoners of the French.

Following this incident the 1st and 2nd Brigade of Guards were quickly on the scene and, with the 3rd Battalion following up, were ordered to regain the sunken road and drive the enemy from the field in its rear, an operation which ultimately proved successful.

Meanwhile Captain Forster and his Company of the 38th were still firmly in possession of the church, although under increasing pressure and suffering casualties from the persistent sniping of the attackers.

"The smashing of the windows from the balls together with the thunder of the cannon in a peaceable room like a church," observed Edmund Wheatley, "quite bewildered me."

Burning houses cast a lurid glare on the scene and the smoke-filled streets resounded to the explosions of muskets and the cries of the combatants, as, in the darkness and confusion, various groups fired on each other as well as the enemy. Against strengthening opposition, the Guards battled their way through the suburbs using bayonet, sword or the butt end of a musket in frequent encounters in which quarter was neither asked or given.

Around the church the fighting reached a pitch of ferocity reminiscent of Albuera and in the space of less than an hour a brass cannon in the churchyard was taken and lost on no less than six occasions. Towards the end of the action the moon rose to disclose a frightful scene of slaughter. In the churchyard and around the cannon corpses were piled in heaps. A French artilleryman, his head cloven to the jaw, lay across the gun's barrel still grasping a sponging staff. In a semicircle around him lay the bodies of several redcoats whose skulls had been smashed from the blows of a blunt instrument.

Only after daybreak did the Guards and a brigade of the King's German Legion, pressing in from each side, finally drive the garrison back behind the walls of Bayonne, where General Thouvenot, after accepting Marshal Soult's instructions to cease hostilities and recognize the Bourbons, finally surrendered his sword on 26 April.

The conflict had been of relatively short duration, just three hours, but in that time more than 800 British troops had become casualties. The sunken road and the cobbled streets of St Etienne were so covered with the dead and wounded and so intermixed that Lieutenant Gleig found it difficult to estimate the number. Entering the church, he discovered the body of General Hay who had been shot while directing a counter-attack. He had paid with his life for his misguided belief that hostilities were over pending official confirmation and that therefore caution could be relaxed.

Several hundred Frenchmen had also fallen victim, but when the British officers expressed their regret at the needless loss of life the French contemptuously brushed aside their commiserations with the comment, "*Une petite promenade de militaire*".

An official end to the war was declared on 27 April when the British celebrated Bonaparte's defeat in time-honoured fashion.

"Joy beamed on every face, and made the tongue eloquent," wrote Thomas Pococke. "We sang and drank that whole night."

Many French soldiers, resenting the celebrations, made no attempt to disguise the misery they felt at the fall of their idol. British officers, who were obliged for their own safety to enter Bayonne in groups, discovered that friendly overtures were met with coldness and an air of bitter resentment. No longer did the wartime spirit of soldierly camaraderie exist which had once permitted George Gleig to wade across a disputed stream with his rod and line as an enemy picket watched his progress with interest, but it was perhaps some consolation to Gleig and his comrades that, in sharp contrast to the military, a cordial welcome was extended to them by the civil population of southern France. Food and wine were cheap and plentiful and the novelty of a strange uniform, especially the kilt, was sufficient to attract the attention of a host of pretty girls.

Wrote one young Ensign: "Our entry and reception in Toulouse was something magnificent; the whole population seemed seized with a sudden passion for the Bourbons and the English. From every window in the town the white flag or some other emblem of loyalty was exhibited in the shape of flags or carpets, in shawls or even sheets."

The transformation in their fortunes was endorsed by Captain

Blakeney: "Our army might now be said to live in clover," enthused the officer from the 28th Regiment. "We had good rations, and the wines of the country were both pleasant and cheap."

Within a few days of the débâcle at Bayonne Napoleon took leave of his Old Guard and departed for exile on the island of Elba. He was to remain in captivity for almost ten months until, learning of the rising tide of discontent with the rule of the restored Bourbons, he evaded a cordon of British frigates to land with a dedicated group of supporters on French soil on 1 March 1815. The rest is history. Within weeks of his defeat at Waterloo he was again a prisoner, this time aboard the *Bellerophon* on a long sea journey to St. Helena in the South Atlantic, there to remain until his death in 1821.

In later years Napoleon was to acknowledge that his 'Spanish Ulcer', as he termed the war in the Peninsula, had played a major part in his downfall. The inadvisability of undertaking a campaign in Russia before his Generals had subdued the Spanish people and wrested the Peninsula from the British was emphasized by a General who was an aide-de-camp to Marshal André Masséna. Referring to the war in Spain, General Baron de Marbot wrote in his memoirs: "I am convinced that Napoleon in the end would have established his brother triumphantly on the throne of Spain if he had been content to finish this war before going to Russia. The Peninsula received no support, save from England, and England, in spite of the recent success of her armies, was so exhausted by the incessant demands of men and money for the Peninsula that the House of Commons was on the point of refusing the necessary subsidies for a new campaign. But at the moment of our return from Portugal rumours had got about of the design formed by Napoleon of attacking Russia at home, and the English Parliament authorized the continuance of the war."

Now that it was all over after more than six years at a cost to the Treasury of £100 million sterling, Britain's magnificent Peninsular army was considered surplus to requirements. Veterans of many bloody encounters with the French on the sun-baked plains of Andalusia or in the chilly mists of the Pyrenees soon found themselves on crowded transports bound for America, there to face an equally skilful enemy in the bayous of Louisiana. Others, less fortunate, sailed on what was to become, for many, a disease-ridden existence in the fever islands of the East or West Indies. The more fortunate were transported across France to the ports of Calais or Bordeaux through a countryside untouched by war on the first stage of their return to England. Surgeon Walter Henry was happy to be numbered among them: "We left our pleasant quarters near Toulouse on 3 June, to march to Bordeaux, there to embark for England," he wrote. "The marches were short – the inhabitants overwhelmingly civil and we had a ball every night."

Many of the returning veterans harboured feelings which savoured more of apprehension than elation. The average young subaltern's adult life had been one of active campaigning, but the chief topic of conversation on the voyage home was not so much of past battles but of future prospects.

"What on earth did soldiers do in peacetime?" wondered Johnny Kincaid. At best, all he could expect was to be allowed to continue his career on half-pay, and in this respect the officers were considerably better off than the men they had commanded. The ordinary soldier was faced with the bleak prospect of a discharge on a meagre pension with little or no prospect of employment. Sergeant James Hale was perhaps more fortunate in that he was admitted to Chelsea Hospital on a pension of nine pence a day. There was to be no campaign medal to commemorate his years of duty in the Peninsula, for it was not until 1848 that the Military General Service Medal was struck, by which time most of the veterans of Portugal and Spain were no longer on the scene.

In their campaigning years numerous redcoats had formed close relationships with the women of the country and these ladies had shown a remarkable degree of loyalty in sharing the dangers and vicissitudes of their menfolk. At the end of hostilities many of them accompanied their partners to the embarkation ports, together with their children, hoping to be allowed to board the transports, but inevitably they were doomed to disappointment. As William Grattan remarked: "There was much weeping and wailing on the part of the signoras". It was an inviolable rule that only six men in a company of one hundred were permitted to marry, with their wives being taken on the ration strength of the regiment, and the authorities absolutely refused to recognize any other form of co-habitation. Now many of the women, pregnant and almost all destitute, faced a long and arduous journey back to a Catholic home with, at best, an uncertain future and, at worst, the trauma of being driven from the family abode in disgrace. The soldiers, to their credit, did their best to alleviate the women's hardship by raising a small subscription, despite themselves being seven months in arrears of pay. Money, however, could not compensate for severed bonds of affection and, as the vessels put out to sea, a sound which haunted many of Wellington's redcoats for the duration of the voyage drifted after them – the anguished cries of the women and children deserted on the quayside.

Lord Wellington reached Paris on 4 May to great acclaim and to a dukedom on his return to England. There were few criticisms of the Duke's conduct during his campaigning years and perhaps John Mills' opinion was coloured by his experiences during the retreat from Burgos, when he wrote: "You must know that our Noble Marquis is not gifted with much feeling – ambition hardens the heart. He only regards the comforts of his men as far as it is actually necessary to his purposes; all have their faults and this is his."

The men whose gallantry had done much to liberate the peoples of the Peninsula and restore tranquillity to France were left with only the memories of their victories. John Harris, thinking back on his adventures as a Rifleman, wrote: "The field of death and slaughter was no bad place to judge men." Reminiscing in his shoemaker's shop in Soho over the six years which he considered the most memorable of his life, he recalled "comrades long mouldered to dust, I see again performing the acts of heroes".

In achieving those acts the cost in human suffering had been immense. Forty thousand British soldiers were left behind in unmarked graves, 200,000 Frenchmen had suffered a similar fate or had been wounded or taken prisoner by Wellington's troops. Many thousands had been butchered by the guerrillas in Spain or Portugal. The people of those countries, however, had paid an equally stiff price for their freedom. Hundreds of thousands had been killed, many towns reduced to rubble and the economy of each country had been brought almost to the point of collapse. In contrast to Spain and France, which were to be plagued with political unrest for years, Britain emerged from the conflict as the leading military power in Europe with increased prestige and the benefits of a stable government.

At his final confrontation with Napoleon Bonaparte the Duke did not have the advantage of his Peninsula veterans, many of whom had been campaigning in America, where they were instrumental in burning the White House, or garrisoning overseas possessions. Waterloo, the last battle of Wellington's military career, was followed by forty years of peace in Europe during which time the army was allowed to stagnate, due in large measure to the Duke's opposition to any form of growth or development in military affairs, but the earlier victories of his magnificent Peninsula soldiers and his victory at Waterloo enabled a succession of British foreign ministers, Castlereagh in 1814 at the Congress of Vienna and, later, Canning and Palmerston, to play a significant role in the expansion of an Empire without equal and the envy of most other European nations.

There is little evidence to show that the Duke of Wellington ever acknowledged that his fame and success was due in large measure to the men he commanded, but perhaps the thought was with him when, shortly after Waterloo, he was asked by the War Office to suggest a name by which the common soldier might be typified on an Army document shortly to be drafted. The Iron Duke considered for a moment, his memory ranging back over the many battles he had fought in India,

Portugal, Spain and France. One incident came to mind and he recalled an occasion during one of his earlier campaigns when he had paused to speak to a mortally wounded redcoat, a veteran from his own Regiment, the 33rd Foot. He recalled the man's name. "Thomas Atkins," replied the Duke. "Let it be Thomas Atkins."

SELECT BIBLIOGRAPHY

James Anton.	*Retrospect of a Military Life.*	1841.
George Bell.	*Rough Notes by an Old Soldier.* (2 Vols.)	1867.
Charles Boothby.	*Under England's Flag.*	1900.
Robert Blakeney.	*A Boy in the Peninsula War.*	1899.
Thomas Bunbury.	*Reminiscences of a Veteran.*	1861.
Charles Cadell.	*Narrative of the Campaigns of the 28th Regiment.*	1835.
John Cooke.	*Memoirs of the Late War.*	1831.
Edward Costello.	*Adventures of a Soldier.*	1841.
John Cooper.	*Rough Notes of Seven Campaigns.*	1869.
Joseph Donaldson.	*The Eventful Life of a Soldier.*	1827.
George Gleig.	*The Subaltern.*	1825.
Alexander Gordon.	*Recollections of Thirty-nine Years in the Army.*	1898.
William Grattan.	*Adventures with the Connaught Rangers.*	1847.
John Green.	*The Vicissitudes of a Soldier's Life. 1806–1815.*	1827.
John Harris.	*Recollections of Rifleman Harris.*	1848.
William Hay.	*Reminiscences Under Wellington.*	1901.
Philip Haythornthwaite.	*The Armies of Wellington.*	1998.
Richard Henegan.	*Seven Years Campaigning.*	1846.
William Thornton Keep.	*In the Service of the King.* The Letters of William Thornton Keep at Home, Walcheren, and In the Peninsula. (Ed. Ian Fletcher)	1997.
Robert Knowles.	*The War in the Peninsula.* Some Letters of Lieutenant Robert Knowles.	1913.
John Kincaid.	*Random Shots From a Rifleman.*	1835.
	Adventures in the Rifle Brigade.	1830.
Jonathan Leach.	*Rough Sketches of the Life of an Old Soldier.*	1831.
Joseph Lehmann.	*Remember you are an Englishman.*	1977.
William Lawrence.	*The Autobiography of Sergeant William Lawrence.*	1886.
John Mills.	*For King and Country.* The Letters and Diaries of John Mills. Coldstream Guards. 1811–1814. (Ed. Ian Fletcher)	1995.
Charles Napier.	*Life and Opinions of Sir Charles James Napier.*	1857.
John Patterson.	*The Adventures of Captain Patterson.*	1837.

Roger Parkinson.	*The Peninsular War.*	1973.
Joseph Moyle-Sherer.	*Recollections of the Peninsula.*	1823.
George Simmons.	*A British Rifleman.*	1899.
Harry Smith.	*The Autobiography of Sir Harry Smith.*	1910.
Auguste Schaumann.	*On the Road with Wellington.*	1924.
William Surtees.	*Twenty-five Years in the Rifle Brigade.*	1833.
William Tomkinson.	*The Diary of a Cavalry Officer in the Peninsula and Waterloo Campaigns.*	1894.
William Warre.	*Letters from the Peninsula.*	1909.
William Wheeler.	*The Letters of Private Wheeler.* (Ed. B.N. Liddell Hart)	1951.

INDEX

Abrantes, 24, 25, 57, 62, 67, 68, 135
Adur, River, 204, 206, 207, 208, 209
Agueda, River, 102, 128, 139, 134
Albuera, 114, 121, 122, 135, 140, 217
Alexander, Tzar, 1
Almarez, 60, 76, 78, 147
Almeida, 24, 26, 62, 81, 82, 91, 99, 101,
    102, 103, 104, 110, 111, 112
Anson, Maj-Gen. George, 185, 186, 213,
    214
Anstruther, Brig-Gen. Robert, 16, 17, 26
Anton, Sergeant James, 10, 198, 199, 205,
    206, 207, 214
Astorga, 28, 31, 35, 47

Badajoz, 24, 60, 77, 79, 103, 113, 122, 124,
    132, 133, 135; storming of, 137, 139,
    141, 142, 143, 145, 146, 192
Baird, Gen. Sir David, 24, 25, 27, 28, 29,
    37, 55
Barossa, 94, 95, 96, 98
Bayonne, 1, 26, 168, 177, 181, 182, 199,
    207, 219; besieged, 204, 205, 209, 210,
    211, 216, 217, 218
Bell, Ensign George, 11, 63, 75, 128; at
    Badajos, 143; at Vitoria, 176; at
    Sorauren, 183, 187; ?????, 167, 181,
    202, 209, 215
Bembibre, 37, 39
Benevente, 28, 33, 34, 35
Beresford, Gen. William Carr, 26, 62, 63,
    64, 66, 77, 91, 103; at Albuera, 113,
    114, 116, 117, 118, 120, 121, 122, 149,
    197, 207, 212, 213; and troops, 198,
    209, 211, 214
Berthier, Marshal Louis-Alexandre, 28
Bessières, Marshal Jean-Baptiste, 27, 102,
    106
Betanzos, 46, 47

Bidassoa, River, 2, 180, 181, 182, 184, 187,
    188, 193, 195
Bingham, Maj. George Ridout, 164, 178
Bonaparte, Joseph, 68, 69, 70, 71, 74, 93,
    156, 157, 158, 168, 167, 178; at Vitoria,
    170, 172, 176, 177, 178; and troops,
    161, 163, 166, 169, 180, 181
Bonaparte, Napoleon, 1, 2, 3; and Spain, 4,
    26, 27, 30, 34, 35, 38, 51, 59, 60, 80,
    112, 131, 179, 181, 193, 201, 215; and
    Russia, 146, 165; abdication, 216, 218,
    219, 221
Bonnet, Gen. Pierre Françoise, 150, 153,
    154; is wounded, 155
Boothby, Captain Charles, 25, 26, 27, 35,
    53, 57, 66, 71; is wounded, 77
Bragge, Lieut William, 63, 159, 164
Brown, Colonel, 95, 96, 98
Bugeaud, Lieut Thomas, 3
Bunbury, Ensign Thomas, 57, 65, 71, 72,
    95, 97, 98, 204
Burgos, 27, 28, 155, 157, 158, 159, 160,
    161, 163, 167, 220
Burrard, Lt-Gen. Sir Harry, 14, 15, 18, 19
Busaco, 84, 87, 89

Cadell, Maj. Charles, 37, 39, 43, 44, 198
Cadiz, 93, 94, 95, 98, 114, 165
Campbell, Gen. Alexander, 104
Castanos, Gen. Don Francisco, 22, 27, 28,
    114
Castello Branco, 24
Ciudad Rodrigo, 24, 26, 27; falls to
    Massena, 80, 81, 82, 102, 103, 104,
    110, 112, 124, 125; besieged, 127, 128,
    133, 135, 142, 146, 148, 161, 163, 165,
    192

Clausel, Gen. Bertrand, 153, 154, 155, 157, 158, 165, 182, 184, 185, 186, 199, 203, 204, 207

Close, Ensign Edward, 116, 120, 215, 216

Coa, River, 104, 107, 126

Coimbra, 24, 64, 83, 84, 87, 89

Colbert, Gen. Auguste, 38, 40

Colborne, Lt-Col John, 113, 116, 117, 120, 195, 196, 197

Cole, Lt-Gen. Hon. Lowry, 117, 118, 153, 184, 185, 187, 207

Cooke, Captain John, 9, 26, 132, 140, 190, 191, 199, 213

Cooper, Sergeant John, 9, 10, 24, 75, 78, 114, 115, 117, 118, 144: ????115, 117, 118, 144, 175, 176, 185, 207, 208

Corunna, 20, 24, 25, 27, 28, 31, 42, 43, 45, 46, 50, 51, 53, 56, 57, 59, 60, 90, 158

Costello, Rifleman Edward, 63, 68, 75, 82, 99, 107, 130, 132, 138, 140, 143, 162, 174, 178

Crauford, Maj.-Gen. Robert, 31, 33, 36, 47, 48, 49, 74, 82, 86, 87, 104, 108; 130; death of, 131, 133; and Light Brigade, 73, 78, 80, 81, 90, 117, 130

Cuesta, Gen. Don Gregorio, 60, 67, 68, 69, 70, 71, 73, 74, 75, 76, 77

Dalhousie, Lt-Gen. George Ramsay, 173, 187

Dalrymple, Lt-Gen. Sir Hew, 14, 19, 20, 51

Delaborde, Gen. Henri François, 7, 8, 13, 66

d'Erlon, Marshal Jean Baptiste, 137, 174, 181, 182, 183, 184, 197, 207

Donaldson, Private Joseph, 89, 101, 104, 109, 131, 132, 157

Douro, River, 28, 60, 64, 66, 149, 158, 161, 163, 165, 185

Duhesme, Gen. Philibert, 3

Du Point, Gen., Pierre, 3

Ebro, River, 22, 167, 168, 182

Elvas, 24, 113, 134, 136, 144, 145

Elvina, 50, 53, 54, 55, 56

Esla, River, 33, 34, 166

Erskine, Maj.-Gen. Sir William, 104

Fane, Maj.-Gen. Henry, 16, 26

Fernyhough, Lieut Robert, 154, 164

Field, Lieut W., 83, 93, 106, 110

Forlorn Hope, 123, 124, 130, 138

Fort Conception, 106

Fort Napoleon, 147

Fort Ragusa, 147

Foy, Gen. Maximilien Sebastian, 65, 66, 155, 180

Fuentes de Onoro, 103, 104, 106, 108, 110, 174, 180

Gavin, Ensign William, 6, 37

Gazan, Gen. Honoré, 118, 174, 181

Girard, Gen. Jean Baptiste, 114, 116, 118

Gleig, Lieut George, 10, 39, 137, 189, 192, 193, 201, 202, 203, 205, 209, 213, 216, 218

Gordon, Captain Alexander, 24, 25, 27, 29, 30, 34, 35, 36, 38, 39, 40, 50

Graham, Lt-Gen. Sir Thomas, 55, 93, 94, 95, 96, 116, 131, 165, 168, 170, 177, 182, 185, 189, 190; and troops, 98, 173, 174, 181, 191

Grattan, Lieut William, 8, 91, 104, 109, 110, 111, 131, 132, 140, 142, 144, 205, 220

Green, Private John, 40, 41, 43, 78, 137, 138, 150, 153, 156, 167, 174, 176, 186

Guadiana, River, 68, 122, 124, 134, 135, 142

Hale, Sergeant James, 46, 58, 220

Harley, Captain John, 191, 192

Harris, Rifleman Jonathan, 9, 10, 15, 16, 17, 18, 33, 41, 43, 48, 49, 104, 221

Hay, Ensign William, 87, 216

Hawker, Lieut Peter, 5, 26, 66, 76

Henegan, Sir Richard, 6, 60, 96, 101, 167, 178, 191, 199, 200

Henry, Surgeon Walter, 136, 142, 144, 170, 215, 219

Hill, Lt-Gen. Sir Rowland, 62, 71, 147, 158, 161, 162, 163, 165, 168, 172, 181, 183, 184, 185, 205, 207, 208; and troops, 173, 194, 199, 202, 203, 209, 210, 212, 215

Hope, Lt-Gen. Sir John, 31, 35, 56, 204, 206, 207, 209, 216, 217

Hough, Lieut Henry, 156

Jourdan, Marshal Jean Baptiste, 74, 170, 172, 176, 177, 180, 181

Junot, General Jean Andoche, 2, 4, 15, 16, 17, 18, 19, 20, 28, 51, 102, 106

Keep, Ensign William Thornton, 165, 176, 183, 201; wounded, 204, 205

Kellerman, General François, 18, 19

Kincaid, Captain John, 99, 123, 124, 125, 126, 130, 131, 138, 139, 142, 143, 144, 149, 157, 165, 167, 168, 173, 174, 175, 184, 193, 220

King's German Legion, 6, 71, 73, 95, 106, 155, 160, 209, 212, 218
Kempt, Maj.-Gen. Sir James, 136, 173, 174, 197
Keogh, Ensign Edward, 97
Knowles, Lieut Robert, 120, 126, 127, 141, 154

Landsheit, Sergeant Norberton, 15
La Pena, General Manuel, 93, 94, 95, 96, 98
Lapisse, General Pierre, 62, 64, 72; death of, 73
Lawrence, Sergeant William, 11, 23, 61; at Badajoz, 137, 138, 139, 144, 145, 175, 176, 213
Leach, Captain Jonathan, 5, 8, 23, 81, 82, 85, 87, 110, 162
Lefebvre-Desnouttes, Gen. Charles, 26, 34, 35
Leira, 6, 7, 62, 101
Leith, Lt-Gen. Sir James, 141, 152, 153, 190, 191
Leval, General, 96, 97
Lewin, Captain Harry Ross, 18, 19, 63, 111, 112, 127, 150, 154, 160, 161, 163, 208
Lisbon, 2, 7, 8, 13, 14, 15, 18, 19, 20, 22, 23, 24, 35, 57, 60, 61, 62, 63, 76, 77, 80, 90, 102, 103, 158, 165
Loison, General Louis Henry, 8, 13, 86, 102
Lugo, 28, 43, 44, 45, 46, 66

McCarthy, Captain, 136, 138, 139, 142
Madrid, 3, 25, 28, 38, 68, 69, 70, 74, 76, 155, 157, 158, 161, 162, 165, 167
Maemphel, Joseph, 3, 88, 91, 111
Malcom, Lieut John, 195, 214
Marmont, Marshal Auguste Frédéric Louis, 100, 112, 123, 125, 126, 128, 130, 145, 146, 148, 149; is wounded, 155
Masséna, Marshal André, 80, 81, 82, 83, 84, 85, 87, 90, 91, 99, 104, 106, 108, 111; and troops, 89, 90, 101, 102, 103, 106, 110, 112, 219
Masterton, Sergeant, 97, 98
Maya Pass, 181, 182, 183, 184, 185, 187
Medellin, 68, 71
Merida, 147
Mills, Ensign John, 67, 102, 110, 127, 132, 146, 148, 149, 156, 159, 160, 162, 220
Mondego Bay, 5
Mondego, River, 24, 83, 99, 100
Moore, Lt-Gen. Sir John, 4, 11, 13, 14, 15, 21; as C-in-C, 22, 24, 25, 26, 27, 28, 29, 30, 58, 87; in retreat, 31, 34, 35, 36, 38, 39, 44, 45, 50, 53, 54; death of, 55,

56; memorial to, 59; and troops, 24, 25, 33, 40, 43, 46, 50, 57, 62
Mortier, Marshal Edouard Adolphe, 28, 68
Montbrun, General Louise Pierre, 125
Murat, Marshal Joachim, 3
Murray, General Sir John, 196

Napier, Major Charles, 40, 53, 54, 55
Napier, Major George, 45, 54, 55, 74, 87, 90, 91, 129, 130, 133
Napier, Major William, 81, 108, 119, 197
Neale, Adam, 6, 19, 20, 42, 49
Ney, Marshal Michel, 66, 68, 81, 82, 86, 99, 102
Nive, River, 199, 202, 203, 204
Nivelle, River, 194, 195, 197, 198

Obidos, 7
Oporto, 60, 65, 66
Orthez, 206, 207, 208

Pack, Maj.-Gen. Sir Dennis, 130, 153, 159, 161, 185
Paget, Lt-Col Henry, 24, 29, 31, 46, 53, 54, 55, 163
Pakenham, Maj.-Gen. Hon. Edward, 126, 151, 152, 153, 187, 202
Pamplona, 168, 177, 179, 180, 181, 182, 184, 185, 187, 194
Patterson, Captain John, 19, 26, 46, 147
Phillipon, General Armand, 122, 124, 135, 138, 142
Picton, Lt-Gen. Sir Thomas, 86, 130, 132; is wounded, 141, 151; and troops, 104, 106, 109, 125, 131, 137, 141, 173, 174, 185, 207, 212
Plunket, Rifleman Thomas, 19, 35, 40, 63, 78, 79
Pococke, Private Thomas, 15, 23, 31, 34, 39, 41, 46, 47, 50, 56, 100, 106, 108, 109, 110, 172, 195, 218
Posa Velha, 104, 106, 107, 110
Pyrenees, 61, 165, 168, 179, 181, 182, 187, 188, 189, 193, 195, 202, 219

Ramsey, Captain Norman, 108
Reille, General Honoré, 170, 180, 181, 182, 184, 186, 203, 204, 207
Reynier, General Jean Louis, 86, 102, 103
Rice, Major Samuel, 100, 121, 143, 149
Robertson, Seargeant D., 38, 57
Rockets, 93, 206, 213, 214
Rolica, 7
Romana, General Pedro Caro, 27, 28, 30, 35, 36, 40, 60

Roncesvalles, 181, 182, 184, 194
Ruffin, General François, 73, 94, 96; death of, 98

Sabugal, 103
Sahagun, 29, 30
Salamanca, 24, 26, 27, 28, 103, 110, 112, 125, 145, 146, 154, 158, 159, 160, 161, 163, 165
Sanchez, Don Julian, 61
San Sebastian, 179, 180, 181, 182, 185, 187, 188, 189, 193
Santarem, 91, 99
Schaumann, Commissary August, 6, 20, 22, 23, 33, 34, 36, 41, 42, 45, 47, 50, 56, 76, 83, 84, 99, 100, 170, 175, 177, 202
Sherer, Lieut Joseph Moyle-, 84, 113, 116, 118, 119, 120, 121, 161, 180, 182, 183
Simmons, Lieut George, 67, 74, 80, 81, 82, 99, 100, 102, 103, 122, 129, 140, 157, 188, 194, 202, 208
Smith, Lieut Harry, 139, 142, 174, 196
Soult, Marshal Nicolas Jean-de-Dieu, 26, 28, 29, 36, 38, 44, 45, 51, 52, 56, 59, 62, 64, 65, 67, 74, 76, 103; at Albuera, 113, 114, 116, 117, 121, 122, 123, 124, 128, 137, 145, 146, 148, 161, 163; in the Pyrenees, 181, 182, 185, 187, 194, 201, 203, 204, 205, 206, 207, 208, 211, 218; and troops, 44, 57, 60, 66, 68, 77, 147, 188, 209, 215
Stepney, Lieut Cowell John, 101, 106
Stewart, Brig.-Gen. Hon Charles, 71, 72, 108, 116, 182, 187
Suchet, Marshal Louis Gabriel, 158
Surtees, Q.M.S. William, 25, 27, 33, 49, 94, 97, 143, 144, 174, 195, 202

Tagus, River, 5, 22, 63, 70, 76, 79, 146, 147, 161
Tagus Valley, 25, 62, 68, 102, 126, 165
Talavera, 67, 69, 70, 71, 74, 137
Thomières, General Jean Guillaume, 150, 152, 155
Thouvenot, General Pierre, 216, 217, 218

Tomkinson, Captain William, 63, 64, 80, 89, 90, 91, 107, 148, 167
Tormes, 149
Torres Vedras, 8, 15, 79, 90, 91
Toulouse, 208, 211, 212, 215, 218, 219

Valladolid, 3, 4, 24, 25, 26, 27, 80, 155, 158, 162
Vera, 179
Victor, Marshal Claud, 26, 62, 64, 67, 68, 69, 70, 71, 72, 73, 94, 96; and troops, 93, 94, 98
Vigo, 24, 36, 47, 49, 60
Villafranca, 36, 37, 38, 41, 43, 45, 46, 90
Villatte, General Eugene, 172
Vimiero, 13, 15, 21, 23, 31, 39, 41, 62
Vitoria, 167, 168, 170, 175, 176, 178, 181, 182, 208

Warre, Captain William, 20, 27, 90, 148
Wellesley, Sir Arthur, 5, 7, 8, 13, 14, 15, 19, 20, 21, 58, 62, 63, 64, 65, 67, 68, 70, 71, 73, 74, 76, 77, 78; elevated to peerage, 79; and tactics, 11, 12, 16; and troops, 6, 18, 66
Welington, 1st Duke of, 61, 81, 82, 83, 84, 91, 93, 106, 107, 110, 111, 113, 121, 122, 123, 124, 125, 132, 134; at Badajoz, 135, 137, 139, 140, 141, 143, 144, 145; at Salamanca, 146, 147, 148, 150, 151, 152, 153, 154, 155, 157, 158, 164; at Vitoria, 168, 169, 173, 175, 177, 178; in the Pyrenees, 180, 181, 182, 184, 185, 186, 187, 188; in France, 193, 194, 196, 197, 201, 202, 204, 206, 207, 211, 213, 215; is wounded, 208; learns of peace, 216, 222; and troops, 80, 89, 90, 100, 103, 104, 129, 141, 159, 160, 162, 165, 166, 167, 195, 199, 203, 205, 210, 220, 221
Wheatley, Ensign Edmund, 195, 202, 208, 215, 216, 217
Wheeler, Corporal William, 63, 101, 102, 118, 122, 135, 149, 156, 162, 178, 198

Zadorra, River, 168, 170, 172, 173